THE ELEM

HUMA

DE CORPORE POLITICO

THOMAS HOBBES was born in Malmesbury in Wiltshire in 1588. Well taught in local schools and, from his own reports, ill educated at Oxford, he was employed as tutor and secretary by the Earl of Devonshire for much of his life. His three tours of the Continent before 1640 introduced him to the new learning of Galileo and others, and established the connections necessary for his sojourn in Paris, 1640–51, during the English Civil Wars.

His first original work was *The Elements of Law* (1640). Its arguments concerning nature, man, and society were redeployed and extended in *De Cive* (1642), *Leviathan* (1651), and *De Corpore* (1655), as well as in numerous other fiercely controversial publications.

Popularly condemned for his political philosophy, his analysis of morality, and his 'atheism', his works were nevertheless widely read in England and Europe. After the Restoration in 1660 he survived his own notoriety under the protection of Charles II and the Earl of Devonshire. He died at Hardwick Hall in 1679.

PROFESSOR J. C. A. GASKIN is a graduate of Oxford University and a Fellow of Trinity College Dublin. His publications include *The Quest for Eternity* (1984), *Hume's Philosophy of Religion* (1988 and 1993), and *Varieties of Unbelief* (1989). He has previously edited a volume of David Hume's works on religion for World's Classics. The spell of Hobbes originally fell upon him when in the sixth form of the City of Oxford High School.

THE WORLD'S CLASSICS

THOMAS HOBBES

The Elements of Law Natural and Politic

PART I

Human Nature

PART II

De Corpore Politico

WITH

Three Lives

Edited with an Introduction by
J. C. A. GASKIN
Fellow of Trinity College Dublin

Oxford   New York

OXFORD UNIVERSITY PRESS

1994

Oxford University Press, Walton Street, Oxford OX2 6DP

Oxford New York Toronto
Delhi Bombay Calcutta Madras Karachi
Kuala Lumpur Singapore Hong Kong Tokyo
Nairobi Dar es Salaam Cape Town
Melbourne Auckland Madrid
and associated companies in
Berlin Ibadan

Oxford is a trade mark of Oxford University Press

Translations and Editorial material © *J. C. A. Gaskin 1994*

First published as a World's Classics paperback 1994

British Library Cataloguing in Publication Data
Data available

Library of Congress Cataloging in Publication Data
Hobbes, Thomas, 1588–1679.
[Human nature]
The elements of law, natural and politic: part I, Human nature, part II, De corpore
politico; with Three lives/Thomas Hobbes; edited with an introduction by
J. C. A. Gaskin.
p. cm.—(World's classics)
This work was originally published in 1650 as two separate books, Human nature,
and De corpore politico. Human nature contained the first 13 chapters, De Corpore
politico contained chapters 14 thru 19 of the first work, and chapters 20 thru 29.
The present edition considers chapters 1 thru 19 as part 1, Human nature, and
chapters 20 thru 29 as part 2, De corpore politico. Included in this work are
chapters from Hobbes' De corpore, translations of His Verse life, and Prose life,
and an abstract of John Aubrey's Brief life. Includes bibliographical references.
1. Natural law. 2. Political science—Early works to 1800.
I. Hobbes, Thomas, 1588–1679. De corpore politico. 1994.
II. Gaskin, J. C. A. (John Charles Addison) III. Title. IV. Title:
De corpore politico. V. Series.
JC153.H55 1994 171'.2—dc20 93–38333
ISBN 0–19–283121–6

1 3 5 7 9 10 8 6 4 2

Typeset by Best-set Typesetter Ltd., Hong Kong
Printed in Great Britain by BPC Paperbacks Ltd
Aylesbury, Bucks.

PREFACE

It has been for long more difficult to read Hobbes than to read about him. This deplorable state of affairs is because—with the signal exception of *Leviathan*—most of his works are difficult to find outside great libraries. The present volume is some attempt to put that right. *The Elements of Law* is Hobbes's first major work, one of his most succinct and challenging, and an anticipation of much for which he is famous in *Leviathan*.

The introduction briefly sets *The Elements of Law* in its historical context and makes a somewhat more extensive attempt to explain, and occasionally to comment upon, Hobbes's grand system of philosophy—a system not immediately apparent from *The Elements of Law* read in isolation. The chapters from *De Corpore* are appended because of their striking relevance to some of the early chapters in *The Elements of Law*, their intrinsic interest, and the chronic unavailability of the original work.

I am grateful to the Bodleian Library for facilitating the republication of their very rare copy of the 1680 translation of Hobbes's 'Verse Life', and to Mary Lyons for her scholarly and stylish attention to the new translation of Hobbes's 'Prose Life'. These autobiographies, never before published together in translation, along with the abstract of John Aubrey's 'Brief Life', form a unique collection of material on Hobbes.

My enthusiasm for Hobbes will show at times. Despite the almost medieval attitudes evident in, for example, his chapters on servants and on children in *De Corpore Politico*, his perception of what man is, and of the political and moral problems to which our nature leads us, is profound and enduring. He sees clearly when he sees man as a creature of restless desires that cease only in death. He sees clearly when he describes the life that would result from the unrelenting pursuit of our individual self-interests. He sees better than many when he argues that political order, almost any *order*, is preferable to the murderous confusion which we could instance all too easily from recent history. What is more, Hobbes was writing when the new sciences of quantity and number were taking over from an entirely different authoritarian medieval synthesis, and he was emphatically on the side of the new sciences. In his enthusiasm Hobbes exposes their philosophical base with a clear confidence from which we now tend to shrink, and his confidence is more thought-provoking than the caution of a thousand lesser men and women of more recent vintage. In effect he argues that there is only one real world, that the sciences describe it, and that religion must be contained within that world.

In the preparation of this volume I am obliged to the Arts and Social Sciences Fund of Dublin University. I am also very much indebted to the help of Charles Benson, Keeper of Early Printed Books in the Library of Trinity College Dublin and to Professor William Lyons for his critical reading of my Introduction at a time when the demands of other work were very pressing. Finally, but most particularly, I wish to record my debt to the Trustees of the Chatsworth Settlement and the Duke and Duchess of Devonshire for permitting me to examine the Hobbes manuscripts still at Chatsworth, and for the assistance of Michael Pearman and others in the Library there. Hobbes himself was enormously beholden to the Cavendish family, as was Tönnies in his original work on *The Elements of Law* in the 1880s. And the debt of succeeding generations of Hobbes scholars continues to accumulate.

J. C. A. GASKIN

CONTENTS

CONTENTS

SCHEME OF REFERENCE

The Elements of Law	*The Elements of Law Natural and Politic*, the whole twenty-nine chapters of the present text.
Human Nature	Part I of the present text (Chapters I to XIX).
De Corpore Politico	Part II of the present text (Chapters XX to XXIX). Note that what we know as *The Elements of Law* was originally published in 1650 (and for long afterwards) as two separate books bearing the titles of the constituent parts. In the present volume *Human Nature* refers to the first nineteen chapters here printed, not to the first thirteen chapters published in 1650 as *Human Nature*. Similarly *De Corpore Politico* here refers to Chapters XX to XXIX, not to the work as published in 1650, which contained Chapters XIV to XXIX.
De Cive	*Philosophical Rudiments concerning Government and Society* (1651), the English version of *De Cive* (1642), conventionally referred to by its Latin title. Quotations are from the text edited by Howard Warrender (Oxford, 1983) with modernized spelling.
Leviathan	*Leviathan; or, The Matter, Form and Power of a Commonwealth Ecclesiastical and Civil* (1651). Quotations are from the first edition with modernized spelling.
De Corpore	*Elements of Philosophy, the First Section concerning Body* (1656), the English version of *De Corpore* conventionally referred to by its Latin title and not to be confused with Part II of *The Elements of Law*. Quotations are from volume i of the *English Works of Thomas Hobbes*, ed. W. Molesworth (London, 1839).

In all but one of Hobbes's main works the chapter numbers run continuously from start to finish ignoring the Parts of the work. The one exception is *The Elements of Law* as hitherto published, where a new sequence of chapter numbers commences at whatever the printer or editor has decided should be its parts. Following a suggestion made by Howard Warrender in his fine edition of the English version of *De Cive* (p. 10 n. 4), I have numbered the chapters in this edition in one continuous sequence of roman numerals I to XXIX.

Again, in all Hobbes's main works with the exception this time of *Leviathan*, the paragraphs (or 'articles' as Hobbes sometimes calls them) are numbered within each chapter in arabic numerals. This, in conjunction with single runs of chapter numbers in roman numerals for each work, gives a very convenient and reasonably precise means of standard reference. Thus *De Cive*, X. 8 means *De Cive*, Chapter X, paragraph 8 in any edition. In the case of *Leviathan*, there being no paragraph numbers, nor any standard edition to which it is convenient to give page reference, I give only the chapter number in roman numerals.

INTRODUCTION

HOBBES was a powerful writer: menacingly terse, eloquent, orderly, forceful, and vivid. He was also a powerful philosopher: one who assimilated the violently conflicting intellectual and political currents of his time and gave to them, by means of a relatively few basic principles tenaciously and perceptively argued, a new, widely applicable, unorthodox, and, some would say, thoroughly pernicious resolution.

The resolution included a consistent solution to the political problems of his contemporaries and, for that matter, to the problems of all societies threatened by the miseries of internal strife and civil war. It also involved an analysis of human nature and motivation calculated to show how the unbridled pursuit of our individual aversions and desires would result in the war of every man against every man; how that state is avoided by a mutual compact which establishes a body politic; what the body politic is, and how it could relapse back into the state of war if the compact were broken.

But Hobbes is not only of interest as a political philosopher. He also set out, as a substantial preamble to his philosophy of civil society, a fascinating account of science, and of general philosophical problems concerned, among others, with sense perception, causation, free will, materialism, and language. These are immensely interesting in their own right, and could well have rivalled Descartes's as departure-points for modern philosophy if Hobbes had been more careful in their development, or less suspect to his immediate successors on account of his authoritarian political philosophy, his apparent subversion of morality, and his alleged atheism. (I say 'apparent' and 'alleged' for reasons to which I will return.)

Hobbes[1] was born in 1588 in Malmesbury in Wiltshire.

---

[1] Further information concerning Hobbes's life will be found in the 'Three Lives', below, and in the Chronology.

His first work was a translation, published in 1628, of Thucydides' *History of the Peloponnesian War*. It was at least in part intended as a cautionary tale of civil war addressed to his increasingly fractious and rebellious countrymen. His first substantial, original work was *The Elements of Law Natural and Politic*, written in or shortly before 1640. It was circulated immediately in manuscript copies, but not actually printed until 1650 when it appeared as two separate books with the titles *Human Nature* and *De Corpore Politico* respectively.

The Elements of Law is in fact the 'little Treatise in English' mentioned by Hobbes in his *Considerations upon the Reputation, Loyalty, Manners, and Religion of Thomas Hobbes*, which he published in 1662 in answer to Dr Wallis, one of his critics. Hobbes wrote

When the Parliament sat, that began in April 1640, and was dissolved in May following, and in which many Points of the Regal Power, which were necessary for the Peace of the Kingdom, and the Safety of his Majesty's Person, were disputed and denied, Mr. Hobbes wrote a little Treatise in English, wherein he did set forth and demonstrate, That the said Power and Rights were inseparably annexed to the Sovereignty; which Sovereignty they did not then deny to be in the King; but it seems understood not, or would not understand that Inseparability. Of this Treatise, Though not printed, many Gentlemen have Copies, which occasioned much Talk of the Author; and had not his Majesty dissolved the Parliament, it had brought him into Danger of his Life.

The Elements of Law was thus written under the threat of civil war although it fastidiously avoids specific reference to current events. It was, moreover, written when Hobbes was 52 years old: an age which the majority of his contemporaries never attained and which today, without earlier publications, would guarantee academic obscurity and handsome encouragements to an early and unproductive retirement. In Hobbes's case, however, *The Elements of Law* was merely the first and, according to many critics, the clearest and most accessible statement of what was to become the grand philosophical system continued in *De Cive* (1642), *Leviathan* (1651), *De Corpore* (1655), and *De Homine* (1657). The system was also defended (along with some of its more useless eccentricities)[2] and enlarged in numerous tracts: for example, in Hobbes's controversy with Bramhall concerning necessity and free will, in the quasi-historical work *Behemoth* (an account of the history and causes of the Civil Wars in England 1640–60), and in *A Dialogue between a Philosopher and a Student of the Common Laws of England* (concerned with the extent to which common law had limited or could limit the king's authority). The parts of the grand system omitted or given small space in *The Elements* are chiefly the long discussions of the relation of religion to the civil authority which occur both in *De Cive* and in the latter half of *Leviathan*, the logic and mechanistic philosophy set out in *De Corpore*, the concern with mathematics also conspicuous in *De Corpore*, and the account of optics in *De Homine*.

The Elements of Law has thus considerable claims as the primary source for Hobbes's main ideas, as the most succinct presentation of them, and as an epitome of those parts of his philosophy which have most enduring value.

These virtues do not, however, make *The Elements of Law* a quick read. Hobbes seldom ekes out what he has to say. His argument is often dense in texture. He expects his readers to remember or refer back to what has gone before and to go on drawing conclusions out of his first principles or definitions. The result would justify a voluminous commentary. All I can attempt in the present edition is some indication of the place of *The Elements of Law* in Hobbes's overall scheme of thought, a look at a few of its main ideas, and some indication of the problems it raised and the criticisms it provoked when the text was printed and widely circulated along with other works by Hobbes in the 1650s.

Political and Religious Strife

Hobbes's life, 1588–1679, could almost have been designed to coincide with the strife which divided the political, re-

---

[2] e.g. Hobbes's hapless attempt to square the circle in *De Corpore*, XX, and the fruitless and absurd controversy in which this involved him with the Oxford mathematicians Seth Ward (1617–89) and John Wallis (1618–1703). See Croom Robertson, *Hobbes* (Edinburgh, 1886), 167–85.

ligious, philosophical, and scientific structures and theories we call medieval from those we call modern. In the first decades of his life the Catholic and Aristotelian synthesis of religion and philosophy, with its attendant view of nature as part of a divinely purposeful cosmos, was under challenge throughout Europe. The challenge came from the new sciences opened up by Copernicus and Kepler and so effectively championed by Galileo. It came from the revival of ancient sceptical philosophy resulting from the first printing of a Latin text of Sextus Empiricus in the 1560s and, a little later, from the re-emergence of the ideas of Greek atomism and materialism through new interest in the works of Lucretius and Diogenes Laertius. And, most violently, it came from the various movements towards reformation in religion.

Religious strife had broken out long before 1640 between Roman Catholic and Protestant in Germany, France, and the Low Countries, and between Protestant and other Reformed sects in Scotland. Conflict was also developing in England, between the traditional sovereign powers and those who for economic, social, or religious reasons felt justified as individuals in defying authority even to the point of civil insurrection. In a phrase of Churchill's, 'the furious winds of religious strife' were blowing across northern Europe. Conflicting dogmas became the daily diet of political and religious controversy. Man's sense of sin—always assiduously cultivated by Christianity but hitherto systematically absolved by the Roman Church—became, with Protestantism, an intense personal search for the means of salvation, a salvation that concerned an individual's life in all eternity, and took proportionately little care of earthly felicity, secular authority, or the peace of civil society.

In this strife Hobbes took clear positions. He rejected the medieval science and Aristotelianism still lingering at Oxford when he was an undergraduate. He whole-heartedly affirmed the new sciences which were eventually to result in the Newtonian synthesis. He adopted philosophical views—much in evidence in the first half of the *The Elements of Law*—which were in perfect accord with the new sciences, and he deployed those views by methods which were intensely rationalistic, but whose outcome was the first real flowering of the empiricism with which English-language philosophy was ever after to be associated. In science and philosophy Hobbes was a radical. But in religion and politics, despite his emphatic rebuttal of Roman Catholicism in the final chapter of. *Leviathan*, he is a species of conservative. He employed all his intellectual might in resisting the disintegration of civil society, which he saw as a consequence of men and women seeking individual religious salvation, or following unrestrained their natural self-interest.

In Britain the storm gathered for thirty years after Hobbes's departure from Oxford in 1608 as companion-tutor to the young Cavendish (in 1626 to become the second Earl of Devonshire). Hobbes watched it both from within the politically significant Cavendish family and as an acquaintance of men of power and responsibility including Francis Bacon (philosopher, royal sycophant, and Lord Chancellor). Widely travelled in Europe, Hobbes would also have been acutely aware of the intellectual and religious currents that were moving against the old order on the Continent.

In 1629 Charles I dissolved his increasingly unco-operative Parliament and began the period of peaceful and economical personal rule that was eventually ended by sheer shortage of revenue. In November 1638 the first clear defiance of the sovereign authority of the King took place in Edinburgh when the General Assembly of Scotland refused to dissolve on the demands of the King's Commissioners. Charles turned to a new English Parliament for help. It was not forthcoming. The Parliament was dissolved in May 1640 (the same month Hobbes dedicated *The Elements of Law* to his then patron, the Earl of Newcastle), and the conflicts about the legal status of the King's actions, his law-making and revenue-raising powers, and the nature of the religious settlement imposed by Laud were ready to boil over into civil war.

Hobbes's overmastering concern in the later chapters of his 'little Treatise in English' with the nature of law, covenants, oaths, sovereignty, private conscience, the causes of rebellion, and the foundation of and need for a body politic is thus wholly understandable in its historical context. It is similar to the concerns of Milton, Coke, Hooker, Filmer, Pym, and other great English writers of the period. The difference is that much of what Hobbes has to say has a depth and value that was not extinguished with the circumstances that occasioned it.

Hobbes's Grand Philosophical System in Three Parts

There is no hint in *The Elements of Law* that Hobbes saw either *Human Nature* or *De Corpore Politico* as parts of some greater structure than themselves. His declared object, in the paragraphs that stand for a preface, is an understanding of human nature, of 'what is a body politic, and what it is we call a law'. The objective, stated in 'The Epistle Dedicatory', is to reduce the doctrine of justice and policy 'to the rules and infallibility of reason' and to build thereon 'the truth of cases in the law of nature' for the avoidance of mutual fear and the preservation of peace and the state (or 'commonwealth' as Hobbes normally calls it). Two years later Hobbes published *De Cive*, a book which amplifies and adds mainly to the political theory outlined in the latter half of *The Elements of Law*. However, in the second Latin edition of *De Civê*, published in Amsterdam in 1647, Hobbes added a 'Preface to the Reader'. In it, in the words of the English version of 1651, the idea of a sequence of philosophical dissertations is first proposed:

I was studying Philosophy for my mind's sake, and I had gathered together its first Elements in all kinds, and having digested them into three Sections by degrees, I thought to have written them so as in the first I would have treated of a body, and its general properties; in the second of man and his special faculties, and affections; in the third, of civil government and the duties of Subjects: Wherefore the first Section would have contained the first Philosophy, and certain elements of Physics; in it we would have considered the reasons of Time, Place, Cause, Power, Relation, Proportion, Quantity, Figure and motion. In the second we would have been conversant about imagination, Memory, intellect, ratiocination, appetite, Will, good and Evil, honest and dishonest, and the like.

The third section is *De Cive*. Hobbes's summary of it in the Preface is also a description of what had already been his main concerns in the later chapters of *The Elements of Law*:

I demonstrate in the first place, that the state of men without civil society (which state we may properly call the state of nature) is nothing else but a mere war of all against all; and in that war all men have equal right unto all things; Next, that all men as soon as they arrive to understanding of this hateful condition, do desire (even nature itself compelling them) to be freed from this misery. But that this cannot be done except by compact, they all quit that right which they have unto all things. Furthermore I declare, and confirm what the nature of compacts is; how and by what means the right of one might be transferred unto another to make their compacts valid; also what rights, and to whom they must necessarily be granted for the establishing of Peace, I mean what those dictates of reason are, which may properly be termed the Laws of Nature.

What Hobbes is proposing, and what he actually executed in his works, though not in the order stated in *De Cive*, is a philosophical progression which would start with natural bodies and the most fundamental principles of the natural sciences, move on to man and an account of his sense perception, language, reasoning, psychological nature, and morality, and conclude with an account of civil society or the 'body politic'. In the later work, *De Corpore*, I. 9, a very similar progression of philosophy is described in different terms (see below pp. 192–3).

The systematic rather than chronological order of Hobbes's philosophical works, with repetitions and overlaps,[3] is thus:

1. First philosophy, BODY or BODY NATURAL: *De Corpore* (Latin, 1655; English, 1656), leading to

---

[3] A more detailed comparison of the extent to which their contents overlap with the two Parts of *The Elements of Law* can be seen on pp. xliv–xlvi, below. Most of Hobbes's main publications appeared in both Latin and English, but it is preferable to speak of the Latin (or English) *versions* rather than of translations, as some of the versions were not translated by Hobbes himself, and when they were, alterations were sometimes made by him.

2. MAN: *Human Nature* (the first Part of the English manuscript, 1640, of *The Elements of Law*, first printed in English, 1650); *Leviathan*, Part I (English, 1651; Latin, 1668); *De Homine* (Latin only, 1657), leading to

3. COMMONWEALTH or BODY POLITIC: *De Corpore Politico* (the second Part of the English manuscript of 1640 of *The Elements of Law*, first printed in English, 1650); *De Cive* (Latin, 1642; English, 1651); *Leviathan*, Parts II–IV (English, 1651; Latin, 1668).

However, since Hobbes first dealt with 2 and 3 in *The Elements of Law* without reference to and perhaps without thought of 1, then published an extension of 3 in *De Cive* without reference to either 1 or 2, and then redeveloped both 2 and 3 very effectively in *Leviathan* before eventually supplying 1 in *De Corpore*, seventeen years after *The Elements of Law*, it is a serious question in what real sense, if any, Hobbes's declared order is a progression, or his philosophy a system.

The Methods of the Grand System

What Hobbes actually says (for example, in *De Corpore*, VI. 6) is that '*after* physics we must come to moral philosophy' (my emphasis). Why 'after' and how necessarily 'after'? Three considerations govern the order: first, the scope or basicness of the subject-matter; secondly, the structure required by following Hobbes's paradigm for clear reasoning; thirdly, Hobbes's use of what he calls the 'synthetic' and the 'analytic' methods.

In the first place Hobbes takes it that a small number of carefully defined conceptions and laws are basic to all accounts of the universe in the sense that their scope extends to everything that is, or could be, a part of the material universe: the universe of 'body'.[4] But what is a conception?

[4] Hobbes's quest for a single, or at most a very few, ultimate explanatory principles was neither new nor an aspiration which perished with 17th-century mechanics. It was anticipated by the Presocratic philosophers' search for an archē or origin (an explanatory source which could not be given, and needed no further explanation). It has been succeeded by the quest of modern theoretical physics for

In *De Corpore*, VIII. 2, Hobbes struggles to explain that an 'accident' of a bodily thing is that 'by means of which it works in us a conception of itself'. The *accident* is that which the bodily thing actually is or has. The *conception* is our construct of the thing caused by the way its accidents act upon our senses. 'Conception' is, however, a portmanteau word having a number of usages which Hobbes does not always consistently distinguish. Conceptions are (1) the contents of our experience when and however these contents are actually being caused by the accidents of external bodily things acting upon our senses, *and* (2) those contents as they remain accessible to us in memories, dreams, imaginations, and so on, *and* (3) whatever it is that we have when we understand a word, or phrase, or other discrete part of a language; when, in Hobbes's terminology, we understand a name. Hobbes commonly uses the word 'phantasm' for conceptions 1 and 2, although he is inclined to employ the word 'image' for the subclass of phantasms associated with vision. Occasionally he adopts the word 'idea' as a synonym for 'conception' in all or any of the senses 1 to 3.

The conceptions which principally interest Hobbes as basic are those of body, motion, and endeavour. (See *De Corpore*, IV. 5.) The laws of the universe of body or matter are very fundamental laws of motion, particularly the law of inertia. Hobbes takes it as obvious that the scope or range of application of these laws is so great that, if we are to have an orderly and structured knowledge of the universe, or of *anything*, we must begin with an understanding of them, and of certain other philosophical conceptions that are almost equally basic.[5] Thus an understanding of the basic mechanics of body *comes before* and is presupposed by an understand-

a set of laws and entities which would be minimal and ultimate in the sense that all other laws, and the existence of all other entities, could be derived from it, and could be derived from no simpler set.

[5] In a similar way it might still be said that physics and chemistry are 'basic' sciences in ways in which metallurgy and geology are not. A proper understanding of the latter pair presupposes some knowledge of the former, and not vice versa. Again, some conception of, for example, number, is presupposed by all the sciences. If anything is to be understood, number and computation must be understood first.

ing of human nature. And similarly an understanding of human nature, including the mechanics of perception, of neural physiology, and of the resulting mechanistic psychology of aversions and desires, comes before an understanding of that which human nature sustains, threatens, and occasions: namely, commonwealth or the body politic. Hence the rationale of the order BODY, MAN, COMMONWEALTH. The whole hierarchical sequence is set out in *De Corpore*, VI. 17 (see pp. 209–10).

In the second place, we know from John Aubrey's anecdote (p. 235, below), and from Hobbes's own statements (see 'Prose Life', pp. 246 f.), that he was hugely impressed by his comparatively late discovery of the techniques of demonstration used in Euclidian geometry. The conspicuous characteristic of the system is the logically decisive derivation of certain truths or 'theorems', themselves by no means self-evident or trivial, from definitions and a few 'common notions' or axioms (very general, virtually self-evident propositions such as 'the whole is greater than its parts'). It is a system that preserves truth and yields certainties. If the initial definitions and axioms are accepted as true, the theorems must be accepted as true by any rational being. The discipline of the system is hard, but for the presentation of a body of knowledge the gain in terms of clarity and deductive certainty is great. Thus Hobbes applied the discipline wherever possible in his accounts of body, man, and commonwealth. Hence the prevalence of very tightly structured, interrelated definitions in all of Hobbes's main works starting with *The Elements of Law*. Hence the sense of a progression of definitions: 'motion' must be defined before 'endeavour' because motion figures in the definition of endeavour; 'endeavour' must be defined before the passions (so perceptively detailed in *Human Nature*, IX, and in *Leviathan*, IV) because 'endeavour' has to be understood in the accounts of the passions. Hence the frequency of appeals back to what 'hath already been proved' in such-and-such a place. Hence the progression from fundamental conceptions of widest application concerning body and motion to those of narrower application concerning human nature and commonwealth.

But, finally, there is a reason why the three sections of the grand system may be developed out of logical order. It is that the 'synthetic method', the deductive synthesis leading from earlier principles and definitions to new truths, is in practice mixed with, and augmented by, a quite different method, the 'analytic method', which involves direct observation, or sense experience, or introspection. In *De Corpore*, VI. 7, Hobbes remarks:

For the causes of the motions of the mind are known, not only by ratiocination [reasoning], but also by the experience of every man that takes the pains to observe those motions within himself.

And in the Introduction to *Leviathan*, more specifically:

Read thyself... was... meant... to teach us, that for the similitude of the thoughts, and Passions of one man, to the thoughts, and Passions of another, whosoever looketh into himself, and considereth what he doth when he does *think*, *opine*, *reason*, *hope*, *fear*, etc., and upon what grounds; he shall thereby read and know, what are the thoughts, and Passions of all other men, upon the like occasions.

These are both examples of the employment of the *analytic* method. The difference between the analytic and the synthetic method is summarized in the Table of Contents for Chapter VI of *De Corpore*: 'That method of civil and natural science, which proceeds from sense to principle, is *analytic*, and again that, which begins at principle, is *synthetical*.' The synthetic method is nearer to the pattern of geometrical deduction in as much as it consists in deriving consequences from definitions (or from what is already established), or in deducing effects from observed causes, where the causes are already described in terms of general principles or definitions. The analytic method, on the other hand, is used when the synthetic method is not possible because of the unstructured knowledge of the investigator, or the urgent priority of the subject in hand. If the dogs of war are at the gate, it is more urgent to set out *ad hoc* peace proposals than to synthesize these with fundamental truths about the nature of reality! The analytic method consists in working back from the immediate data of experience to a cause or to an explanatory structure of definitions. Hobbes himself either mixes the two methods (he affirms in *De Corpore*, VI. 3, that this is normal practice), or, particularly in deploying the second and third sections of his system, he simply makes a brief gesture towards fundamental principles and then uses the analytic method. Such brief gestures may be seen in *Human Nature*, II. 7, and in the first sentence of *De Cive*.

The overall influence of these considerations on Hobbes's grand system is thus to set up a paradigm. The paradigm is a synthetic deductive system following the model of Euclidian demonstration and employing definitions, common notions, and derived theorems. When the paradigm cannot be exactly followed, it can be augmented by the analytic method,[6] itself still as far as possible subject to the rigour of logical presentation and clear definitions. But what, according to Hobbes, is this much employed device, a *definition*?

Definitions

Hobbes's earliest account of language is in *Human Nature*, V. In simple terms he regards language as names added together by association. Each name 'is the voice of a man, arbitrarily imposed, for a mark to bring to his mind some conception [image, idea, or understanding] concerning the thing on which it is imposed' (V. 2). (His later account in *De Corpore*, II. 4, makes it clear that the mark must somehow bring to *our* minds a *shared* conception. Language is between people, not solipsistic.) But, on occasions, it is necessary to be particular clear about exactly what conception a compounded name[7] brings to mind. Or it may be

---

[6] Readers who are acquainted with Kant's more philosophically familiar use of the words 'analytic' and 'synthetic' will recognize that Hobbes's use is entirely different from Kant's. Hobbes's use is somewhat nearer to the still-surviving common usage of the words 'analysis' and 'synthesis'. Hobbes's deductive–synthetic method could be said to aim at a *synthesis* of all knowledge into one ordered system. His analytic method is *analysis* of particular experience designed to discover its causes or to bring the experience under general rules or descriptions.

[7] A compounded name is one which contains several conceptions, as 'bird' contains the conceptions 'feathered', 'bipedal', 'beaked', etc. On Hobbes's showing most names will be compounded and therefore capable of explication.

necessary to introduce a new compounded name to unite conceptions previously separated. (For example, 'endeavour' as introduced by Hobbes in *De Corpore*, XV. 2.) Or it may be necessary, especially when teaching or communicating knowledge, to separate a compounded name into its component conceptions so that the compounded name is more clearly conceived than before. *Human Nature*, IX, has a mass of such compounded names unpacked into their components as part of Hobbes's explication of the passions. In all such cases definitions of names are used.

The full account of definitions is printed below. It is in *De Corpore*, VI. 13–17. In brief a definition is 'a proposition whose predicate [i.e. the set of defining names, usually on the right-hand side, known as the *definiens*] resolves the subject [i.e. the compounded name to be defined, known as the *definiendum*] when it may; and when it may not, it exemplifies [gives an example of] the same' (*De Corpore*, VI. 14). Apart from certain technical requirements which Hobbes sets out, for example that the *definiens* contain more names than the *definiendum* (synonyms are not definitions), the primary requirements of a definition are that it should be clear and agreed.

To be clear and agreed, the *definiens* must 'resolve' the *definiendum* in such a way that the receiver of the definition has conceptions called to mind by the names in the *definiens* which are similar to, but clearer than, the conception he originally had of the compounded name in the *definiendum*. The *definiens* must also convey the same conception to the receiver of the definition as it does to the giver of the definition: a requirement which, we should note, cannot be known to be satisfied until later use shows agreement in the way in which the defined term is being employed.

The Grand System: BODY

An infelicity of the grand system is that the scope of the three parts is not strictly delineated. Large subjects straddle the parts, or can appear in more than one. Thus it is far from clear whether and why Hobbes's chapters on logic, epistemology, and what we would now call general philo-sophy (notably *Human Nature*, I–VI; *Leviathan*, I–V; *De Corpore*, I, II, VI, IX, and X) should fit under BODY ('first philosophy') or MAN. At the other junction in the system there is again no decisive reason for placing accounts of the state of war and of natural laws under MAN rather than COMMONWEALTH, or vice versa.[8]

Nevertheless, what Hobbes regarded as the fundamental principles of his first philosophy, and of all true accounts of things, is unambiguous. The first principles are body, certain related conceptions, and motion. These, or some under-standing of them, are taken for granted in *The Elements of Law*, for example in XI. 4, where Hobbes merely explains that 'spirit' means a natural body that 'worketh not on the senses; but that filleth up the place which the image of a visible body might fill up', and earlier it is assumed that motion is 'all that is real' (II. 7) as the cause of sensation.

The first principles, taken for granted in *The Elements of Law*, profoundly influence the way in which Hobbes expects us to look at the world. They are unpacked in *De Corpore*. Body is 'that, which having no dependence upon our thought, is coincident or coextended with some part of space' (VIII. 1). Note that Hobbes is not saying what body in itself *is* despite his very occasional use of the word 'matter' as if it referred to something distinct from 'body' (see, for example, *De Corpore*, VI. 8). In particular he is not following his friend Pierre Gassendi's revival of ancient atomism as an account of the hidden structures of body. Hobbes is saying that *something* exists independently of our conceptions, and this something (and its parts, if it has any) has the quasi-geometrical properties of 'magnitude' or 'extension' or oc-cupies 'that which some call *real* space' (*De Corpore*, VIII. 4). But he is also making a claim of colossal philosophical, scientific, and religious significance: namely that nothing

---

[8] This ambiguity gives some rationale to the *original* way in which *Human Nature* (then Chs. I–XIII) and *De Corpore Politico* (then Chs. XIV–XXIX) appeared in print. Chs. I–XIII do indeed round off Hobbes's account of general philosophy and, in a loose sense, human nature; Chs. XIX–XXIX are, as a whole, concerned with commonwealth.

other than body exists. The claim is expressed in a passage of unrivalled force and clarity in *Leviathan*, XLVI:

the *Universe*, that is the whole mass of all things that are, is Corporeal, that is to say, Body; and hath the dimensions of Magnitude, namely Length, Breadth and Depth: also every part of Body, is likewise Body, and hath the like dimensions; and consequently every part of the Universe, is Body; and that which is not Body, is no part of the Universe: And because the Universe is All, that which is no part of it is *Nothing*; and consequently *no where*.

Let us call this claim 'one-world realism'. It does not re-affirm the ancient axiom of Epicurus that the universe consists of void space and matter in the form of tiny indestructible particles.[9] But it revives in a quite dramatic way a philosophical view particularly associated with Epicurus, and particularly inimical to the Christian tradition. The view is that one and only one reality exists. The view is flatly contrary to Plato's, Descartes's, and most religious accounts of reality as dualistic: body *and* spirit, perishable flesh *and* immortal soul, this world *and* the next world, material substance *and* immaterial substance. (The last formulation is the one Hobbes most often attacks.) Hobbes's rejection of matter–spirit dualism, and his emphatic affirmation of the one-world realism that lies at the heart of most modern science and was also fundamental to all ancient atomism, re-created a problem which has never since been properly solved. One-world realism is difficult, perhaps impossible, to reconcile with the supposed reality of gods, spirits, and

[9] Epicurean atomism presents a number of difficulties for the mechanistic physics emerging in the 17th century. First, it implied the possibility that mechanical laws could operate across a void; that, for example, gravity could operate without any medium through which or by means of which its pull could be exerted. Secondly, atomism had various materialistic and anti-religious implications with which, incidentally, Hobbes was later saddled, and which Gassendi tried to counter in his *Syntagma Philosophicum* (1658), his revival of atomism, by insisting that God and the soul were outside the scope of atomistic explanations. As will be seen, for Hobbes, God and the soul are one with the universe of 'body'. But since he does not say what body *is*, he can claim that he has not reduced God (as the Epicureans did) to an elusive cluster of atoms *in* the universe, nor given to atoms the eternity and ultimacy reserved to God in the Christian scheme of things. See Howard Jones, *The Epicurean Tradition* (London, 1989), Chs. 7 and 8.

human souls. In short it is incompatible with religion as commonly understood.

But body, that which has magnitude and is ultimately all that exists, has at least one real quality. It moves, and movement is ultimate in the sense that it is incapable of further explanation: 'the causes of universal things . . . have all but one universal cause, which is motion . . . and motion cannot be understood to have any other cause besides motion' (*De Corpore*, VI. 5).

Motion is a continual relinquishing of one place, and acquiring of another . . . I say a continual relinquishing, because no body, how little soever, can totally and at once go out of its former place into another (*De Corpore*, VIII. 10).

And body moves according to certain universal principles. One is the law of inertia, which Hobbes, writing before Newton's definitive codification, struggles to express:

Whatsoever is at rest will always be at rest, unless there be some other body besides it, which by endeavouring to get into its place by motion, suffers it no longer to remain at rest. . . . In like manner, whatsoever is moved will always be moved, except there be some other body beside it . . . (*De Corpore*, VIII. 19, and cf. *Leviathan*, II, second paragraph).

Another principle is the one now usually expressed as 'To every action there is an equal and opposite reaction'. Hobbes tries to grasp this in *De Corpore*, XV. 2, and again in XXV. 2: 'All resistance is endeavour opposite to another endeavour, that is to say, reaction.'

However, not all motion is observable. Some things have parts too tiny to be observed or move too quickly for us to observe the movement. 'Thought is quick.' Therefore a conception is required of movement over a point of time and space which is tending to nothing. Such a conception is Hobbes's 'endeavour'. This is not endeavour in the ordinary sense in which a man may endeavour to eat a mutton chop or read a novel by Proust, but

I define ENDEAVOUR to be *motion made in less space and time than can be given*; that is *less than can be determined or assigned by exposition or number*; that is, *motion made through the length of a point, and in an instant or point of time* (*De Corpore*, XV. 2).

Hobbes adds that the *definiens* does not refer to geometrically defined points, 'for there is no such thing in nature'. It refers to points too small to be actually divided or too numerous to be actually numbered.

Hobbes's conception 'endeavour' is important in his system and in general. Used a little later by Leibniz, it is one of the first hints that led to the development of the differential calculus: 'endeavour' is distance tending to nothing divided by time tending to nothing.[10]

So body, motion, endeavour, and the laws of motion are the fundamental principles of first philosophy. In *De Corpore* Hobbes develops from them accounts of other physical conceptions (movement, speed, etc.). He also introduces certain mathematical and logical conceptions (number, addition, subtraction, identity, and so on) and certain philosophical conceptions (proposition, truth, cause, sensation, etc.). In the case of the philosophical conceptions, much of the material is anticipated in the early chapters of *Human Nature*. The remainder of *Human Nature* is concerned with the second section of Hobbes's grand system, man, and *De Corpore Politico* with the third, commonwealth.

The Grand System: MAN and COMMONWEALTH

The overall structure of Hobbes's argument in *The Elements of Law* is as follows. First there is an analysis of human nature: an account of what the natural human being really is. Secondly, there is an account of the state of war: what life would be like if human beings acted without restraint in accordance with the way they really are. Thirdly, there is an account of the rational precepts we have to adopt if we are to avoid the misery of the state of war. Finally, and mainly in *De Corpore Politico*, there is an account of commonwealth, of the means of enforcing natural laws within a body

[10] See G. C. Robertson, 'Leibniz and Hobbes', *Mind*, 1888.

politic, and of the influences which tend to destroy the body politic and return its members to the war of each against every man.

In *Human Nature*, Vll. 1–2, Hobbes makes a very quick reference[11] to a conventional distinction between 'vital motions' and 'animal motions'. Vital motions are the involuntary movements of the body performed as part of the process of being alive—heartbeats, breathing, bowel movements, and so on. Animal motions are voluntary motions including speaking, eating, and most movements of our limbs. Now, Hobbes explains, sensation is caused by a movement in the object proceeding to us. The movement conveys motion to the nerve-endings at the surface of a sense-organ (fingertips, retina, ear-drum, and so on). This motion is then conveyed as *endeavour*, via the nerves, to the brain 'which motion not stopping there, but proceeding to the heart, of necessity must there either help or hinder that motion which is called vital'. If it assists the vital motions, a feeling of pleasure occurs. If it retards them, a feeling of pain occurs. Pleasure is provocation to move towards that which causes the pleasure; pain is provocation to move away. The internal beginning of such movement is endeavour, and is felt as desire or fear. Such endeavours show themselves as animal movement towards or away from the object, and 'Every man, for his own part, calleth that which pleaseth, and is delightful to himself, GOOD; and that EVIL which displeaseth him' (*Human Nature*, VII. 3).

Hobbes's account is mechanistic and, we might be inclined to say, simplistic. But it is by no means wholly implausible. Consider how well it appears to describe what happens when one accidentally touches a hot stove, or anticipates attack from a dangerous person or animal, or sees a particularly attractive member of the opposite sex, or is offended by a plate of nut cutlets. The last two examples are particularly illuminating because sexual and gastronomic tastes evidently differ, and it is fundamental to Hobbes's thesis that *all* desires and aversions are the desires and aversions

---

[11] See also *Leviathan*, IV, first paragraph, and *De Corpore*, XXV. 1–4.

of individuals, and therefore actually do, or in principle always could, differ. The things which an individual calls 'good' or 'evil' are relative to that individual: 'For these words Good, Evil, and Contemptible, are ever used with relation to the person that useth them: There being nothing simply and absolutely so; nor any common rule of Good and Evil, to be taken from the nature of the objects themselves' (*Leviathan*, VI). (As will be seen in *Human Nature*, XVII, 14, Hobbes does allow for a conception of good and evil known to 'all men by reason'. But that is much later, and not a man's primary conception.) The outcome of all this is to attach personal ethics on to psychology, psychology on to physiology, and physiology, via an account of sense perception, on to the physics of motion.

Other outcomes include two of Hobbes's most characteristic contributions to philosophy. One is his reductionist account of perception. The other is his egoistic or 'selfish' ethics. The core of his account of perception is that 'conceptions or apparitions are nothing really, but motion in some internal substance of the head'. Hobbes is not, I think, saying anything so categorically confusing and implausible as 'conceptions *are experienced as* an internal motion in the experiencer's head'. He is saying that a complete causal explanation of the experiencing of a conception is given by reference to motions and endeavours. Hobbes, as already pointed out, emphatically held that the universe is body and nothing but body, that body moves, and that movement is according to certain laws. Hence the ultimate account we can give of anything, including human thoughts and conceptions, must be in those terms. But those terms do not exclude or make unduly problematical the reality that you and I do not report or experience the motions which are conceptions in us in the same terms which we use in giving an account of them as motions in bodies.

The account of ethics seems to reduce apparently altruistic virtues, including some conspicuously Christian virtues, to egoism or exercises of covert self-interest. Look, for examples, at the definition of pity in *Human Nature*, IX. 10, or the account of charity in IX. 17:

There is yet another passion sometimes called love, but more properly good will or CHARITY. There can be no greater argument to a man of his own power[12] than to find himself able, not only to accomplish his own desires, but also to assist other men in theirs: and this is that conception wherein consisteth charity.

There is much of this sort of thing in Hobbes. It can be taken to say both that men are normally pursuing their own selfish ends whether they appear to be doing so or not, and, more radically, that, because of the mechanistic psychology Hobbes uncovers in *Human Nature*, men and women in fact cannot do other than follow their own devices and desires *whatever* they appear to be doing or allege they are doing. Thus moral teaching either inculcates hypocrisy or asks the psychologically impossible:[13] 'every man's end being some good to himself' (XXIV. 4). A picture of the consequences for society, the rat race, is given in the extended metaphor which concludes Chapter IX. It is a portrait of human nature as it really is according to Hobbes, and as it would show itself if the bonds of society broke or had never been formed. It is also, we may think, a prophetic portrait. Life will be a race which 'we must suppose to have no other goal, nor no other garland, but being foremost, and in it'. It will be a race in which felicity is 'Continually to out-go the next before. . . . And to forsake the course is to die.'

But what would be the result if human beings actually did behave without any fear of restraint and in accordance with the natural passions Hobbes uncovers? The result would be the terrible condition he calls 'the estate of war' or 'the state of nature'. It is described in *Leviathan*, XIII, in a passage whose concluding words are the best known in English philosophy:

In such condition, there is no place for Industry; because the fruit thereof is uncertain: and consequently no Culture of the Earth, no

---

[12] See *Human Nature*, IV. 1, and, more especially, *Leviathan*, X: 'The POWER *of a Man* (to take it Universally) is his present means, to obtain some future apparent Good.'

[13] A brief account of such moral realism in the literature of the Restoration which Hobbes influenced can be found in B. Willey, *The Seventeenth Century Background* (London, 1934).

Navigation, nor use of the commodities that may be imported by Sea; no commodious Building; no Instruments of moving, and removing such things as require much force; no Knowledge of the face of the Earth; no account of Time; no Arts; no Letters; no Society; and which is worst of all, continual fear, and danger of violent death; And the life of man, solitary, poor, nasty, brutish, and short.

This description puts darkness and shadow into the structure already in place in *Human Nature*, XIV: 'the estate of men in this natural liberty is the estate of war'. But why should such natural liberty produce such a horrific result even given the mechanistic psychology Hobbes describes? The answer is given with power and simplicity in a single sentence in Hobbes's Preface to *De Cive*:

I set down for a Principle by experience known to all men, and denied by none, to wit, that the dispositions of men are naturally such, that except they be restrained through fear of some coercive power, every man will distrust and dread each other, and as by natural right he may, so by necessity he will be forced to make use of the strength he hath, towards the preservation of himself.

And the result will be the war of each against every man, which is of all conditions the worst: the most replete with pain and fear of death, and the most damaging to the attainment of any of our wants. 'Reason therefore dictateth to every man for his own good, to seek after peace' (*Human Nature*, XIV. 14). But how is this peace to be sought?

First, by using our reason, 'wherein we can agree' (not our passions wherein we conflict) to identify the conditions that must be observed in order to avoid the estate of war. These conditions are the precepts of reason which Hobbes calls 'natural laws' and which he sets out in *Human Nature*, XV–XVII. (I say *which Hobbes calls* because they do not have the august cosmic or divine ancestry of the old Stoic and Roman Catholic concepts of natural law. They are merely *conditions*, discoverable by the light of natural reason, for avoiding a dreadful human condition—the war of each against all—albeit incidentally confirmed by the law of God, as Hobbes seeks to show in Chapter XVIII.) They 'declare unto us the ways of peace, where the same may be obtained, and of defence where it may not'. They are 'the dictates of natural reason, and also moral laws, because they concern men's manners and conversation one towards another'.

Secondly, peace is to be sought by instituting and defending a civil society or body politic which has power to enforce the rational precepts for the avoidance of war when those precepts are against an individual's natural inclinations:

It remaineth therefore still that consent (by which I understand the concurrence of many men's wills to one action) is not sufficient security for their common peace, without the erection of some common power, by the fear whereof they may be compelled both to keep the peace amongst themselves, or to join their strengths together, against a common enemy. (*Human Nature*, XIX. 6)

The common power, be it monarch or council of men, however constituted, is the sovereign to whom some at least of the natural freedoms that an individual has are yielded by covenant, and for his advantage in avoiding the estate of war.

At this point, *De Corpore Politico*, the last ten chapters of *The Elements of Law*, commences. It contains an account of how a commonwealth is instituted and of the varieties of commonwealth and their possible disadvantages. There is an analysis of the nature of rebellion, family authority, and, in Chapter XXV, of the problem of conflict 'when the commands of God and man shall differ'. These chapters, from our perspective, do not have the universality and comparative timelessness of *Human Nature*. But they are of the most vivid historical interest—a product of Hobbes's foresight of impending strife and his prescription for its avoidance.

God, Religion, and the Castigation of Mr Hobbes

Feared for the power of his arguments and fearful of their consequences for himself, much quoted but more often misquoted and abused, Hobbes was subjected to a stream of refutations[14] in the form of books, pamphlets, and sermons from the early 1650s, when his writings became widely know, until after the end of the century. Apart from the polemical complaint that he wrote scandalously well for someone so obviously in league with the Devil, there were three main charges: that he subverted morality, that he sanctioned tyranny, and that he either was himself an atheist or at the very least facilitated atheistical views.

The charge that Hobbes subverted morality derived from what David Hume was later to characterize as Hobbes's 'selfish hypothesis': that it is psychologically impossible to act voluntarily against one's own interests (hence, whatever the appearances of selfishness or altruism, all actions are in reality motivated by various forms of self-interest) and that the words 'good', 'evil', and the like are used primarily to describe what suits or does not suit the interests of the person using the words. (Hence no thing or action is good or evil in itself, and there is no common measure of good and evil to be taken from the nature of things.) Both premisses of the selfish hypothesis are in *The Elements of Law*, and both reappear, with only a slight softening of the first, in *Leviathan*. Their influence in standard interpretations of Hobbes shows in the many attempts to reconcile morality and self-interest which are evident in the works of Shaftesbury, Mandeville, Butler, Hutcheson, Hume, and other writers on moral philosophy in the first half of the eighteenth century. Their influence still shows in almost all undergraduate essays on Hobbes where the motivation of self-interest is usually seen as the only realistic account of human action. But the full story is not quite as crudely subversive of morality as a short statement of the selfish hypothesis would make it appear.

Hobbes's account of morality starts from the natural character of a human being when he or she is *not* part of a body politic. At that point, and it is the point at which superficial criticism tends to stop, it is indeed the case that

---

[14] S. J. Mintz, *The Hunting of Leviathan* (Cambridge, 1962) gives an account of the criticism directed at Hobbes in the period 1650–1700.

'Every man, for his own part calleth that which pleaseth and is delightful to himself, good; and that evil which displeaseth him' (VII. 3) and nothing is 'absolutely' good, nor is there any common measure of good and evil. But (XVII. 14 and XX. 10) a common measure does exist when a body politic is in being. The common measure is then the law of the body politic—the 'civil law' as Hobbes usually calls it. When the civil law is at variance with what an individual will naturally do according to his or her private self-interest, the institutions which hold sovereign power will enforce the civil law by means of whatever fear and coercion is required. Thus fear makes self-interest accord with civil law. Why will the sovereign power enforce the civil law? Because the desire for such enforcement is the fundamental reason why men ever give up their 'natural liberty' and form a body politic in the first place. And the civil law itself is not arbitrary. It is the universal right reason of the laws of nature—the conditions for avoiding the estate of war—expressed and interpreted (for the avoidance of ambiguity and dispute) through the particular reason of the sovereign power in each body politic.

So in a body politic, the usual but not the 'natural' condition of mankind, there are non-self-referring laws, namely the civil laws. Civil laws are particularizations of natural laws. Natural laws are, as Hobbes points out, moral laws since they regulate conduct between men.

But two difficulties are at once evident. One is what regulates morality in situations too personal and private, or too individual, to be controlled by civil laws. The other, the political difficulty, is what happens when the sovereign power enforces civil laws clearly at variance with laws of nature of the sort identified by Hobbes in Chapters XVI and XVII, or itself acts contrary to the laws of nature.

Several partial answers to the first difficulty are provided by Hobbes himself. In the anecdote preserved by Aubrey (see p. 242) Hobbes gave money to a distressed old man because 'I was in pain to consider the miserable condition of the old man; and now my alms, giving him some relief, doth also ease me.' This is to say that, at least sometimes, acting according to one's own aversion to pain (in a broad sense) or desire for pleasure *includes* avoiding the discomfort of acting badly towards other people. As Hobbes puts it: there is a special pleasure in giving pleasure to others (*Human Nature*, IX. 15). Hobbes does not develop this observation, but it is a pointer to the road later taken by Shaftesbury and Hume: namely that benevolence, or the joy in giving joy to others, is a basic human motive along with, and not ultimately explicable in terms of, self-interest.

Even in the terms of Hobbesian mechanistic psychology, what he says here gives some content to private morality although the content is not exactly what, in other discussions of morality, one might look for or expect. What is more, Hobbes seems to suggest that we can go a little further. People, unlike animals (XIX. 7), have a conception of right and wrong distinct from pleasure and pain. The conception is derived from our rational (not psychological) recognition of the conditions necessary for peaceful living, that is from our recognition of the laws of nature. But if the laws of nature are also, as Hobbes is anxious to show, the laws of God, then the rational conception of right and wrong combines, to enforce private morality, with whatever motivation (e.g. hope of salvation) is provided by belief in God. This looks like an excellent solution to the problem of private morality. But Hobbes is extremely wary of it because of his vivid personal experience replicated by others throughout the Christian era—that unless my belief in God can be so regulated as not to conflict with your belief in God, religion produces more civil strife than private morality.

The political difficulty relating to action by the sovereign power, contrary to the natural laws, leads directly to the general charge that Hobbes defends tyranny. The charge is largely justified. Hobbes gave an account of the state which was in general so conservative that it could be used to defend almost any tyranny providing only the tyranny was efficiently keeping the peace at home and repelling enemies abroad, and so politically latitudinarian that it could justify submission to whatever form of government was securely established.

In its historical context, *The Elements of Law* justified monarchy (for which Hobbes clearly had a strong personal preference), and defended the King's sovereignty before the Civil Wars and his claimed law-making powers. But the defence was simply that monarchy was more stable and reliable than various democratic alternatives. It was not the favoured royalist grounds of the divine right of kings. After the Civil Wars, the same arguments justified submission to Cromwellian rule. In a situation of political uncertainty such a political philosophy clearly made its author suspect. It was as if, in a modern context, Hobbes's account of commonwealth had been used by the Channel Islanders in the Second World War to justify both an initial allegiance to the British Crown *and* co-operation with the invaders who became the *de facto* sovereign power in 1940. (Such a case is explicitly made in *De Corpore Politico*, XXI. 15).

The extent to which one could acquiesce in *de facto* sovereignty ought, if Hobbes is right, to depend upon an assessment of the awfulness of the alternative, the estate of war. As he puts it (*De Corpore Politico*, XXIV. 1) 'The benefit is . . . the peace and preservation of every particular man, than which it is not possible there can be a greater.' And indeed the estate of war (in Somalia, the Sudan, and the former Yugoslavia in the 1990s, for example) could be so terrible than no likely tyranny could be worse. But in other situations the uncertain outcome of human events can make such an assessment look like disloyalty or even treason. What is more, one is left with the uncomfortable feeling that some tyrannies have indeed been worse than the estate of war, and Hobbes makes no allowance for this. He thus attracted hostility from Royalists, who wanted an immovable defence of monarchy, *and* from those who wanted (and in 1688 achieved) constitutional limitations on royal power.

But Hobbes's supposed atheism was worse than his politics. To be charged with atheism in seventeenth-century Europe was an exceedingly serious matter. The epithet 'atheist' was deeply offensive. It provoked hostility, and the charge carried a variety of nasty legal penalties. Hobbes

vigorously denied both that he was one and that his publications carried any such implication. The real truth about
his personal religious beliefs is impossible to establish with
certainty. The implications of what he published cannot,
however, be qualified by their author's private views, and
although one reading (let us call it reading A) might confirm
a knowledgeable but unemphatic and minimal commitment
to Christian beliefs, another (reading B), if it does not entail
outright atheism, certainly raises very serious problems for
conventional religion.

Reading A. In the first place Hobbes's knowledge of the
Bible is evidently magisterial by any modern standard that
could be used. Like an erudite evangelist with a foot in your
door, he can justify almost any position he wants to defend
by elaborate, exhaustive, and apparently sincere citation of
scripture. The process can be seen in *The Elements of Law*,
XVIII, XXV, and XXVI. When one looks further, for an
affirmation of the essentials of Christianity, this also can be
found. There is a God, because effects imply causes till we
come to 'the first cause of all causes' (XI. 2). The fundamental and necessary point of faith required for salvation is
'that Jesus is the Messiah, that is, the Christ' and what
follows from that. But even reading A suggests a certain
minimalism of commitment to religion. Yes, philosophical
conclusions must accord wth *some* version of holy writ, but
perhaps because that is the only way they can be made
acceptable to Hobbes's readers. Yes, there is the fundamental requirement for salvation, but the rest is mere
'superstruction' (XXV) and can be decided by 'such as have
sovereign authority' (XXVI. 11). Yes, a man must act
according to his private conscience (namely his 'opinion of
evidence', VI. 8) when he is free to do so, 'And whatsoever
is done contrary to private conscience, is then a sin, when
the laws have left him to his own liberty, *and never else*'
(XXV. 12; my emphasis). Yes, religion is of enormous
importance in human affairs and is the main subject in the
last third of *De Cive* and the latter half of *Leviathan*. But in
all this Hobbes leaves the impression that religion is of

concern, not so much because it is the true and only path to salvation and eternal life, but because given anything more than a restricted and minimal function within the civil law, religion is a threat to the peace and order of society. Freed from the restraint of civil law and left to conflicting interpretations, it is a way to return the body politic to the estate of war—a way vividly manifested among Hobbes's Christian contemporaries and perhaps not entirely without example in more recent times where religions divide communities and promote strife.

Reading B. Apart from the impression that Hobbes is struggling to defend a species of religion which would be acceptable to sincere believers without threatening the existence of the body politic, it is clear in *Leviathan*, and already evident in *The Elements of Law*, that his fundamental philosophical and scientific position sits very badly indeed with religious belief. His one-world realism (see above, p. xxv) appears to debar us from all conventional talk of God and human immortality. This reading needs explication.

According to Hobbes, we know that there is a God because a 'first cause of all causes' is required (XI. 2), and in *Leviathan*, XII, 'there must be . . . one First Mover; that is a First, and an Eternal cause of all things; which is that which men mean by the name of God'. But although men may *mean* this by the word 'God', Hobbes himself appears elsewhere to destroy the very possibility of an *argument* to a First Mover: 'motion cannot be understood to have any other cause besides motion' (*De Corpore*. VI. 5). This is to lay himself open to the charge of Stratonian atheism—the opinion that the natural world (the only world there is according to Hobbes) contains within itself the reasons why things are as they are. There is no 'external' creative design. What is worse, this 'God' that *means* to men 'a First Mover' is 'incomprehensible':

and consequently all his attributes signify our inability and defect of power to conceive any thing concerning his nature, and not any conception of the same. (*Human Nature*, XI. 2)

And whereas we attribute to God Almighty, seeing, hearing, speaking, knowing, loving, and the like; by which names we understand something in the men to whom we attribute them, we understand nothing by them in the nature of God. (XI. 3)

Moreover, one-world realism makes it impossible for this incomprehensible First Mover to be a supernatural spirit. *Nothing* can be supernatural. So 'spirit' must be understood in a rather surprising way as 'a body natural, but of such subtlety that it worketh not on the senses; but that filleth up the place which the image of a visible body might fill up' (XI. 4). And 'though Scripture acknowledge spirits, yet doth it nowhere say, that they are incorporeal, meaning thereby, without dimensions and quantity' (XI. 5).

This is to imply a most unorthodox theology. For one thing it makes talk of God as creator, immanent in but not a part of the physical universe, all but impossible. For another, it invites pseudo-scientific quests for God as an elusive natural entity. More radically, within the usual terms of reference of one-world realism, not to have any effects on the senses is not to exist. It is difficult for Hobbes to shrug off this implication by the claim in *De Corpore*, I. 8, that philosophy excludes theology. It never had excluded theology in Christian history. A similar difficulty is encountered with immortality. The conceptual scheme within which immortality is usually spoken about refers to the human individual as body *and* soul; the latter, a non-natural and non-bodily entity, having the potentiality to survive corporeal death. But Hobbes's one-world realism, as with God, can only mean that this 'soul' is some sort of insensible, undetectable natural body. The subject is only hinted at in *The Elements of Law* but is thoroughly examined in *Leviathan*, XXXVIII, in a way entirely consonant with *The Elements of Law*. The chapter argues in detail that the scriptures show that 'salvation shall be on earth . . . when God shall reign,' and

That the Soul of man is in its own nature Eternal, and a living Creature independent on the body; or that any mere man is Immortal, otherwise than by the Resurrection in the last day . . . is a doctrine not apparent in Scripture.

It is probably a fair comment[15] that resurrection in the last day was sufficiently distant and conditional to be safely admitted into Hobbes's scheme of things. But the first paragraph of the chapter gives an exceedingly illuminating reason why, apart from consistency with his one-world realism, it matters so much to have hell-fire and heaven more remote from human affairs than Christianity would normally have had them:

The maintenance of Civil Society, depending on Justice; and Justice on the power of Life and Death, and other less Rewards and Punishments residing in them that have the Sovereignty of the Commonwealth; It is impossible a Commonwealth should stand, where any other than the Sovereign, hath a power of giving greater rewards than Life; and of inflicting greater punishments than Death. Now seeing *Eternal life* is a greater reward, than the *life present*; and *Eternal torment* a greater punishment than the *death of Nature*; It is a thing worthy to be well considered, of all men that desire (by obeying Authority) to avoid the calamities of Confusion, and Civil War, what is meant in holy Scripture by *Life Eternal*, and *Torment Eternal*. (*Leviathan*, XXXVIII and cf. *The Elements of Law*, XXVI. 10, the final sentence)

Hobbes's first concern in dicussing immortality is with the ways of civil peace, and the avoidance of the evils of the estate of war here on earth. If immortality threatens peace, then it is our view of immortality that must be adjusted.

So in conclusion, although Hobbes could certainly argue that his works do not entail atheism, it is clear that his primary concern is not to glorify God, or advance his kingdom here on earth, or to make vivid and urgent man's concern with what needs to be done to secure his immortal salvation. Hobbes's primary concern is to give religion a content and legal footing whose *first* objective is the peace of society. In the process he gives religion an interpretation which is both arguably scriptural, contrary to Christian tradition, possibly incredible, and primarily concerned to accord with the one-world realism of the new sciences.

If we ask of Hobbes himself how he viewed religion and

[15] See Willey, *The Seventeenth Century Background*, 98.

belief in God we can get no certain answer. He fended off Mersenne's attempt to administer the sacrament according to the Roman rite in 1647 when it was thought Hobbes was dying. He then accepted it according to the English rite. There is ample evidence that he found the prospect of death particularly abhorrent throughout his long life (see, for example, *The Elements of Law*, XIV. 6). But we cannot know whether he loved life so much that he hated the thought of oblivion, or feared the process of dying, or was apprehensive of an issue from death in the hands of the Lord God. Perhaps more significantly he is prone, particularly in *Leviathan*, to exceptionally waspish comments about religion. A famous one pops up apparently gratuitously in *Leviathan*, VI: '*Fear* of power invisible, feigned by the mind, or imagined from tales publickly allowed, *Religion*; not allowed, *Superstition*', and again, in chapter XXXII of *Leviathan*, Hobbes remarks:

For it is with the mysteries of our Religion, as with wholesome pills for the sick, which swallowed whole, have the virtue to cure; but chewed, are for the most part cast up again without effect.

These and others seem to come from the heart. If they do not, it is hard to see why he should have indulged them at his own risk. It may be that the real Hobbes slips out in *Leviathan*, XLIV, when he speaks of 'Phantasms of the brain, without any real nature of their own, distinct from human fancy: such as are dead mens Ghosts, and Fairies, and other matter of old Wives tales.' It is certain that Hobbes was not a man whose spiritual temperature was on a constant high or which rapidly reached boiling-point in defence of religion. He saw the destruction and strife it caused as a more real thing than the salvation and joy it could remotely promise on the last day. This is not to say Hobbes was an atheist—merely that he was a precursor of the modern secular world that gives priority to human affairs.

In his first publication, the translation of Thucydides, Hobbes speaks of Anaxagoras in his introductory essay in terms which may well have applied better to himself, though with the merciful exception of the last clause: 'Anaxagoras;

whose opinions, being a strain above the apprehension of the vulgar, procured him the estimation of an atheist: which name they bestowed upon all men that thought not as they did of their ridiculous religion, and in the end cost him his life.' Hobbes lived unmolested because he had friends in very high places, because of the extraordinary affection he elicited from all who knew him whatever their opinion of his philosophy, and because the fashion for burning opponents of Christianity was on the wane.

In the end I suspect that Hobbes's approval-rating is directly proportional to the civil violence of the times in which his readers live. Thus in the violence of the seventeenth century James Harrington thought him 'the best writer, at this day, in all the world'. In the complacent peace of the mid-eighteenth century David Hume remarked that 'he is much neglected'. In the *civil* peace of the first half of the twentieth century Bertrand Russell conceded that 'he is still worth refuting'. But yesterday (or was it tomorrow?) I heard a citizen of Afghanistan (or was it Yugoslavia or will it be somewhere else?) saying 'Better peace under a tyranny than bloodshed under a democracy'—and *that* is pure Hobbes.

THE ELEMENTS OF LAW
COMPARED WITH THE CONTENTS
OF HOBBES'S OTHER WORKS

IT has already been emphasized that *Human Nature* and *De Corpore Politico*, the two Parts of *The Elements of Law*, were Hobbes's earliest systematic statements of what, by 1647, he had come to regard as the second and third sections of his Grand System. But the ideas first set out in *The Elements of Law* were not abandoned in later statements. They reappear and are developed or modified in *De Cive* (1642), *Leviathan* (1651), *De Corpore* (1655), and, to a much lesser extent, in *De Homine* (1657).

In broad terms, *Human Nature*, Chapters II to XIII, is reworked as Chapters I to XII of *Leviathan*, and some of the early chapters on general philosophical topics are again taken further in parts of *De Corpore*. *Human Nature*, Chapters XIV to XIX, and most of *De Corpore Politico*, are reworked both in *De Cive*, Chapters I to XIV, and in *Leviathan*, mainly in Chapters XIII to XIX. More specific overlaps between the contents of *The Elements of Law* and Hobbes's other main philosophical works can be seen in the following Table of Contents. Roman numerals refer to chapters, arabic numerals to paragraphs or sections of chapters. But note that Hobbes is not merely recycling the wording of *The Elements of Law* in his later work. He seldom self-quotes. What one finds is similar subject-matter rephrased or developed in the light of historical or intellectual pressures. *De Homine* is not included in the comparison, as its contents (much concerned with optics and physiology) add very little to the psychology Hobbes set out most thoroughly in *Human Nature* seventeen years earlier.

Elements of Law English MS, 1640 English, 1650 (London)	De Cive Latin, 1642 (Paris) English, 1651 (London)	Leviathan English, 1651 (London) Latin, 1668 (Amsterdam)	De Corpore Latin, 1655 (London) English, 1656 (London)
Human Nature			
I Preface, introduction	—	—	— —
II Sense perception		I	XXV. 1–6
III Imagination, dreams		II	XXV. 7–11
IV Thought, experience, expectation of future		III	II
V Words, names, language	—	IV	Scattered paras.
VI Knowledge, evidence, belief, science	—	V	
VII Love, aversion, pain, etc.	—	VI (early part)	XV. 2 XXV. 12
VIII Power, honour, reverence	—	VIII, IX (bits)	
IX The passions		VI (latter part)	—

X Intelligence and madness	—	VIII (bits)	—
XI God and spirits	XV. 14	XI (end of) XXXI (middle of)	—
XII The will etc.	—	VI (middle)	X (related philosophical topics)
XIII Consent, persuasion, etc.	—	Scattered paras.	—
XIV The state of nature etc.	I	XIII	—
XV Transfer of rights, oaths, and convenants	XII (para)	XIV (para)	—
XVI Laws of nature	III	XV	—
XVII More laws of nature	III	XV	—
XVIII Laws of nature as divine laws	IV	No specific chapter	—
XIX The causes of a body politic	V	XVII	—

Continued

	Elements of Law English MS, 1640 English, 1650 (London)	De Cive Latin, 1642 (Paris) English, 1651 (London)	Leviathan English, 1651 (London) Latin, 1668 (Amsterdam)	De Corpore Latin, 1655 (London) English, 1656 (London)
De Corpore Politico				
XX Requisites for a commonwealth	VI	XVIII		—
XXI Three sorts of commonwealth	VII	XIX		—
XXII Lords and servants	VIII	XX		—
XXIII Power within families	IX	XX		—
XXIV Disadvantages of types of government	X, XII (bits)	XIX (bits)		—
XXV Religion and private judgement	XV (bits)	XX (bits) XLIII (bits)		—
XXVI Authority in religion	XVI. 13, 16	—		—
XXVII Causes of rebellion	XII	XVII (bits)		—
XXVIII Duties of sovereign power	XIII	XXIX (bits) XXX		—
XXIX Kinds of laws	XIV	XXVI		—

A NOTE ON THE TEXTS

The Elements of Law

The copy text is, with certain corrections, that established by Ferdinand Tönnies in 1889. Tönnies pointed out in his preface that the early printing history of *The Elements of Law Natural and Politic* resulted in the first editions being unsupervised by Hobbes and containing numerous misreadings. The whole work had been written before May 1640, but was at first only 'published' in the old sense of being circulated among friends in a number of manuscript copies. In 1650 Hobbes was still in Paris at the end of his long sojourn during the Civil War. In that year someone, with or without his authority, but certainly without his supervision, published two separate books from a manuscript of *The Elements of Law*.

The first to be issued, to give its full title, was *Human Nature: or, The Fundamental Elements of Policy. Being a discovery of the faculties, acts, and passions of the soul of man, from their original causes; according to such philosophical principles as are not commonly known or asserted*. This was printed twice in 1650 (at the beginning and end of the year). It contains the first thirteen chapters of Part I of *The Elements of Law*.

The second was *De Corpore Politico: or the Elements of Law, Moral and Politic. With discourses upon moral heads; as Of the law of nature. Of oaths and covenants. Of several kinds of government. With the changes and revolutions of them*. This was issued in the middle of 1650. A second edition (printed twice) appeared in 1652. Both editions contain Chapters XIV to XIX of Part I of *The Elements of Law* together with all ten chapters of Part II (Chapters XX to XXIX of the present volume).

The only other recorded publication of *Human Nature* and *De Corpore Politico* in the seventeenth century was in a composite volume, a so-called 'third edition', published in

1684 under the very confusing title *Tripos in Three Parts*: the 'third part' being one of Hobbes's essays on necessity which had no significant philosophical connection with either of the other alleged parts. This volume, together with the splendid folio volume of Hobbes's moral and political works published in London in 1750, and vol. iv of Sir William Molesworth's edition of *The English Works of Thomas Hobbes* (1840), all treat *Human Nature* and *De Corpore Politico* as related but separate works, and none of them make any reference to the surviving manuscripts.

Such reference was finally made by Tönnies in 1889. It established beyond dispute that the two separately published works are the successive parts of one and the same work, and that the wording in printed editions, contrived to separate them (see the explanatory notes to p. 77 of the present volume), is not in Hobbes's manuscript copies. In preparing his edition Tönnies corrected the previously printed text to accord with his reading of the manuscripts. The result is certainly a vast improvement and all that the philosopher or general reader is ever likely to want, but it is not perfect. It is, for example, almost impossible from his variant readings (not reproduced in the present volume) to reconstruct any one of the manuscripts, or to understand why one reading should be preferred to another. More important, Tönnies has adopted a somewhat high-handed attitude to Hobbes's punctuation. A full examination of these matters must await the volume in the new critical edition of Hobbes's philosophical works being published by Oxford University Press, but in the present text I have taken the opportunity to restore (silently) some of Hobbes's punctuation where his intention is clear in his manuscript. For no apparent reason Tönnies is particularly defective—even with regard to wording—in Hobbes's Epistle Dedicatory. This now reads as Hobbes wrote it. Tönnies also took the decision, rightly I think, to modernize the spelling and modify the use of capital letters. I have followed this policy in all but one of the texts reproduced in this volume. Such modernization removes some of the quaintness and period flavour, but it facilitates attention to what is important without in any way altering the sense, as revised punctuation is liable to do.

For reasons explained in my Scheme of Reference (p. x) I have numbered the chapters in *The Elements of Law* in accordance with Hobbes's *usual* practice: that is to say, in *one* continuous sequence of roman numerals from start to finish ignoring the Parts. I have also gathered Hobbes's analytical Table of Contents for each chapter into one comprehensive table at the front of the text. In practical terms this greatly speeds up skimming the contents for the location of a topic or argument, and it is what Hobbes himself has done or sanctioned in the principal manuscripts.

De Corpore

The English version of *De Corpore* (*Elements of Philosophy, the First Section concerning Body*) was published in 1656 and never again printed in Hobbes's lifetime. It is a work of interest in the history of science and of importance in Hobbes's general philosophy. It was not reprinted in the folio of 1750 and, since Molesworth's edition of 1840, has been virtually unobtainable. The chapters here reproduced are from Molesworth's edition.

Three Lives

Three contemporary accounts of the life of Thomas Hobbes, 'the philosopher of Malmesbury', were published together in Latin in 1681, two years after his death, by 'R.B.' (Richard Blackbourn, a friend of Hobbes's admirer John Aubrey, himself author of the famous collection of biographical notes later published in various forms and generally referred to as *Aubrey's Brief Lives*). The three are: Dr Blackbourn's Latin 'Actual Life' based on notes and memos by Aubrey; a short prose life written in the third person but dictated by Hobbes in 1676 or at the very least written under his personal direction in 1676 at the request of John Aubrey; and a verse life, 'Vita Carmine Expressa', consisting of 188 elegiac couplets written by Hobbes himself in 1672 and first published in Latin in 1679.

In the present volume the 'Prose Life' is newly translated by Mary Lyons from the copy preserved by John Aubrey with one lacuna made good from wording supplied in the 1681 printing. The 'Verse Life' is an anonymous translation published in 1680 in London. I am grateful to the Bodleian Library for facilitating my transcription of their very rare copy, whose spelling and other oddities are reproduced in the present volume. The text has, as far as I can establish, never been printed since 1680. I have not attempted to reproduce Blackbourn's 'Actual Life'. Instead, I have assembled most of the material in Aubrey's 'Brief Life', which was itself the source for Dr Blackbourn. It is necessarily a selection in the present context because Aubrey's 'Life' is not an ordered and finished work, but semi-random notes, memos, and observations from which Aubrey intended to construct a life. The reader who wishes to see almost exactly what Aubrey wrote, and see it in full, should consult *'Brief Lives', chiefly of Contemporaries, set down by John Aubrey, between the years 1669 and 1696*, ed. Andrew Clark (Oxford, 1898), i. 321–95.

SELECT BIBLIOGRAPHY

A LARGE number of books have been written on Hobbes in the past hundred years or so. None substitute for a careful reading of his own magnificent prose and tightly constructed arguments. A few so overload him with analysis and idiosyncratic interpretation that sight of the fiery urgency and power of the original writings is all but lost. But some are immensely helpful.

The best general account of his life and publications is still *Hobbes* by G. Croom Robertson (Edinburgh, 1886) followed by Leslie Stephens' pleasantly readable *Hobbes* (London, 1904). Among recent work an excellent introduction is provided by *Hobbes: Morals and Politics* by D. D. Raphael (London, 1977) and another in *Hobbes* by R. Tuck (Oxford, 1989). The former provides an outstandingly useful assessment of other major books on Hobbes under the heading 'Interpretations'. Four books which survey the whole area, but in greater detail, are: *Hobbes* by Richard Peters (Harmondsworth, 1956), *Hobbes's System of Ideas* by J. W. N. Watkins (London, 1965), *The Anatomy of Leviathan* by F. S. McNeilly (London, 1968), and *Hobbes* by T. Sorel (London, 1986).

An influential account of his political philosophy is *The Political Philosophy of Hobbes* by Leo Strauss (Oxford, 1936). A different but stimulating view of Hobbes can be found in *The Political Theory of Possessive Individualism* by C. B. Macpherson (Oxford, 1962), 1–107.

On Hobbes's scientific work and his philosophy of science the standard and essential work is F. Brandt, *Thomas Hobbes's Mechanical Conception of Nature* (Copenhagen, 1928, and English translation, London, same year).

His philosophy of religion is ill served by publications but *Hobbes Studies*, ed. K. C. Brown (Oxford, 1965) contains an essay by W. B. Glover together with a number of other interesting contributions on a variety of topics and interpretations. A. P. Martinich's *The Two Gods of Leviathan*

(Cambridge, 1992) provides an interesting account of Hobbes as a religious conservative.

Hobbes's own works, as I remarked in my Preface, are, with the exception of *Leviathan*, difficult to find in popular editions. The standard set remains *The English Works of Thomas Hobbes*, ed. Sir William Molesworth (11 vols.; London, 1839) together with his edition of the Latin works (5 vols.; London, 1845).

CHRONOLOGY

1588   Birth of Thomas Hobbes at Malmesbury, Wiltshire, on Good Friday, 5 April: 'His mother fell in labour with him upon the fright of the invasion of the Spaniards'—Aubrey.

1592–1602   Educated to high standards in Greek and Latin at local schools.

1602–8   Magdalen Hall, Oxford. Awarded BA in February 1608. Dislikes Oxford's Aristotelianism.

1608–28   Hobbes employed by Sir William Cavendish (created first Earl of Devonshire 1618) as tutor to his son and later as the first Earl's own secretary.

1610–14[?]   Hobbes's *first* visit to Continent.

1621–6   Conversations with Francis Bacon (forerunner of British empiricist tradition in philosophy).

1628   Hobbes's translation of Thucydides' *History of the Peloponnesian War* published.
Leaves the Cavendish family's employment as a result of economies made after death of first Earl.

1629–30   Hobbes's *second* visit to Continent as travelling tutor to the son of Sir Gervase Clinton. Probably in this period Hobbes became vividly aware both of methods of proof and deduction in Euclidian geometry and of the significance of the question 'What is sensation?'

1630   Re-employed by Cavendish family, with whom he retained connections until the end of his life.
Earliest assignable date for composition of short Latin thesis relating sensation to varieties of movement (latest possible date: 1637).

1634–6   Hobbes's *third* visit to Continent: befriended by Marin Mersenne (clerical patron of new learning in France); via Mersenne offered objections to Descartes's *Meditations* before its publication; friend of Gassendi, the apologist for an Epicurean atomist account of nature; met and admired Galileo and others.

1640   'My little Treatise in English', namely *Elements of Law, Natural and Politic* (containing *Human Nature* and *De Corpore Politico*), written and widely circulated among friends in MS copies.

1640–51   Sojourn in France, to which Hobbes fled at the end of 1640 in anticipation of civil war in England and in apprehension of the dangers to himself inherent in his doctrines as expressed in the 'little Treatise'.

1642   *De Cive* (an expanded version of *De Corpore Politico*) published in Latin in Paris.

1645/6   First conversation with Bramhall, Bishop of Derry, concerning liberty and necessity.

1646–7   Tutor to future Charles II then taking refuge in Paris.

1647   Severe illness: receives sacrament according to rite of Church of England from future Bishop of Durham.

1647–50   *Leviathan* written in France.

1648   Meets Descartes in Paris. Mersenne dies and Hobbes begins to feel unsafe in Paris because of his hostility to Roman Catholicism.

1650   *Human Nature* and *De Corpore Politico* published in print in London, possibly without Hobbes's authority.

1651   *Leviathan* published in London.
            De Cive published in English version in London.

1652   Hobbes returns to England.

1654–63   Controversy with Bishop Bramhall concerning liberty and necessity published and developed.

1655   *De Corpore* published in Latin.

1656   *De Corpore* published in English (do *not* confuse with *De Corpore Politico*, the second Part of *The Elements of Law*).

1656–78   Published controversy with Oxford mathematician Seth Ward and John Wallis concerning Hobbes's claim in Ch. XX of *De Corpore* to have 'squared the circle'. Hobbes manifestly worsted.

1658   *De Homine* published in Latin. (An original work repeating some of the ideas from, but not a version of, *Human Nature*, and including much new material on optics.)

1660   Hobbes befriended by Charles II after Restoration, welcomed at Court and given a pension (sometimes paid).

1666   House of Commons seeks information about 'Mr Hobbes's *Leviathan*' in relation to its bill against atheism. Aubrey reports that about this time 'some of the bishops made a motion to have the good old gentleman burnt for a heretic'.
A Dialogue between a Philosopher and a Student of the Common Laws of England written at instigation of Aubrey. Published 1681.

1668   *Behemoth* (a history of the Civil Wars, 1640–60) written but, at wish of the King, not published.

1673   Translation into English of *Odyssey* published: 'I had nothing else to do.'

1675–9 At Chatsworth and Hardwick Hall in semi-retirement under protection of Cavendish family.

1676   Translation of *Iliad* added to new edition of *Odyssey*.

1679   Thomas Hobbes died at Hardwick Hall on 4 December and was buried at parish church of Ault Hucknall.
Behemoth published.

THE ELEMENTS OF
LAW NATURAL AND
POLITIC

HOBBES'S CHAPTERS AND TABLE OF CONTENTS

PART II. DE CORPORE POLITICO

[Hobbes does not specify contents for *Human Nature* Chapter II, paragraphs 1 and 3, Chapter VII, paragraph 4, or Chapter VIII, paragraph 8.]

TO

TO

THE RIGHT HONOURABLE

WILLIAM, *Earl of Newcastle,**

GOVERNOR *to the* PRINCE HIS HIGHNESS,

one of HIS MAJESTY'S MOST HONOURABLE PRIVY COUNCIL

THE EPISTLE DEDICATORY

My most honoured Lord,

FROM the two principal parts of our nature, Reason and Passion, have proceeded two kinds of learning, mathematical and dogmatical. The former is free from controversies and dispute, because it consisteth in comparing figures and motion only; in which things truth and the interest of men, oppose not each other. But in the later there is nothing not disputable, because it compareth men, and meddleth with their right and profit; in which as oft as reason is against a man, so oft will a man be against reason. And from hence it comes, that they who have written of justice and policy in general do all invade each other, and themselves, with contradiction. To reduce this doctrine to the rules and infallibility of reason, there is no way, but first, to put such principles down for a foundation, as passion not mistrusting may not seek to displace. And afterward to build thereon the truth of cases in the law of nature (which hitherto have been built in the air) by degrees, till the whole be inexpugnable. Now (my Lord) the principles fit for such a foundation, are those which I have heretofore acquainted your Lordship withal in private discourse; and which, by your command I have here put into method. To examine cases thereby, between sovereign and sovereign, or between sovereign and subject, I leave to them, that shall find leisure, and encouragement thereto. For my part, I present this to your Lordship, for the true, and only foundation of such science. For the style, it is therefore the worse, because whilst I was writing I consulted more with logic, than with rhetoric. But for the doctrine, it is not slightly proved; and the conclusions thereof, are of such nature, as for want of them, government and peace have been nothing else, to this day, but mutual fear. And it would be an incomparable benefit to commonwealth, that every man held the opinions concerning law and policy, here delivered. The ambition therefore of this book, in seeking by your Lordship's countenance, to insinuate itself with those whom the matter it containeth most nearly concerneth, is to be excused. For myself, I desire no greater honour, than I enjoy already in your Lordship's known favour; unless it be, that you would be pleased in continuance thereof, to give me more exercise in your commands; which, as I am bound by your many great favours, I shall obey, being

My most honoured Lord
Your Lordship's most humble and obliged Servant
THO HOBBES

May 9, 1640

PART I
HUMAN NATURE

CHAPTER I

THE GENERAL DIVISION OF MAN'S NATURAL FACULTIES

1. THE true and perspicuous explication of the Elements of Laws, Natural and Politic, which is my present scope, dependeth upon the knowledge of what is human nature, what is a body politic, and what it is we call a law. Concerning which points, as the writings of men from antiquity downward have still increased, so also have the doubts and controversies concerning the same, and seeing that true knowledge begetteth not doubt, nor controversy, but knowledge; it is manifest from the present controversies, that they which have heretofore written thereof, have not well understood their own subject.

2. Harm I can do none though I err no less than they. For I shall leave men but as they are in doubt and dispute. But intending not to take any principle upon trust, but only to put men in mind what they know already, or may know by their own experience, I hope to err the less; and when I do, it must proceed from too hasty concluding, which I will endeavour as much as I can to avoid.

3. On the other side, if reasoning aright I win not consent (which may very easily happen) from them that being confident of their own knowledge weigh not what is said, the fault is not mine but theirs. For as it is my part to show my reasons, so it is theirs to bring attention.

4. Man's nature is the sum of his natural faculties and powers, as the faculties of nutrition, motion, generation, sense, reason, &c. For these powers we do unanimously call natural, and are contained in the definition* of man, under these words, animal and rational.

5. According to the two principal parts of man, I divide his faculties into two sorts, faculties of the body, and faculties of the mind.

6. Since the minute and distinct anatomy of the powers of the body is nothing necessary to the present purpose, I will only sum them up into these three heads, power nutritive, power motive, and power generative.

7. Of the powers of the mind there be two sorts, cognitive or imaginative or conceptive; and motive. And first of the cognitive.

8. For the understanding of what I mean by the power cognitive, we must remember and acknowledge that there be in our minds continually certain images or conceptions* of the things without us, insomuch that if a man could be alive, and all the rest of the world annihilated, he should nevertheless retain the image thereof, and of all those things which he had before seen and perceived in it; every man by his own experience knowing that the absence or destruction of things once imagined, doth not cause the absence or destruction of the imagination itself. This imagery and re-presentations of the qualities of things without us is that we call our cognition, imagination, ideas, notice, conception, or knowledge of them. And the faculty, or power, by which we are capable of such knowledge, is that I here call power cognitive, or conceptive, the power of knowing or conceiving.

CHAPTER II
THE CAUSE OF SENSE

1. HAVING declared what I mean by the word conception, and other words equivalent thereunto, I come to the con-ceptions themselves, to show their difference, their causes, and the manner of their production as far as is necessary for this place.

2. Originally all conceptions proceed from the actions of the thing itself, whereof it is the conception. Now when

the action is present, the conception it produceth is called SENSE, and the thing by whose action the same is produced is called the OBJECT of sense.

3. By our several organs we have several conceptions of several qualities in the objects; for by sight we have a conception or image composed of colour or figure, which is all the notice and knowledge the object imparteth to us of its nature by the eye. By hearing we have a conception called sound, which is all the knowledge we have of the quality of the object from the ear. And so the rest of the senses also are conceptions of several qualities, or natures of their objects.

4. Because the image in vision consisting in colour and shape is the knowledge we have of the qualities of the object of that sense; it is no hard matter for a man to fall into this opinion, that the same colour and shape are the very qualities themselves; and for the same cause, that sound and noise are the qualities of the bell, or of the air. And this opinion hath been so long received, that the contrary must needs appear a great paradox; and yet the introduction of species visible and intelligible* (which is necessary for the maintenance of that opinion) passing to and fro from the object, is worse than any paradox, as being a plain impossibility. I shall therefore endeavour to make plain these four points:*

(1) That the subject wherein colour and image are inherent, is not the object or thing seen.

(2) That that is nothing without us really which we call an image or colour.

(3) That the said image or colour is but an apparition unto us of that motion, agitation, or alteration, which the object worketh in the brain or spirits, or some internal substance of the head.

(4) That as in conception by vision, so also in the conceptions that arise from other senses, the subject of their inherence is not the object, but the sentient.

5. Every man hath so much experience as to have seen the sun and other visible objects by reflection in the water

and in glasses, and this alone is sufficient for this conclusion: that colour and image may be there where the thing seen is not. But because it may be said that notwithstanding the image in the water be not in the object, but a thing merely phantastical, yet there may be colour really in the thing itself; I will urge further this experience: that divers times men see directly the same object double, as two candles for one, which may happen by distemper, or otherwise without distemper if a man will, the organs being either in their right temper, or equally distempered. The colours and figures in two such images of the same thing cannot be inherent both therein, because the thing seen cannot be in two places: one of these images thereof is not inherent in the object. But seeing the organs of sight are then in equal temper or equal distemper, the one of them is no more inherent than the other, and consequently neither of them both are in the object; which is the first proposition mentioned in the precedent section.

6. Secondly, that the image of any thing seen by reflection in glass or water or the like, is not any thing in or behind the glass, or in or under the water, every man may prove to himself; which is the second proposition.

7. For the third, we are to consider first, that upon every great agitation or concussion of the brain, as it happeneth from a stroke, especially if the stroke be upon the eye, whereby the optic nerve suffereth any great violence, there appeareth before the eyes a certain light, which light is nothing without, but an apparition only, all that is real being the concussion or motion of the parts of that nerve.* From which experience we may conclude, that apparition of light without, is really nothing but motion within. If therefore from lucid bodies there can be derived motion, so as to affect the optic nerve in such manner as is proper thereunto, there will follow an image of light somewhere in that line by which the motion was last derived unto the eye; that is to say, in the object, if we look directly on it, and in the glass or water, when we look upon it in the line of reflection, which in effect is the third proposition, namely, That image and colour is but an apparition unto us of that motion,

agitation, or alteration, which the object worketh in the brain, or spirits, or some internal substance in the head.

8. But that from all lucid, shining and illuminated bodies, there is a motion produced to the eye, and, through the eye, to the optic nerve, and so into the brain, by which that apparition of light or colour is effected, is not hard to prove. And first, it is evident that the fire, the only lucid body here on earth, worketh by motion equally every way; insomuch as the motion thereof stopped or inclosed, it is presently extinguished, and no more fire. And farther, that that motion, whereby the fire worketh, is dilatation, and contraction of itself alternately, commonly called scintillation or glowing, is manifest also by experience. From such motion in the fire must needs arise a rejection or casting from itself of that part of the medium which is contiguous to it, whereby that part also rejecteth the next, and so successively one part beateth back the other to the very eye; and in the same manner the exterior part of the eye (the laws of refraction still observed) presseth the interior. Now the interior coat of the eye is nothing else but a piece of the optic nerve, and therefore the motion is still continued thereby into the brain, and by resistance or reaction of the brain, is also a rebound in the optic nerve again, which we not conceiving as motion or rebound from within, think it is without, and call it light; as hath been already shewed by the experience of a stroke. We have no reason to doubt, that the fountain of light, the sun, worketh any other wise than the fire, at least in this matter, and thus all vision hath its original from such motion as is here described. For where there is no light, there is no sight; and therefore colour also must be the same thing with light, as being the effect of lucid bodies: their difference being only this, that when the light cometh directly from the fountain to the eye, or indirectly by reflection from clean and polite bodies, and such as have no particular motion internal to alter it, we call it light. But when it cometh to the eyes by reflection from uneven, rough, and coarse bodies, or such as are affected with internal motion of their own, that may alter it, then we call it colour; colour and light differing only in this, that the one is pure, the other a

perturbed light. By that which hath been said, not only the truth of the third proposition, but also the whole manner of producing light and colour, is apparent.

9. As colour is not inherent in the object, but an effect thereof upon us, caused by such motion in the object, as hath been described: so neither is sound in the thing we hear, but in ourselves. One manifest sign thereof is: that as a man may see, so also he may hear double or treble, by multiplication of echoes, which echoes are sounds as well as the original; and not being in one and the same place, cannot be inherent in the body that maketh them. Nothing can make any thing in itself: the clapper hath not sound in it, but motion, and maketh motion in the internal parts of the bell so the bell hath motion, and not sound. That imparteth motion to the air; and the air hath motion, but not sound. The air imparteth motion by the ear and nerves to the brain; and the brain hath motion* but not sound. From the brain it reboundeth back into the nerves outward, and thence it becometh an apparition without, which we call sound. And to proceed to the rest of the senses, it is apparent enough, that the smell and taste of the same thing, are not the same to every man, and therefore are not in the thing smelt or tasted, but in the men. So likewise the heat we feel from the fire is manifestly in us, and is quite different from the heat that is in the fire. For our heat is pleasure or pain, according as it is extreme or moderate; but in the coal there is no such thing. By this the fourth and last of the propositions is proved (viz.) That as in conception by vision, so also in the conceptions that arise from other senses, the subject of their inherence is not the object, but the sentient.

10. And from thence also it followeth, that whatsoever accidents or qualities our senses make us think there be in the world, they are not there, but are seemings and apparitions only. The things that really are in the world without us, are those motions by which these seemings are caused. And this is the great deception of sense, which also is by sense to be corrected. For as sense telleth me, when I see directly, that the colour seemeth to be in the object; so also sense telleth me, when I see by reflection, that colour is not in the object.

CHAPTER III

OF IMAGINATION AND THE KINDS THEREOF

1. As standing water put into motion by the stroke of a stone, or blast of wind, doth not presently give over moving as soon as the wind ceaseth, or the stone settleth: so neither doth the effect cease which the object hath wrought upon the brain, so soon as ever by turning aside of the organ the object ceaseth to work; that is to say, though the sense be past, the image or conception remaineth; but more obscurely while we are awake, because some object or other continually plieth and soliciteth our eyes, and ears, keeping the mind in a stronger motion, whereby the weaker doth not easily appear. And this obscure conception is that we call PHANTASY or IMAGINATION: imagination being (to define it) conception remaining, and by little and little decaying from and after the act of sense.

2. But when present sense is not, as in SLEEP, there the images remaining after sense (when there be any) as in dreams, are not obscure, but strong and clear, as in sense itself. The reason is, because that which obscured and made the conceptions weak, namely sense, and present operation of the objects, is removed. For sleep is the privation of the act of sense, (the power remaining) and dreams are the imaginations of them that sleep.

3. The causes of DREAMS* (if they be natural) are the actions or violence of the inward parts of a man upon his brain, by which the passages of sense, by sleep benumbed, are restored to their motion. The signs by which this appeareth to be so, are the differences of dreams proceeding from the different accidents of man's body. Old men being commonly less healthful and less free from inward pains, are thereby more subject to dreams, especially such dreams as be painful: as dreams of lust, or dreams of anger, according as the heart, or other parts within, work more or less upon the brain, by more or less heat. So also the descent of different sorts of phlegm maketh one to dream of different tastes of meats or drinks. And I believe there is a reciprocation of motion from the brain to the vital parts, and

back from the vital parts to the brain; whereby not only imagination begetteth motion in those parts; but also motion in those parts begetteth imagination like to that by which it was begotten.* If this be true, and that sad imaginations nourish the spleen, then we see also a cause, why a strong spleen reciprocally causeth fearful dreams. And why the effects of lasciviousness may in a dream produce the image of some person that hath caused them. If it were well observed, whether the image of the person in a dream be as obedient to the accidental heat of him that dreameth, as waking his heat is to the person, and if so, then is such motion reciprocal. Another sign that dreams are caused by the action of the inward parts, is the disorder and casual consequence of one conception or image to another: for when we are waking, the antecedent thought or conception introduceth, and is cause of the consequent, as the water followeth a man's finger upon a dry and level table. But in dreams there is commonly no coherence (and when there is, it is by chance), which must proceed from this, that the brain in dreams is not restored to its motion in every part alike; whereby it cometh to pass, that our thoughts appear like the stars between the flying clouds, not in the order which a man would choose to observe them in, but as the uncertain flight of broken clouds permit.

4. As when the water, or any liquid thing moved at once by divers movements, receiveth one motion compounded of them all; so also the brain or spirits therein, having been stirred by divers objects, composeth an imagination of divers conceptions that appeared singly to the sense. As for example, the sense sheweth us at one time the figure of a mountain, and at another time the colour of gold; but the imagination afterwards hath them both at once in a golden mountain. From the same cause it is, there appear unto us castles in the air, chimeras, and other monsters which are not in *rerum natura*,* but have been conceived by the sense in pieces at several times. And this composition is that which we commonly call FICTION of the mind.

5. There is yet another kind of imagination, which for clearness contendeth with sense, as well as a dream; and

that is, when the action of sense hath been long or vehement: and the experience thereof is more frequent in the
sense of seeing, than the rest. An example whereof is, the
image remaining before the eye after a steadfast looking
upon the sun. Also, those little images that appear before
the eyes in the dark (whereof I think every man hath
experience, but they most of all, that are timorous or
superstitious) are examples of the same. And these, for
distinction sake, may be called PHANTASMS.

6. By the senses (which are numbered according to the
organs to be five) we take notice (as hath been said already)
of the objects without us; and that notice is our conception
thereof: but we take notice also some way or other of our
conceptions. For when the conception of the same thing
cometh again, we take notice that it is again; that is to say,
that we have had the same conception before; which is as
much as to imagine a thing past; which is impossible to
sense, which is only of things present. This therefore may be
accounted a sixth sense, but internal, not external, as the
rest, and is commonly called REMEMBRANCE.

7. For the manner by which we take notice of a conception past, we are to remember, that in the definition of
imagination, it is said to be a conception by little and little
decaying, or growing more obscure. An obscure conception
is that which representeth the whole object together, but
none of the smaller parts by themselves; and as more or
fewer parts be represented, so is the conception or representation said to be more or less clear. Seeing then the
conception, which when it was first produced by sense, was
clear, and represented the parts of the object distinctly; and
when it cometh again is obscure, we find missing somewhat
that we expected; by which we judge it past and decayed.
For example, a man that is present in a foreign city, seeth
not only whole streets, but can also distinguish particular
houses, and parts of houses; departed thence, he cannot
distinguish them so particularly in his mind as he did, some
house or turning escaping him; yet is this to remember the
city; when afterwards there escapeth him more particulars,
this is also to remember, but not so well. In process of time,

the image of the city returneth, but as of a mass of building only, which is almost to have forgotten it. Seeing then remembrance is more or less, as we find more or less obscurity, why may not we well think remembrance to be nothing else but the missing of parts, which every man expecteth should succeed after they have a conception of the whole? To see at great distance of place, and to remember at great distance of time, is to have like conceptions of the thing: for there wanteth distinction of parts in both; the one conception being weak by operation at distance, the other by decay.*

8. And from this that hath been said, there followeth, that a man can never know he dreameth; he may dream he doubteth, whether it be a DREAM or no: but the clearness of the imagination representeth every thing with as many parts as doth sense itself, and consequently, he can take notice of nothing but as present; whereas to think he dreameth, is to think those his conceptions past, that is to say, obscurer than they were in the sense: so that he must think them both as clear, and not as clear as sense; which is impossible.

9. From the same ground it proceedeth, that men wonder not in their dreams at places and persons, as they would do waking: for waking, a man would think it strange to be in a place wherein he never was before, and remember nothing of how he came there. But in a dream, there cometh little of that kind into consideration. The clearness of conception in a dream, taketh away distrust, unless the strangeness be excessive, as to think himself fallen from on high without hurt, and then most commonly he awaketh.

10. Nor is it impossible for a man to be so far deceived, as when his dream is past, to think it real: for if he dream of such things as are ordinarily in his mind, and in such order as he useth to do waking, and withal that he laid him down to sleep in the place where he findeth himself when he awaketh (all which may happen) I know no κριτήριον* or mark by which he can discern whether it were a dream or not, and do therefore the less wonder to hear a man sometimes to tell his dream for a truth, or to take it for a vision.

CHAPTER IV

OF THE SEVERAL KINDS OF DISCURSION OF THE MIND

1. THE succession of conceptions in the mind, their series or consequence of one after another, may be casual and incoherent, as in dreams for the most part; and it may be orderly, as when the former thought introduceth the latter; and this is discourse of the mind. But because the word discourse is commonly taken for the coherence and consequence of words, I will (to avoid equivocation) call it DISCURSION.*

2. The cause of the coherence or consequence of one conception to another, is their first coherence, or consequence* at that time when they were produced by sense. As for example: from St. Andrew the mind runneth to St. Peter, because their names are read together; from St. Peter to a stone, for the same cause; from stone to foundation, because we see them together; and for the same cause, from foundation to church, from church to people, and from people to tumult. And according to this example, the mind may run almost from any thing to any thing. But as to the sense the conception of cause and effect succeed one another; so may they after sense in the imagination. And for the most part they do so. The cause whereof is the appetite of them, who, having a conception of the end, have next unto it a conception of the next means to that end. As when a man, from the thought of honour to which he hath an appetite, cometh to the thought of wisdom, which is the next means thereto; and from thence to the thought of study, which is the next means to wisdom, etc.

3. To omit that kind of discursion by which we proceed from any thing to any thing, there are of the other kind divers sorts. As first in the senses: there are certain coherences of conceptions, which we may call RANGING. Examples whereof are: a man's casting his eye upon the ground, to look about for some small thing lost; the hounds casting about at a fault in hunting; and the ranging of spaniels. And herein we take a beginning arbitrarily.

4. Another sort of discursion is, when the appetite giveth a man his beginning, as in the example before adduced: where honour, to which a man hath appetite, maketh him to think upon the next means of attaining it, and that again of the next, &c. And this the Latins call *sagacitas*, SAGACITY, and we may call it hunting or tracing, as dogs trace the beast by the smell, and men hunt them by their footsteps; or as men hunt after riches, place, or knowledge.

5. There is yet another kind of discursion beginning with appetite to recover something lost, proceeding from the present backward, from the thought of the place where we miss it, to the thought of the place from whence we came last; and from the thought of that, to the thought of a place before, till we have in our mind some place, wherein we had the thing we miss: and this is called REMINISCENCE.

6. The remembrance of the succession of one thing to another, that is, of what was antecedent, and what consequent, and what concomitant, is called an EXPERIMENT; whether the same be made by us voluntarily, as when a man putteth any thing into the fire, to see what effect the fire will produce upon it; or not made by us, as when we remember a fair morning after a red evening. To have had many experiments, is that we call EXPERIENCE, which is nothing else but remembrance of what antecedents have been followed with what consequents.

7.* No man can have in his mind a conception of the future, for the future is not yet. But of our conceptions of the past, we make a future; or rather, call past, future relatively. Thus after a man hath been accustomed to see like antecedents followed by like consequents, whensoever he seeth the like come to pass to any thing he had seen before, he looks there should follow it the same that followed then. As for example: because a man hath often seen offences followed by punishment, when he seeth an offence in present, he thinketh punishment to be consequent thereto. But consequent unto that which is present, men call future. And thus we make remembrance to be prevision or conjecture of things to come, or EXPECTATION or PRESUMPTION of the future.

8. In the same manner, if a man seeth in present that which he hath seen before, he thinks that that which was antecedent to what he saw before, is also antecedent to that he presently seeth. As for example: he that hath seen the ashes remain after the fire, and now again seeth ashes, concludeth again there hath been fire. And this is called CONJECTURE of the past, or presumption of fact.

9. When a man hath so often observed like antecedents to be followed by like consequents, that whensoever he seeth the antecedent, he looketh again for the consequent; or when he seeth the consequent, he maketh account there hath been the like antecedent; then he calleth both the antecedent and the consequent, SIGNS one of another, as clouds are a sign of rain to come, and rain of clouds past.

10. This taking of signs from experience, is that wherein men do ordinarily think, the difference stands between man and man in wisdom, by which they commonly understand a man's whole ability or power cognitive. But this is an error; for these signs are but conjectural; and according as they have often or seldom failed, so their assurance is more or less; but never full and evident; for though a man hath always seen the day and night to follow one another hitherto; yet can he not thence conclude they shall do so, or that they have done so eternally. Experience concludeth nothing universally. If the signs hit twenty times for once missing, a man may lay a wager of twenty to one of the event; but may not conclude it for a truth. But by this it is plain, that they shall conjecture best, that have most experience: because they have most signs to conjecture by; which is the reason that old men are more prudent, that is, conjecture better, *cæteris paribus*,* than young. For, being older, they remember more; and experience is but remembrance. And men of quick imagination, *cæteris paribus*, are more prudent than those whose imaginations are slow: for they observe more in less time. And PRUDENCE is nothing else but conjecture from experience, or taking signs of experience warily, that is, that the experiments from which one taketh such signs be all remembered; for else the cases are not alike, that seem so.

11. As in conjectural things concerning past and future, it

is prudence to conclude from experience, what is likely to come to pass, or to have passed already; so is it an error to conclude from it, that is so or so called. That is to say, we cannot from experience conclude, that any thing is to be called just or unjust, true or false, nor any proposition universal whatsoever, except it be from remembrance of the use of names imposed arbitrarily by men. For example: to have heard a sentence given* (in the like case the like sentence a thousand times) is not enough to conclude that the sentence is just (though most men have no other means to conclude by); but it is necessary, for the drawing of such conclusion, to trace and find out, by many experiences, what men do mean by calling things just and unjust, and the like. Farther, there is another caveat to be taken in concluding by experience, from the tenth section of the second chapter; that is, that we conclude not such things to be without, that are within us.

CHAPTER V

OF NAMES, REASONING, AND DISCOURSE OF THE TONGUE

1. SEEING the succession of conceptions in the mind are caused (as hath been said before) by the succession they had one to another when they were produced by the senses; and that there is no conception that hath not been produced immediately before or after innumerable others, by the innumerable acts of sense; it must needs follow, that one conception followeth not another, according to our election, and the need we have of them, but as it chanceth us to hear or see such things as shall bring them to our mind. The experience we have hereof, is in such brute beasts, which, having the providence to hide the remains and superfluity of their meat, do nevertheless want the remembrance of the place where they hid it, and thereby make no benefit thereof

in their hunger. But man, who in this point beginneth to advance himself above the nature of beasts, hath observed and remembered the cause of this defect, and to amend the same, hath imagined and devised to set up a visible or other sensible mark, the which when he seeth again, may bring to his mind the thought he had when he set it up. A MARK therefore is a sensible object which a man erecteth voluntarily to himself, to the end to remember thereby somewhat past, when the same is objected to his sense again. As men that have passed by a rock at sea, set up some mark, whereby to remember their former danger, and avoid it.

2. In the number of these marks, are those human voices (which we call the names or appellations of things) sensible to the ear, by which we recall into our mind some conceptions of the things to which we give those names or appellations. As the appellation white bringeth to remembrance the quality of such objects as produce that colour or conception in us. A NAME or APPELLATION* therefore is the voice of a man, arbitrarily imposed, for a mark to bring to his mind some conception concerning the thing on which it is imposed.

3. Things named, are either the objects themselves, as man; or the conception itself that we have of man, as shape or motion; or some privation, which is when we conceive that there is something which we conceive, not in him. As when we conceive he is not just, not finite, we give him the name of unjust and infinite, which signify privation or defect either in the thing named, or in us that give the name. And to the privations themselves we give the names injustice and infiniteness. So that here be two sorts of names: one of things, in which we conceive something, or of the conceptions themselves, which are called POSITIVE; the other of things wherein we conceive privation or defect, and those names are called PRIVATIVE.

4. By the advantage of names it is that we are capable of science, which beasts, for want of them, are not; nor man, without the use of them: for as a beast misseth not one or two out of her many young ones, for want of those names of order, one, two, three, &c., which we call number; so

neither would a man, without repeating orally, or mentally, the words of number, know how many pieces of money or other things lie before him.

5. Seeing there be many conceptions of one and the same thing, and for every several conception we give it a several name; it followeth that for one and the same thing, we have many names or attributes; as to the same man we give the appellations of just, valiant, &c., for divers virtues, and of strong, comely, &c., for divers qualities of the body. And again, because from divers things we receive like conceptions, many things must needs have the same appellation. As to all things we see, we give the same name of visible; and to all things we see moved, we give the appellation of moveable. And those names we give to many, are called UNIVERSAL to them all; as the name man to every particular of mankind: such appellations as we give to one only thing, are called individual, or SINGULAR; as Socrates, and other proper names; or, by circumlocution, as: he that writ the Iliad, for Homer.

6. This universality of one name to many things, hath been the cause that men think that the things themselves are universal. And do seriously contend, that besides Peter and John, and all the rest of the men that are, have been, or shall be in the world, there is yet somewhat else that we call man, (viz.) man in general, deceiving themselves by taking the universal, or general appellation, for the thing it signifieth.* For if one should desire the painter to make him the picture of a man, which is as much as to say, of a man in general; he meaneth no more, but that the painter shall choose what man he pleaseth to draw, which must needs be some of them that are, have been, or may be, none of which are universal. But when he would have him to draw the picture of the king, or any particular person, he limiteth the painter to that one person himself chooseth. It is plain therefore, that there is nothing universal but names; which are therefore also called indefinite; because we limit them not ourselves, but leave them to be applied by the hearer: whereas a singular name is limited or restrained to one of the many things it signifieth; as when we say, this man,

pointing to him, or giving him his proper name, or by some such other way.

7. The appellations that be universal, and common to many things, are not always given to all the particulars, (as they ought to be) for like conceptions and considerations in them all; which is the cause that many of them are not of constant signification, but bring into our minds other thoughts than those for which they were ordained. And these are called EQUIVOCAL.* As for example, the word faith sometimes signifieth the same with belief; sometimes it signifieth particularly that belief which maketh a Christian; and sometimes it signifieth the keeping of a promise. Also all metaphors are (by profession) equivocal. And there is scarce any word that is not made equivocal by divers contextures of speech, or by diversity of pronunciation and gesture.

8. This equivocation of names maketh it difficult to recover those conceptions for which the name was ordained; and that not only in the language of other men, wherein we are to consider the drift, and occasion, and contexture of the speech, as well as the words themselves; but also in our own discourse, which being derived from the custom and common use of speech, representeth not unto us our own conceptions. It is therefore a great ability in a man, out of the words, contexture, and other circumstances of language, to deliver himself from equivocation, and to find out the true meaning of what is said: and this is it we call UNDERSTANDING.*

9. Of two appellations, by the help of this little verb IS, or something equivalent, we make an AFFIRMATION or NEGATION, either of which in the Schools we call also a proposition, and consisteth of two appellations joined together by the said verb is: as for example, this is a proposition: man is a living creature; or this: man is not righteous; whereof the former is called an affirmation, because the appellation living creature is positive; the latter a negation, because not righteous is privative.

10. In every proposition, be it affirmative or negative, the latter appellation either comprehendeth the former, as in

this proposition, charity is a virtue, the name of virtue comprehendeth the name of charity (and many other virtues besides), and then is the proposition said to be TRUE or TRUTH: for, truth, and a true proposition, is all one. Or else the latter appellation comprehendeth not the former; as in this proposition, every man is just, the name of *just* comprehendeth not every man; for *unjust* is the name of the far greater part of men. And then the proposition is said to be FALSE, or falsity: falsity and a false proposition being the same thing.

11. In what manner of two propositions, whether both affirmative, or one affirmative, the other negative, is made a SYLLOGISM,* I forbear to write. All this that hath been said of names or propositions, though necessary, is but dry discourse: and this place is not for the whole art of logic, which if I enter further into,* I ought to pursue: besides, it is not needful; for there be few men which have not so much natural logic, as thereby to discern well enough, whether any conclusion I shall hereafter make, in this discourse, be well or ill collected: only thus much I say in this place, that making of syllogisms is that we call RATIOCINATION or reasoning.

12. Now when a man reasoneth from principles that are found indubitable by experience, all deceptions of sense and equivocation of words avoided, the conclusion he maketh is said to be according to right reason; but when from his conclusion a man may, by good ratiocination, derive that which is contradictory to any evident truth whatsoever, then is he said to have concluded against reason: and such a conclusion is called absurdity.

13. As the invention of names hath been necessary for the drawing of men out of ignorance, by calling to their remembrance the necessary coherence of one conception to another; so also hath it on the other side precipitated men into error: insomuch, that whereas by the benefit of words and ratiocination they exceed brute beasts in knowledge; by the incommodities that accompany the same they exceed them also in errors. For true and false are things not incident to beasts, because they adhere to propositions and language;

nor have they ratiocination, whereby to multiply one untruth by another: as men have.

14. It is the nature almost of every corporeal thing, being often moved in one and the same manner, to receive continually a greater and greater easiness and aptitude to the same motion; insomuch as in time the same becometh so habitual, that to beget it, there needs no more than to begin it. The passions of man, as they are the beginning of all his voluntary motions,* so are they the beginning of speech, which is the motion of his tongue. And men desiring to shew others the knowledge, opinions, conceptions, and passions which are within themselves, and to that end having invented language, have by that means transferred all that discursion of their mind mentioned in the former chapter, by the motion of their tongues, into discourse of words; and *ratio*, now, is but *oratio*,* for the most part, wherein custom hath so great a power, that the mind suggesteth only the first word, the rest follow habitually, and are not followed by the mind. As it is with beggars, when they say their *paternoster*, putting together such words, and in such manner, as in their education they have learned from their nurses, from their companions, or from their teachers, having no images or conceptions in their minds answering to the words they speak. And as they have learned themselves, so they teach posterity. Now, if we consider the power of those deceptions of sense, mentioned chapter II section 10, and also how unconstantly names have been settled, and how subject they are to equivocation, and how diversified by passion, (scarce two men agreeing what is to be called good, and what evil; what liberality, what prodigality; what valour, what temerity) and how subject men are to paralogism* or fallacy in reasoning, I may in a manner conclude, that it is impossible to rectify so many errors of any one man, as must needs proceed from those causes, without beginning anew from the very first grounds of all our knowledge, sense; and, instead of books, reading over orderly one's own conceptions: in which meaning I take *nosce teipsum** for a precept worthy the reputation it hath gotten.

CHAPTER VI

OF KNOWLEDGE, OPINION, AND BELIEF

1. THERE is a story somewhere, of one that pretended to have been miraculously cured of blindness, wherewith he was born, by St. Alban or other St., at the town of St. Alban's; and that the Duke of Gloucester being there, to be satisfied of the truth of the miracle, asked the man, What colour is this? who, by answering, It is green, discovered himself, and was punished for a counterfeit: for though by his sight newly received he might distinguish between green, and red, and all other colours, as well as any that should interrogate him, yet he could not possibly know at first sight, which of them was called green, or red, or by other name. By this we may understand, there be two sorts of knowledge, whereof the one is nothing else but sense, or knowledge original (as I have said at the beginning of the second chapter), and remembrance of the same; the other is called science or knowledge of the truth of propositions, and how things are called, and is derived from understanding. Both of these sorts are but experience; the former being the experience of the effects of things that work upon us from without; and the latter the experience men have of the proper use of names in language.* And all experience being (as I have said) but remembrance, all knowledge is re-membrance: and of the former, the register we keep in books, is called history; but the registers of the latter are called the sciences.

2. There are two things necessarily implied in this word knowledge;* the one is truth, the other evidence; for what is not true, can never be known. For let a man say he knoweth a thing never so well, if the same shall afterwards appear to be false, he is driven to a confession, that it was not knowledge, but opinion. Likewise, if the truth be not evident, though a man holdeth it, yet is his knowledge of it no more than theirs that hold the contrary. For if truth were enough to make it knowledge, all truths were known: which is not so.

3. What truth is, hath been defined in the precedent chapter; what evidence is, I now set down. And it is the concomitance of a man's conception with the words that signify such conception in the act of ratiocination.* For when a man reasoneth with his lips only, to which the mind suggesteth only the beginning, and followeth not the words of his mouth with the conceptions of his mind, out of a custom of so speaking; though he begin his ratiocination with true propositions, and proceed with perfect syllogisms, and thereby make always true conclusions; yet are not his conclusions evident to him, for want of the concomitance of conception with his words. For if the words alone were sufficient, a parrot might be taught as well to know a truth, as to speak it. Evidence is to truth, as the sap is to the tree, which so far as it creepeth along with the body and branches, keepeth them alive; when it forsaketh them, they die. For this evidence, which is meaning with our words, is the life of truth; without it truth is nothing worth.

4. Knowledge, therefore, which we call SCIENCE,* I define to be evidence of truth, from some beginning or principle of sense. For the truth of a proposition is never evident, until we conceive the meaning of the words or terms whereof it consisteth, which are always conceptions of the mind; nor can we remember those conceptions, without the thing that produced the same by our senses. The first principle of knowledge therefore is, that we have such and such conceptions; the second, that we have thus and thus named the things whereof they are conceptions; the third is, that we have joined those names in such manner, as to make true propositions; the fourth and last is, that we have joined those propositions in such manner as they be concluding. And by these four steps the conclusion is known and evident, and the truth of the conclusion said to be known. And of these two kinds of knowledge, whereof the former is experience of fact, and the latter evidence of truth: as the former, if it be great, is called prudence, so the latter, if it be much, hath usually been called, both by ancient and modern writers, SAPIENCE or wisdom: and of this latter, man only is capable; of the former, brute beasts also participate.

5. A proposition is said to be supposed, when, being not evident, it is nevertheless admitted for a time, to the end, that joining to it other propositions, we may conclude something; and so proceed from conclusion to conclusion, for a trail whether the same will lead us into any absurd or impossible conclusion; which if it do, then we know such supposition to have been false.

6. But if running through many conclusions, we come to none that are absurd, then we think the supposition probable; likewise we think probable whatsoever proposition we admit for truth by error of reasoning, or from trusting to other men. And all such propositions as are admitted by trust or error, we are not said to know, but think them to be true: and the admittance of them is called OPINION.

7. And particularly, when the opinion is admitted out of trust to other men, they are said to believe it; and their admittance of it is called BELIEF, and sometimes faith.

8. It is either science or opinion which we commonly mean by the word conscience: for men say that such and such a thing is true upon, or in their consciences; which they never do, when they think it doubtful; and therefore they know, or think they know it to be true. But men, when they say things upon their conscience, are not therefore presumed certainly to know the truth of what they say. It remaineth then, that that word is used by them that have an opinion, not only of the truth of the thing, but also of their knowledge of it. So that conscience, as men commonly use the word, signifieth an opinion, not so much of the truth of the proposition, as of their own knowledge of it, to which the truth of the proposition is consequent. CONSCIENCE therefore I define to be opinion of evidence.

9. Belief,* which is the admitting of propositions upon trust, in many cases is no less free from doubt, than perfect and manifest knowledge. For as there is nothing whereof there is not some cause; so, when there is doubt, there must be some cause thereof conceived. Now there be many things which we receive from report of others, of which it is impossible to imagine any cause of doubt: for what can be opposed against the consent of all men, in things they can

know, and have no cause to report otherwise than they are (such as is a great part of our histories), unless a man would say that all the world had conspired to deceive him. And thus much of sense, imagination, discursion, ratiocination, and knowledge, which are the acts of our power cognitive, or conceptive. That power of the mind which we call motive, differeth from the power motive of the body; for the power motive of the body is that by which it moveth other bodies, which we call strength: but the power motive of the mind, is that by which the mind giveth animal motion to that body wherein it existeth; the acts hereof are our affections and passions, of which I am now to speak.

CHAPTER VII

OF DELIGHT AND PAIN; GOOD AND EVIL

1. IN the eighth section of the second chapter is shewed, how conceptions or apparitions are nothing really, but motion in some internal substance of the head; which motion not stopping there, but proceeding to the heart, of necessity must there either help or hinder that motion which is called vital; when it helpeth, it is called DELIGHT, contentment, or pleasure, which is nothing really but motion about the heart, as conception is nothing but motion within the head; and the objects that cause it are called pleasant or delightful, or by some name equivalent; the Latins have *jucunda, a juvando*, from helping; and the same delight, with reference to the object, is called LOVE: but when such motion weakeneth or hindereth the vital motion, then it is called PAIN; and in relation to that which causeth it, HATRED, which the Latin expresseth sometimes by *odium*, and sometimes by *tædium*.

2. This motion, in which consisteth pleasure or pain, is also a solicitation or provocation either to draw near to the thing that pleaseth, or to retire from the thing that displeaseth. And this solicitation is the endeavour or internal

beginning of animal motion, which when the object delighteth, is called APPETITE; when it displeaseth, it is called AVERSION, in respect of the displeasure present; but in respect of the displeasure expected, FEAR. So that pleasure, love, and appetite, which is also called desire, are divers names for divers considerations of the same thing.

3. Every man, for his own part, calleth that which pleaseth, and is delightful to himself, GOOD; and that EVIL which displeaseth him: insomuch that while every man differeth from other in constitution, they differ also one from another concerning the common distinction of good and evil. Nor is there any such thing as ἀγαθὸν ἁπλῶς, that is to say, simply good. For even the goodness which we attribute to God Almighty, is his goodness to us. And as we call good and evil the things that please and displease; so call we goodness and badness, the qualities or powers whereby they do it. And the signs of that goodness are called by the Latins in one word PULCHRITUDO, and the signs of evil, TURPITUDO; to which we have no words precisely answerable.

4. As all conceptions we have immediately by the sense, are delight, or pain, or appetite, or fear; so are also the imaginations after sense. But as they are weaker imaginations, so are they also weaker pleasures, or weaker pain.

5. As appetite is the beginning of animal motion toward something which pleaseth us; so is the attaining thereof, the END of that motion, which we also call the scope, and aim, and final cause* of the same: and when we attain that end, the delight we have thereby is called FRUITION: so that *bonum* and *finis* are different names, but for different considerations of the same thing.

6. And of ends, some are called *propinqui*, that is, near at hand; others *remoti*, farther off. But when the ends that be nearer attaining, be compared with those that be farther off, they are not called ends, but means, and the way to those. But for an utmost end, in which the ancient philosophers have placed felicity, and have disputed much concerning the way thereto, there is no such thing in this world, nor way to it, more than to Utopia: for while we live, we have desires, and desire presupposeth a farther end.

Those things which please us, as the way or means to a farther end, we call PROFITABLE; and the fruition of them, USE; and those things that profit not, VAIN.

7. Seeing all delight is appetite, and appetite presupposeth a farther end, there can be no contentment but in proceeding: and therefore we are not to marvel, when we see, that as men attain to more riches, honours, or other power; so their appetite continually groweth more and more; and when they are come to the utmost degree of one kind of power, they pursue some other, as long as in any kind they think themselves behind any other. Of those therefore that have attained to the highest degree of honour and riches, some have affected mastery in some art; as Nero in music and poetry, Commodus in the art of a gladiator. And such as affect not some such thing, must find diversion and recreation of their thoughts in the contention either of play, or business. And men justly complain as of a great grief, that they know not what to do. FELICITY, therefore (by which we mean continual delight), consisteth not in having prospered, but in prospering.*

8. There are few things in this world, but either have a mixture of good and evil, or there is a chain of them so necessarily linked together, that the one cannot be taken without the other, as for example: the pleasures of sin, and the bitterness of punishment, are inseparable; as are also labour and honour, for the most part. Now when in the whole chain, the greater part is good, the whole is called good; and when the evil over-weigheth, the whole is called evil.

9. There are two sorts of pleasure, whereof the one seemeth to affect the corporeal organ of sense, and that I call SENSUAL; the greatest whereof is that, by which we are invited to give continuance to our species; and the next, by which a man is invited to meat, for the preservation of his individual person. The other sort of delight is not particular to any part of the body, and is called the delight of the mind, and is that which we call JOY. Likewise of pains, some affect the body, and are therefore called the pains of the body; and some not, and those are called GRIEF.

CHAPTER VIII

OF THE PLEASURES OF THE SENSE; OF HONOUR

1. HAVING in the first section of the precedent chapter presupposed that motion and agitation of the brain which we call conception, to be continued to the heart, and there to be called passion; I have thereby obliged myself, as far forth as I can, to search out and declare, from what conception proceedeth every one of those passions which we commonly take notice of. For the things that please and displease, are innumerable, and work innumerable ways; but men have taken notice of the passions they have from them in a very few, which also are many of them without name.

2. And first, we are to consider that of conceptions there are three sorts, whereof one is of that which is present, which is sense; another, of that which is past, which is remembrance; and the third, of that which is future, which we call expectation: all which have been manifestly declared in the second and the third chapter. And every of these conceptions is pleasure present. And first for the pleasures of the body which affect the sense of touch and taste, as far forth as they be organical, their conception is sense; so also is the pleasure of all exonerations of nature; all which passions I have before named sensual pleasures; and their contraries, sensual pains; to which also may be added the pleasures and displeasures of odours, if any of them shall be found organical, which for the most part they are not, as appeareth by this experience which every man hath, that the same smells, when they seem to proceed from others, displease, though they proceed from ourselves; but when we think they proceed from ourselves, they displease not, though they come from others: the displeasure therefore, in these is a conception of hurt thereby as being unwholesome, and is therefore a conception of evil to come, and not present. Concerning the delight of hearing, it is diverse, and the organ itself not affected thereby. Simple sounds please by continuance and equality, as the sound of a bell or lute: insomuch that it seemeth an equality continued by the

percussion of the object upon the ear, is pleasure; the contrary is called harshness: such as is grating, and some other sounds, which do not always affect the body, but only sometimes, and that with a kind of horror beginning at the teeth. Harmony, or many sounds together agreeing, please by the same reason as unison, which is the sound of equal strings equally stretched. Sounds that differ in any height, please by inequality and equality alternate, that is to say, the higher note striketh twice, for one stroke of the other, whereby they strike together every second time; as is well proved by Galileo, in the first dialogue concerning local motions,* where he also sheweth, that two sounds differing a fifth, delight the ear by an equality of striking after two inequalities; for the higher note striketh the ear thrice, while the other striketh but twice. In the like manner he sheweth, wherein consisteth the pleasure of concord, and the displeasure of discord, in other differences of notes. There is yet another pleasure and displeasure of sounds, which consisteth in consequence of one note after another, diversified both by accent and measure: whereof that which pleaseth is called air. But for what reason succession in one tone and measure is more air than another, I confess I know not; but I conjecture the reason to be, for that some of them may imitate and revive some passion which otherwise we take no notice of, and the other not; for no air pleaseth but for a time, no more doth imitation. Also the pleasures of the eye consist in a certain equality of colour: for light, the most glorious of all colours, is made by equal operation of the object; whereas colour is (perturbed, that is to say) unequal light, as hath been said chap. II, sect. 8. And therefore colours, the more equality is in them, the more resplendent they are. And as harmony is a pleasure to the ear, which consisteth of divers sounds; so perhaps may some mixture of divers colours be harmony to the eye, more than another mixture. There is yet another delight by the ear, which happeneth only to men of skill in music, which is of another nature, and not (as these) conception of the present, but rejoicing in their own skill; of which nature are the passions of which I am to speak next.

3. Conception of the future is but a supposition of the same, proceeding from remembrance of what is past; and we so far conceive that anything will be hereafter, as we know there is something at the present that hath power to produce it. And that anything hath power now to produce another thing hereafter, we cannot conceive, but by remembrance that it hath produced the like heretofore. Wherefore all conception of future, is conception of power able to produce something; whosoever therefore expecteth pleasure to come, must conceive withal some power in himself by which the same may be attained. And because the passions whereof I am to speak next, consist in conception of the future, that is to say, in conception of power past, and the act to come; before I go any farther, I must in the next place speak somewhat concerning this power.

4. By this power I mean the same with the faculties of body and mind, mentioned in the first chapter, that is to say, of the body, nutritive, generative, motive; and of the mind, knowledge. And besides those, such farther powers, as by them are acquired (viz.) riches, place of authority, friendship or favour, and good fortune; which last is really nothing else but the favour of God Almighty. The contraries of these are impotences, infirmities, or defects of the said powers respectively. And because the power of one man resisteth and hindereth the effects of the power of another: power simply is no more, but the excess of the power of one above that of another. For equal powers opposed, destroy one another; and such their opposition is called contention.

5. The signs by which we know our own power are those actions which proceed from the same; and the signs by which other men know it, are such actions, gesture, countenance and speech, as usually such powers produce: and the acknowledgment of power is called HONOUR; and to honour a man (inwardly in the mind) is to conceive or acknowledge, that that man hath the odds or excess of power above him that contendeth or compareth himself. And HONOURABLE are those signs for which one man acknowledgeth power or excess above his concurrent in another. As for example:—Beauty of person, consisting in a

lively aspect of the countenance, and other signs of natural heat, are honourable, being signs precedent of power generative, and much issue; as also, general reputation amongst those of the other sex, because signs consequent of the same.—And actions proceeding from strength of body and open force, are honourable, as signs consequent of power motive, such as are victory in battle or duel; *et à avoir tué son homme*.—Also to adventure upon great exploits and danger, as being a sign consequent of opinion of our own strength: and that opinion a sign of the strength itself.— And to teach or persuade are honourable, because they be signs of knowledge.—And riches are honourable; as signs of the power that acquired them.—And gifts, costs, and magnificence of houses, apparel, and the like, are honourable, as signs of riches.—And nobility is honourable by reflection, as signs of power in the ancestors.—And authority, because a sign of strength, wisdom, favour or riches by which it is attained.—And good fortune or casual prosperity is honourable, because a sign of the favour of God, to whom is to be ascribed all that cometh to us by fortune, no less than that we attain unto us by industry.— And the contraries, or defects, of these signs are dishonourable; and according to the signs of honour and dishonour, so we estimate and make the value or WORTH of a man. For so much worth is every thing, as a man will give for the use of all it can do.

6. The signs of honour are those by which we perceive that one man acknowledgeth the power and worth of another. Such as these:—To praise; to magnify; to bless, or call happy; to pray or supplicate to; to thank; to offer unto or present; to obey; to hearken to with attention; to speak to with consideration; to approach unto in decent manner, to keep distance from; to give the way to, and the like; which are the honour the inferior giveth to the superior.

But the signs of honour from the superior to the inferior, are such as these: to praise or prefer him before his concurrent; to hear him more willingly; to speak to him more familiarly; to admit him nearer; to employ him rather; to ask his advice rather; to like his opinions; and to give him any gift rather than money, or if money, so much as may not imply his need of a little: for need of little is greater poverty than need of much.* And this is enough for examples of the signs of honour and of power.

7. Reverence is the conception we have concerning another, that he hath a power to do unto us both good and hurt, but not the will to do us hurt.

8. In the pleasure men have, or displeasure from the signs of honour or dishonour done unto them, consisteth the nature of the passions in particular, whereof we are to speak in the next chapter.

CHAPTER IX

OF THE PASSIONS OF THE MIND

1. GLORY, or internal gloriation or triumph of the mind, is that passion which proceedeth from the imagination or conception of our own power, above the power of him that contendeth with us. The signs whereof, besides those in the countenance, and other gestures of the body which cannot be described, are, ostentation in words, and insolency in actions; and this passion, by them whom it displeaseth, is called pride: by them whom it pleaseth, it is termed a just valuation of himself. This imagination of our power and worth, may be an assured and certain experience of our own actions, and then is that glorying just and well grounded, and begetteth an opinion of increasing the same by other actions to follow; in which consisteth the appetite which we call ASPIRING, or proceeding from one degree of power to another. The same passion may proceed not from any conscience of our own actions, but from fame and trust of others, whereby one may think well of himself, and yet be deceived; and this is FALSE GLORY, and the aspiring consequent thereto procureth ill-success. Farther, the fiction (which also is imagination) of actions done by ourselves, which never were done, is glorying; but because it begetteth no appetite nor endeavour to any further attempt, it is

merely vain and unprofitable; as when a man imagineth himself to do the actions whereof he readeth in some romant, or to be like unto some other man whose acts he admireth. And this is called VAIN GLORY: and is exemplified in the fable* by the fly sitting on the axletree, and saying to himself, What a dust do I raise! The expression of vain glory is that we call a wish, which some of the Schoolmen, mistaking for some appetite distinct from all the rest, have called velleity, making a new word, as they made a new passion which was not before. Signs of vain glory in the gesture, are imitation of others, counterfeiting attention to things they understand not, affectation of fashions, captation of honour from their dreams, and other little stories of themselves, from their country, from their names, and the like.

2. The passion contrary to glory, proceeding from apprehension of our own infirmity, is called HUMILITY by those by whom it is approved; by the rest, DEJECTION and poorness; which conception may be well or ill grounded. If well, it produceth fear to attempt any thing rashly; if ill, it may be called vain fear, as the contrary is vain glory, and consisteth in fear of the power, without any other sign of the act to follow, as children fear to go in the dark, upon imagination of spirits, and fear all strangers as enemies. This is the passion which utterly cows a man, that he neither dare speak publicly, nor expect good success in any action.

3. It happeneth sometimes, that he that hath a good opinion of himself, and upon good ground, may nevertheless, by reason of the forwardness which that passion begetteth, discover in himself some defect or infirmity, the remembrance whereof dejecteth him; and this passion is called SHAME, by which being cooled and checked in his forwardness, he is more wary for the time to come. This passion, as it is a sign of infirmity, which is dishonour; so also it is a sign of knowledge, which is honour. The sign of it is blushing, which happeneth less in men conscious of their own defects, because they less betray the infirmities they acknowledge.

4. COURAGE, in a large signification, is the absence of fear in the presence of any evil whatsoever; but in a stricter

and more common meaning, it is contempt of wounds and death, when they oppose a man in the way to his end.

5. ANGER (or sudden courage) is nothing but the appetite or desire of overcoming present opposition. It hath been commonly defined to be grief proceeding from an opinion of contempt; which is confuted by the often experience we have of being moved to anger by things inanimate and without sense, and consequently incapable of contemning us.

6. REVENGEFULNESS is that passion which ariseth from an expectation or imagination of making him that hath hurt us, to find his own action hurtful to himself, and to acknowledge the same; and this is the height of revenge. For though it be not hard, by returning evil for evil, to make one's adversary displeased with his own fact; yet to make him acknowledge the same, is so difficult, that many a man had rather die than do it. Revenge aimeth not at the death, but at the captivity and subjection of an enemy; which was well expressed in the exclamation of Tiberius Cæsar, concerning one, that, to frustrate his revenge, had killed himself in prison: Hath he escaped me?* To kill is the aim of them that hate, to rid themselves of fear; revenge aimeth at triumph, which over the dead is not.

7. REPENTANCE is the passion that proceedeth from opinion or knowledge that the action they have done is out of the way to the end they would attain. The effect whereof is, to pursue that way no longer; but, by consideration of the end, to direct themselves into a better. The first motion therefore in this passion is grief. But the expectation or conception of returning again into the way, is joy. And consequently, the passion of repentance is compounded and allayed of both, but the predominant is joy, else were the whole grief; which cannot be. For as much as he that proceedeth towards the end, conceiveth good, he proceedeth with appetite. And appetite is joy, as hath been said, chap. VII, sect. 3.

8. HOPE is expectation of good to come, as fear is the expectation of evil: but when there be causes, some that make us expect good, and some that make us expect evil,

alternately working in our minds: if the causes that make us expect good, be greater than those that make us expect evil, the whole passion is hope; if contrarily, the whole is fear. Absolute privation of hope is DESPAIR, a degree whereof is DIFFIDENCE.

9. TRUST is a passion proceeding from belief of him from whom we expect or hope for good, so free from doubt that upon the same we pursue no other way. And distrust, or diffidence, is doubt that maketh him endeavour to provide himself by other means. And that this is the meaning of the words trust and distrust, is manifest from this, that a man never provideth himself by a second way, but when he mistrusteth that the first will not hold.

10. PITY is imagination or fiction of future calamity to ourselves, proceeding from the sense of another man's present calamity; but when it lighteth on such as we think have not deserved the same, the compassion is the greater, because then there appeareth the more probability that the same may happen to us. For the evil that happeneth to an innocent man, may happen to every man. But when we see a man suffer for great crimes, which we cannot easily think will fall upon ourselves, the pity is the less. And therefore men are apt to pity those whom they love: for, whom they love, they think worthy of good, and therefore not worthy of calamity. Thence also it is, that men pity the vices of some they never saw before; and therefore every proper man finds pity amongst women, when he goeth to the gallows. The contrary of pity is HARDNESS of heart, proceeding either from slowness of imagination, or from extreme great opinion of their own exemption of the like calamity, or from hatred of all, or most men.

11. INDIGNATION is that grief which consisteth in the conception of good success happening to them whom they think unworthy thereof. Seeing therefore men think all those unworthy whom they hate, they think them not only unworthy of the good fortune they have, but also of their own virtues. And of all the passions of the mind, these two, indignation and pity, are most easily raised and increased by eloquence; for the aggravation of the calamity, and extenuation of the

fault, augmenteth pity. And the extenuation of the worth of the person, together with the magnifying of his success (which are the parts of an orator), are able to turn these two passions into fury.

12. EMULATION is grief arising from seeing one's self exceeded or excelled by his concurrent, together with hope to equal or exceed him in time to come, by his own ability. But, ENVY is the same grief joined with pleasure conceived in the imagination of some ill fortune that may befall him.

13. There is a passion which hath no name, but the sign of it is that distortion of the countenance we call LAUGHTER, which is always joy; but what joy, what we think, and wherein we triumph when we laugh, hath not hitherto been declared by any. That it consisteth in wit, or, as they call it, in the jest, this experience confuteth: for men laugh at mischances and indecencies, wherein there lieth no wit or jest at all. And forasmuch as the same thing is no more ridiculous when it groweth stale or usual, whatsoever it be that moveth laughter, it must be new and unexpected. Men laugh often (especially such as are greedy of applause from every thing they do well) at their own actions performed never so little beyond their own expectation; as also at their own jests: and in this case it is manifest, that the passion of laughter proceedeth from a sudden conception of some ability in himself that laugheth. Also men laugh at the infirmities of others, by comparison of which their own abilities are set off and illustrated. Also men laugh at jests, the wit whereof always consisteth in the elegant discovering and conveying to our minds some absurdity or another. And in this case also the passion of laughter proceedeth from the sudden imagination of our own odds and eminence; for what is else the recommending ourselves to our own good opinion, by comparison with another man's infirmities or absurdity? For when a jest is broken upon ourselves, or friends of whose dishonour we participate, we never laugh thereat. I may therefore conclude, that the passion of laughter is nothing else but a sudden glory arising from sudden conception of some eminency in ourselves, by comparison with the infirmities of others, or with our own

formerly: for men laugh at the follies of themselves past, when they come suddenly to remembrance, except they bring with them any present dishonour. It is no wonder therefore that men take it heinously to be laughed at or derided, that is, triumphed over. Laughter without offence, must be at absurdities and infirmities abstracted from persons, and where all the company may laugh together. For laughing to one's self putteth all the rest to a jealousy and examination of themselves; besides, it is vain glory, and an argument of little worth, to think the infirmities of another sufficient matter for his triumph.

14. The passion opposite hereunto, whose signs are another distortion of the face with tears, called WEEPING, is the sudden falling out with ourselves, or sudden conception of defect; and therefore children weep often; for seeing they think every thing ought to be given unto them which they desire, of necessity every repulse must be a sudden check of their expectation, and puts them in mind of their too much weakness to make themselves masters of all they look for. For the same cause women are more apt to weep than men, as being not only more accustomed to have their wills, but also to measure their power by the power and love of others that protect them. Men are apt to weep that prosecute revenge, when the revenge is suddenly stopped or frustrated by the repentance of the adversary; and such are the tears of reconciliation. Also pityful men are subject to this passion upon the beholding of those men they pity, and suddenly remember they cannot help. Other weeping in men proceedeth for the most part from the same cause it proceedeth from in women and children.

15. The appetite which men call LUST, and the fruition that appertaineth thereunto, is a sensual pleasure, but not only that; there is in it also a delight of the mind: for it consisteth of two appetites together, to please, and to be pleased; and the delight men take in delighting, is not sensual, but a pleasure or joy of the mind, consisting in the imagination of the power they have so much to please. But this name lust is used where it is condemned: otherwise it is called by the general word love; for the passion is one and

the same indefinite desire of the different sex, as natural as hunger.

16. Of love, by which is understood the joy a man taketh in the fruition of any present good, hath been already spoken in the first section of the seventh chapter, under which is contained the love men bear to one another, or pleasure they take in one another's company; and by which men are said to be sociable by nature. But there is another kind of LOVE, which the Greeks call Ἔρως, and is that which we mean, when we say: that man or woman is in love. For as much as this passion cannot be without diversity of sex, it cannot be denied but that it participateth of that indefinite love mentioned in the former section. But there is a great difference between the desire of a man indefinite, and the same desire limited *ad hanc*;* and this is that love which is the great theme of poets. But notwithstanding their praises, it must be defined by the word need; for it is a conception of the need a man hath of that one person desired. The cause of this passion is not always, nor for the most part, beauty, or other quality, in the beloved, unless there be withal hope in the person that loveth: which may be gathered from this: that in great difference of persons, the greater have often fallen in love with the meaner; but not contrary. And from hence it is, that for the most part they have much better fortune in love, whose hopes are built upon something in their person, than those that trust to their expressions and service; and they that care less, than they that care more; which not perceiving many men cast away their services, as one arrow after another; till in the end together with their hopes they lose their wits.

17. There is yet another passion sometimes called love, but more properly good will or CHARITY. There can be no greater argument to a man of his own power, than to find himself able, not only to accomplish his own desires, but also to assist other men in theirs: and this is that conception wherein consisteth charity. In which, first, is contained that natural affection of parents to their children, which the Greeks call Στοργή, as also that affection wherewith men seek to assist those that adhere unto them. But the affec-

tion wherewith men many times bestow their benefits on strangers, is not to be called charity, but either contract, whereby they seek to purchase friendship; or fear, which maketh them to purchase peace. The opinion of Plato concerning honourable love, delivered (according to his custom, in the person of Socrates) in the dialogue intituled *Convivium,** is this: that a man full and pregnant with wisdom, or other virtue, naturally seeketh out some beautiful person, of age and capacity to conceive, in whom he may, without sensual respects, engender and produce the like. And this is the idea of the then noted love of Socrates wise and continent, to Alcibiades young and beautiful; in which love, is not sought the honour, but issue of his knowledge; contrary to common love, to which though issue sometimes follow, yet men seek not that, but to please, and to be pleased. It should therefore be this charity, or desire to assist and advance others. But why then should the wise seek the ignorant, or be more charitable to the beautiful than to others? There is something in it savouring of the use of that time: in which matter though Socrates be acknowledged for continent, yet continent men have the passion they contain, as much or more than they that satiate the appetite; which maketh me suspect this platonic love for merely sensual; but with an honourable pretence for the old to haunt the company of the young and beautiful.

18. Forasmuch as all knowledge beginneth from experience, therefore also new experience is the beginning of new knowledge, and the increase of experience the beginning of the increase of knowledge; whatsoever therefore happeneth new to a man, giveth him hope and matter of knowing somewhat that he knew not before. And this hope and expectation of future knowledge from anything that happeneth new and strange, is that passion which we commonly call ADMIRATION; and the same considered as appetite, is called CURIOSITY, which is appetite of knowledge. As in the discerning faculties, man leaveth all community with beasts at the faculty of imposing names; so also doth he surmount their nature at this passion of curiosity. For when a beast seeth anything new or strange to him, he considereth it so

far only as to discern whether it be likely to serve his turn, or hurt him, and accordingly approacheth nearer it, or flieth from it; whereas man, who in most events remembereth in what manner they were caused and begun, looketh for the cause and beginning of everything that ariseth new unto him. And from this passion of admiration and curiosity, have arisen not only the invention of names, but also the supposition of such causes of all things as they thought might produce them. And from this beginning is derived all philosophy: as astronomy from the admiration of the course of heaven; natural philosophy from the strange effects of the elements and other bodies. And from the degrees of curiosity proceed also the degrees of knowledge among men; for to a man in the chase of riches or authority, (which in respect of knowledge are but sensuality) it is a diversion of little pleasure to consider, whether it be the motion of the sun or the earth that maketh the day, or to enter into other contemplation of any strange accident, than whether it conduce or not to the end he pursueth. Because curiosity is delight, therefore also all novelty is so, but especially that novelty from which a man conceiveth an opinion true or false of bettering his own estate. For in such case they stand affected with the hope that all gamesters have while the cards are shuffling.

19. Divers other passions there be, but they want names; whereof some nevertheless have been by most men observed. For example:* from what passion proceedeth it, that men take pleasure to behold from the shore the danger of them that are at sea in a tempest, or in fight, or from a safe castle to behold two armies charge one another in the field? It is certainly in the whole sum joy, else men would never flock to such a spectacle. Nevertheless there is in it both joy and grief. For as there is novelty and remembrance of own security present, which is delight; so is there also pity, which is grief. But the delight is so far predominant, that men usually are content in such a case to be spectators of the misery of their friends.

20. MAGNANIMITY is no more than glory, of which I have spoken in the first section; but glory well grounded upon

certain experience of power sufficient to attain his end in open manner. And PUSILLANIMITY is the doubt of that; whatsoever therefore is a sign of vain glory, the same is also a sign of pusillanimity: for sufficient power maketh glory a spur to one's end. To be pleased or displeased with fame true or false, is a sign of the same, because he that relieth upon fame, hath not his success in his own power. Likewise art and fallacy are signs of pusillanimity, because they depend not upon our own power, but the ignorance of others. Also proneness to anger, because it argueth difficulty of proceeding. Also ostentation of ancestors, because all men are more inclined to make shew of their own power when they have it, than of another's. To be at enmity and contention with inferiors, is a sign of the same, because it proceedeth from want of power to end the war. To laugh at others, because it is affectation of glory from other men's infirmities, and not from any ability of their own. Also irresolution, which proceedeth from want of power enough to contemn the little differences that make deliberations hard.

21. The comparison of the life of man to a race, though it holdeth not in every point, yet it holdeth so well for this our purpose that we may thereby both see and remember almost all the passions before mentioned. But this race we must suppose to have no other goal, nor no other garland, but being foremost. And in it:

To endeavour is appetite.

To be remiss is sensuality.

To consider them behind is glory.

To consider them before is humility.

To lose ground with looking back vain glory.

To be holden, hatred.

To turn back, repentance.

To be in breath, hope.

To be weary despair.

To endeavour to overtake the next, emulation.

To supplant or overthrow, envy.

To resolve to break through a stop foreseen courage.

To break through a sudden stop anger.
To break through with ease, magnanimity.
To lose ground by little hindrances, pusillanimity.
To fall on the sudden is disposition to weep.
To see another fall, disposition to laugh.
To see one out-gone whom we would not is pity.
To see one out-go we would not, is indignation.
To hold fast by another is to love.
To carry him on that so holdeth, is charity.
To hurt one's-self for haste is shame.
Continually to be out-gone is misery.
Continually to out-go the next before is felicity.
And to forsake the course is to die.

CHAPTER X

OF THE DIFFERENCE BETWEEN MEN IN THEIR DISCERNING FACULTY AND THE CAUSE

1. HAVING shewed in the precedent chapters, that the imagination of men proceedeth from the action of external objects upon the brain, or some internal substance of the head; and that the passions proceed from the alteration there made, and continued to the heart: it is consequent in the next place (seeing the diversity of degree in knowledge in divers men, to be greater than may be ascribed to the divers temper of the brain) to declare what other causes may produce such odds, and excess of capacity, as we daily observe in one man above another. And for that difference which ariseth from sickness, and such accidental distemper, I omit the same, as impertinent to this place, and consider it only in such as have their health, and organs well disposed. If the difference were in the natural temper of the brain, I can imagine no reason why the same should not appear first and most of all in the senses, which being equal both in the wise and less wise, infer an equal temper in the common organ (namely the brain) of all the senses.

2. But we see by experience, that joy and grief proceed

not in all men from the same causes, and that men differ much in constitution of body, whereby, that which helpeth and furthereth vital constitution in one, and is therefore delightful, hindereth and crosseth it in another, and causeth grief. The difference therefore of wits hath its original from the different passions, and from the ends to which their appetite leadeth them.

3. And first, those men whose ends are some sensual delight; and generally are addicted to ease, food, onerations and exonerations of the body, must of necessity thereby be the less delighted with those imaginations that conduce not to those ends, such as are imaginations of honour and glory, which, as I have said before, have respect to the future: for sensuality consisteth in the pleasure of the senses, which please only for the present, and taketh away the inclination to observe such things as conduce to honour; and consequently maketh men less curious, and less ambitious, whereby they less consider the way either to knowledge or to other power; in which two consisteth all the excellency of power cognitive. And this is it which men call DULNESS; and proceedeth from the appetite of sensual or bodily delight. And it may well be conjectured, that such passion hath its beginning from a grossness and difficulty of the motion of the spirits about the heart.

4. The contrary hereunto, is that quick ranging of mind described chap. IV, sect. 3, which is joined with curiosity of comparing the things that come into his mind one with another. In which comparison, a man delighteth himself either with finding unexpected similitude in things, otherwise much unlike, in which men place the excellency of FANCY;* and from thence proceed those grateful similies, metaphors, and other tropes, by which both poets and orators have it in their power to make things please or displease, and shew well or ill to others, as they like themselves; or else in discerning suddenly dissimilitude in things that otherwise appear the same. And this virtue of the mind is that by which men attain to exact and perfect knowledge: and the pleasure thereof consisteth in continual instruction, and in distinction of persons, places, and seasons; it is com-

monly termed by the name of JUDGMENT: for, to judge is nothing else, but to distinguish or discern; and both fancy and judgment are commonly comprehended under the name of WIT, which seemeth a tenuity and agility of spirits, contrary to that restiveness of the spirits supposed in those that are dull.

5. There is another defect of the mind, which men call LEVITY, which betrayeth also mobility in the spirits, but in excess. An example whereof is in them that in the midst of any serious discourse, have their minds diverted to every little jest or witty observation; which maketh them depart from their discourse by parenthesis, and from that parenthesis by another, till at length they either lose themselves, or make their narration like a dream, or some studied nonsense. The passion from which this proceedeth, is curiosity, but with too much equality and indifferency: for when all things make equal impression and delight, they equally throng to be expressed.

6. The virtue opposite to this defect is GRAVITY, or steadiness; in which the end being the great and master-delight, directeth and keepeth in the way thereto all other thoughts.

7. The extremity of dulness is that natural folly which may be called STOLIDITY: but the extreme of levity, though it be a natural folly distinct from the other, and obvious to every man's observation, yet it hath no name.

8. There is a fault of the mind called by the Greeks 'Αμαθία, which is INDOCIBILITY, or difficulty of being taught; the which must needs arise from a false opinion that they know already the truth of that which is called in question. For certainly men are not otherwise so unequal in capacity as the evidence is unequal of what is taught by the mathematicians, and what is commonly discoursed of in other books: and therefore if the minds of men were all of white paper,* they would almost equally be disposed to acknowledge whatsoever should be in right method, and right ratiocination delivered unto them. But when men have once acquiesced in untrue opinions, and registered them as authentical records in their minds; it is no less impossible to speak intelligibly to such men, than to write legibly upon a

paper already scribbled over. The immediate cause therefore of indocibility, is prejudice; and of prejudice, false opinion of our own knowledge.

9. Another, and a principal defect of the mind, is that which men call MADNESS, which appeareth to be nothing else but some imagination of such predominance above all the rest, that we have no passion but from it. And this conception is nothing else but excessive vain glory, or vain dejection; as is most probable by these examples following, which proceed in appearance, every one of them, from some pride, or some dejection of mind. As first we have had the example of one that preached in Cheapside from a cart there, instead of a pulpit, that he himself was Christ, which was spiritual pride or madness. We have had divers examples also of learned madness, in which men have manifestly been distracted upon any occasion that hath put them in remembrance of their own ability. Amongst the learned madmen may be numbered (I think) also those that determine of the time of the world's end, and other such points of prophecy.* And the gallant madness of Don Quixote is nothing else but an expression of such height of vain glory as reading of romants* may produce in pusillanimous men. Also rage and madness of love, are but great indignations of them in whose brains are predominant the contempts of their enemies, or their mistresses. And the pride taken in form and behaviour, hath made divers men run mad, and to be so accounted, under the name of fantastic.

10. And as these are the examples of extremities, so also are there examples too many of the degrees, which may therefore be well accounted follies. As it is a degree of the first, for a man, without certain evidence, to think himself inspired, or to have any other effect in himself of God's holy spirit than other godly men have. Of the second, for a man continually to speak his mind in a *cento** of other men's Greek or Latin sentences. Of the third, much of the present gallantry in love and duel. Of rage, a degree is malice; and of fantastic madness, affectation.

11. As the former examples exhibit to us madness, and the degrees thereof, proceeding from the excess of self-

opinion; so also there be other examples of madness, and the degrees thereof, proceeding from too much vain fear and dejection: as in those melancholy men that have imagined themselves brittle as glass, or have had some other like imagination; and degrees hereof are all those exorbitant and causeless fears, which we commonly observe in melancholy persons.

CHAPTER XI

WHAT IMAGINATIONS AND PASSIONS MEN HAVE, AT THE NAMES OF THINGS SUPERNATURAL

1. HITHERTO of the knowledge of things natural, and of the passions that arise naturally from them. Now forasmuch as we give names not only to things natural, but also to supernatural; and by all names we ought to have some meaning and conception: it followeth in the next place, to consider what thoughts and imaginations of the mind we have, when we take into our mouths the most blessed name of GOD, and the names of those virtues we attribute unto him; as also, what image cometh into the mind at hearing the name of spirit, or the name of angel, good or bad.

2.* Forasmuch as God Almighty is incomprehensible, it followeth that we can have no conception or image of the Deity; and consequently all his attributes signify our inability and defect of power to conceive any thing concerning his nature, and not any conception of the same, excepting only this: *that there is a God.* For the effects we acknowledge naturally, do necessarily include a power of their producing, before they were produced; and that power presupposeth something existent that hath such power; and the thing so existing with power to produce, if it were not eternal, must needs have been produced by somewhat before it; and that again by something else before that: till we come to an eternal, that is to say, to the first power of all powers, and first cause of all causes. And this is it which all men call by the name of GOD: implying eternity, incomprehensibility, and omnipotency. And thus all men that will consider, may naturally know that God is, though not what he is; even as a man though born blind, though it be not possible for him to have any imagination what kind of thing is fire; yet he cannot but know that something there is that men call fire, because it warmeth him.

3. And whereas we attribute to God Almighty, seeing, hearing, speaking, knowing, loving, and the like; by which names we understand something in the men to whom we attribute them, we understand nothing by them in the nature of God. For, as it is well reasoned: Shall not God that made the eye, see? and the ear, hear? so is it also, if we say: shall God that made the eye, not see without the eye? and that made the ear, not hear without the ear? or that made the brain, not know without the brain? or that made the heart, not love without the heart? The attributes therefore given unto the Deity, are such as signify either our incapacity, or our reverence; our incapacity, when we say: incomprehensible and infinite: our reverence, when we give him those names, which amongst us are the names of those things we most magnify and commend, as omnipotent, omniscient, just, merciful, &c. And when God Almighty giveth those names to himself in the Scriptures, it is but ἀνθρωποπαθῶς, that is to say, by descending to our manner of speaking: without which we are not capable of understanding him.

4. By the name of spirit we understand a body natural, but of such subtilty that it worketh not on the senses; but that filleth up the place which the image of a visible body might fill up. Our conception therefore of spirit consisteth of figure without colour; and in figure is understood dimension: and consequently, to conceive a spirit, is to conceive something that hath dimension. But spirits supernatural commonly signify some substance without dimension; which two words do flatly contradict one another. And therefore when we attribute the name of spirit unto God, we attribute it, not as a name of anything we conceive, no more than when we ascribe unto him sense and understanding; but as a

signification of our reverence, who desire to abstract from him all corporeal grossness.

5. Concerning other spirits, which some men call spirits incorporeal, and some corporeal, it is not possible, by natural means only, to come to knowledge of so much, as that there are such things. We who are Christians acknowledge that there be angels good and evil; and that they are spirits, and that the soul of man is a spirit; and that these spirits are immortal. But, to know it, that is to say, to have natural evidence of the same: it is impossible. For all evidence is conception, as it is said chap. VI, sect. 3; and all conception is imagination and proceedeth from sense: chap. III, sect. 1. And spirits we suppose to be those substances which work not upon the sense, and therefore not conceptible. But though the Scripture acknowledge spirits, yet doth it nowhere say, that they are incorporeal, meaning thereby, without dimensions and quantity; nor, I think, is that word incorporeal at all in the Bible; but it is said of the spirit, that it abideth in men; sometime that it dwelleth in them, sometimes that it cometh on them, that it descendeth, and cometh and goeth; and that spirits are angels, that is to say messengers: all which words do consignify locality; and locality is dimension; and whatsoever hath dimension, is body, be it never so subtile. To me therefore it seemeth, that the Scripture favoureth them more, who hold angels and spirits for corporeal, than them that hold the contrary. And it is a plain contradiction in natural discourse, to say of the soul of man, that it is *tota in toto*, and: *tota in qualibet parte corporis*,* grounded neither upon reason nor revelation; but proceeding from the ignorance of what those things are which are called spectra, images that appear in the dark to children, and such as have strong fears, and other strong imaginations, as hath been said chap. III, sect. 5, where I call them phantasms. For taking them to be things really without us, like bodies, and seeing them to come and vanish so strangely as they do, unlike to bodies; what could they call them else, but incorporeal bodies? which is not a name, but an absurdity of speech.

6. It is true, that the heathens, and all nations of the

world, have acknowledged that there are spirits, which for the most part they hold to be incorporeal; whereby it may be thought that a man by natural reason, may arrive, without the knowledge of Scripture, to the knowledge of this; *that spirits are*. But the erroneous collection thereof by the heathens may proceed, as I have said before, from ignorance of the causes of ghosts and phantasms, and such other apparitions. And from thence had the Grecians their number of gods, their number of dæmons good and bad; and for every man his genius; which is not the acknowledging of this truth: that spirits are; but a false opinion concerning the force of imagination.

7. And seeing the knowledge we have of spirits, is not natural knowledge, but faith from supernatural revelation, given to the holy writers of Scripture; it followeth that of inspiration also, which is the operation of spirits in us, the knowledge we have must all proceed from Scripture. The signs there set down of inspiration, are miracles, when they be great, and manifestly above the power of men to do by imposture. As for example: the inspiration of Elias was known by the miraculous burning of his sacrifice. But the signs to distinguish whether a spirit be good or evil, are the same by which we distinguish whether a man or a tree be good or evil: namely actions and fruit. For there be lying spirits wherewith men are inspired sometimes, as well as with spirits of truth. And we are commanded in Scripture, to judge of the spirits by their doctrine, and not of the doctrine by the spirits. For miracles, our Saviour hath forbidden us to rule our faith by them, Matt. 24, 24. And Saint Paul saith, Gal. 1, 8: *Though an angel from heaven preach unto you otherwise, &c. let him be accursed*. Where it is plain, that we are not to judge whether the doctrine be true or no, by the angel; but whether the angel saith true or no, by the doctrine. So likewise, 1 Joh. chap. 4 vers. 1: *Believe not every spirit: for false prophets are gone out into the world*; verse 2: *Hereby shall ye know the spirit of God: every spirit that confesseth that Jesus Christ is come in the flesh, is of God*; verse 3: *And every spirit that confesseth not that Jesus Christ is come in the flesh, is not of God; and this is the*

spirit of Antichrist; verse 15: *Whosoever confesseth that Jesus is the Son of God, in him dwelleth God, and he in God.** The knowledge therefore we have of good and evil inspiration, cometh not by vision of an angel that may teach it, nor by a miracle that may seem to confirm it; but by conformity of doctrine with this article and fundamental point of Christian faith, which also Saint Paul saith 1 Cor. 3, 11, is the sole foundation: that Jesus Christ is come in the flesh.

8. But if inspiration be discerned by this point; and this point be acknowledged and believed upon the authority of the Scriptures: how (may some men ask) know we that the Scripture deserveth so great authority, which must be no less than that of the lively voice of God? that is, how we know the Scriptures to be the word of God? And first, it is manifest: that if by knowledge we understand science infallible and natural, such as is defined in the VI chap. 4 scct., proceeding from sense; we cannot be said to know it, because it proceedeth from the conceptions engendered by sense. And if we understand knowledge as supernatural, we cannot know it but by inspiration; and of that inspiration we cannot judge, but by the doctrine. It followeth therefore, that we have not any way, natural or supernatural, that knowledge thereof which can properly be called infallible science and evidence. It remaineth, that the knowledge we have that the Scriptures are the word of God, is only faith. For whatsoever is evident either by natural reason, or by revelation supernatural, is not called faith; else should not faith cease, no more than charity, when we are in heaven; which is contrary to the doctrine of Scripture. And, we are not said to believe, but to know those things which are evident.

9. Seeing then the acknowledgment of the Scriptures to be the word of God, is not evidence, but faith; and faith, chap. VI, sect. 7, consisteth in the trust we have in other men: it appeareth plainly that the men so trusted, are the holy men of God's church succeeding one another from the time of those that saw the wondrous works of God Almighty in the flesh; nor doth this imply that God is not the worker and efficient cause of faith, or that faith is begotten in man

without the spirit of God; for all those good opinions which we admit and believe, though they proceed from hearing, and hearing from teaching, both which are natural, yet they are the work of God. For all the works of nature are his, and they are attributed to the Spirit of God. As for example Exod. 28, 3: *Thou shalt speak unto all cunning men, whom I have filled with the spirit of wisdom, that they make Aaron's garments for his consecration, that he may serve me in the priest's office*. The faith therefore wherewith we believe, is the work of the Spirit of God, in that sense, by which the Spirit of God giveth to one man wisdom and cunning in workmanship more than to another; and by which he effecteth also in other points pertaining to our ordinary life, that one man believeth that, which upon the same grounds another doth not; and one man reverenceth the opinion, and obeyeth the commands of his superiors, and others not.

10. And seeing our faith, that the Scriptures are the word of God, began from the confidence and trust we repose in the church; there can be no doubt but that their interpretation of the same Scriptures, when any doubt or controversy shall arise, by which this fundamental point, that Jesus Christ is come in the flesh, is not called in question, is safer for any man to trust to, than his own, whether reasoning, or spirit; that is to say his own opinion.

11. Now concerning man's affections to Godward, they are not the same always that are described in the chapter concerning passions. For there, to love is to be delighted with the image or conception of the thing loved; but God is unconceivable; to love God therefore, in the Scripture, is to obey his commandments, and to love one another. Also to trust God is different from our trusting one another. For when a man trusteth a man, chap. IX, sect. 9, he layeth aside his own endeavour; but if we do so in our trust to God Almighty, we disobey him; and how shall we trust to him we disobey? To trust to God Almighty therefore is to refer to his good pleasure all that is above our own power to effect. And this is all one with acknowledging one only God; which is the first commandment. And to trust in Christ is no more, but to acknowledge him for God; which is the fundamental

article of our Christian faith. And consequently to trust, rely, or, as some express it, to cast and roll ourselves on Christ, is the same thing with the fundamental point of faith, namely, that Jesus Christ is the son of the living God.

12. To honour God internally in the heart, is the same thing with that we ordinarily call honour amongst men: for it is nothing but the acknowledging of his power; and the signs thereof the same with the signs of the honour due to our superiors, mentioned chap. VIII, sect. 6 (viz.): to praise, to magnify, to bless him, to pray to him, to thank him, to give oblations and sacrifice to him, to give attention to his word, to speak to him in prayer with consideration, to come into his presence with humble gesture, and in decent manner, and to adorn his worship with magnificence and cost. And these are natural signs of our honouring him internally. And therefore the contrary hereof: to neglect prayer, to speak to him extempore, to come to church slovenly, to adorn the place of his worship less than our own houses, to take up his name in every idle discourse, are manifest signs of contempt of the Divine Majesty. There be other signs which are arbitrary; as, to be uncovered (as we be here) to put off the shoes, as Moses at the fiery bush, and some other of that kind; which in their own nature are indifferent, till to avoid indecency and discord, it be other-wise determined by common consent.

CHAPTER XII

HOW BY DELIBERATION FROM PASSIONS PROCEED MEN'S ACTIONS

1. IT hath been declared already,* how external objects cause conceptions, and conceptions appetite and fear, which are the first unperceived beginnings of our actions: for either the action immediately followeth the first appetite, as when we do any thing upon a sudden; or else to our first appetite there succeedeth some conception of evil to happen unto us by such actions, which is fear, and withholdeth us from

proceeding. And to that fear may succeed a new appetite, and to that appetite another fear, alternately, till the action be either done, or some accident come between, to make it impossible; and so this alternate appetite and fear ceaseth. This alternate succession of appetite and fear, during all the time the action is in our power to do, or not to do, is that we call DELIBERATION; which name hath been given it for that part of the definition wherein it is said that it lasteth so long, as the action whereof we deliberate, is in our power; for so long we have liberty to do or not to do: and deliberation signifieth the taking away of our own liberty.

2. Deliberation therefore requireth in the action deliberated two conditions: one, that it be future; the other, that there be hope of doing it, or possibility of not doing it. For appetite and fear are expectations of the future; and there is no expectation of good without hope; nor of evil without possibility. Of necessaries therefore there is no deliberation. In deliberation the last appetite, as also the last fear, is called WILL (viz.) the last appetite will to do; the last fear will not to do, or will to omit. It is all one therefore to say will and last will: for though a man express his present inclination and appetite concerning the disposing of his goods, by word or writing; yet shall it not be accounted his will, because he hath liberty still to dispose of them otherwise; but when death taketh away that liberty, then it is his will.

3. VOLUNTARY actions* and omissions are such as have beginning in the will; all other are INVOLUNTARY or MIXED. Voluntary such as a man doth upon appetite or fear; involuntary such as he doth by necessity of nature, as when he is pushed, or falleth, and thereby doth good or hurt to another; mixed, such as participate of both; as when a man is carried to prison he is pulled on against his will, and yet goeth upright voluntary, for fear of being trailed along the ground: insomuch that in going to prison, going is voluntary; to the prison, involuntary. The example of him that throweth his goods out of a ship into the sea, to save his person, is of an action altogether voluntary: for, there is nothing there involuntary, but the hardness of the choice, which is not

his action, but the action of the winds; what he himself doth, is no more against his will, than to fly from danger is against the will of him that seeth no other means to preserve himself.

4. Voluntary also are the actions that proceed from sudden anger, or other sudden appetite, in such men as can discern of good and evil; for in them the time precedent is to be judged deliberation. For then also he deliberateth in what cases it is good to strike, deride, or do any other action proceeding from anger or other such sudden passion.

5. Appetite, fear, hope, and the rest of the passions are not called voluntary; for they proceed not from, but are the will; and the will is not voluntary. For a man can no more say he will will, than he will will will, and so make an infinite repetition of the word will; which is absurd, and insignificant.

6. Forasmuch as will to do is appetite, and will to omit, fear; the causes of appetite and of fear are the causes also of our will. But the propounding of benefits and of harms, that is to say, of reward and punishment, is the cause of our appetite and of our fears, and therefore also of our wills, so far forth as we believe that such rewards and benefits, as are propounded, shall arrive unto us. And consequently, our wills follow our opinions, as our actions follow our wills. In which sense they say truly and properly that say the world is governed by opinion.

7. When the wills of many concur to some one and the same action, or effect, this concourse of their wills is called CONSENT; by which we must not understand one will of many men, for every man hath his several will; but many wills to the producing of one effect. But when the wills of two divers men produce such actions as are reciprocally resistances one to the other, this is called CONTENTION: and being upon the persons of one another, BATTLE; whereas actions proceeding from consent are mutual AID.

8. When many wills are involved or included in the will of one or more consenting, (which how it may be, shall be hereafter declared) then is that involving of many wills in one or more called UNION.

9. In deliberations interrupted, as they may be by diversion to other business, or by sleep, the last appetite of such part of the deliberation is called INTENTION, or purpose.

CHAPTER XIII

HOW BY LANGUAGE MEN WORK UPON EACH OTHER'S MINDS

1. HAVING spoken of the powers and acts of the mind, both cognitive and motive, considered in every man by himself, without relation to others; it will fall fitly into this chapter, to speak of the effects of the same powers one upon another; which effects are also the signs, by which one taketh notice of what another conceiveth and intendeth. Of these signs, some are such as cannot easily be counterfeited; as actions and gestures, especially if they be sudden; whereof I have mentioned some for example sake in the ninth chapter, at the several passions whereof they are signs; others there are that may be counterfeited: and those are words or speech; of the use and effect whereof I am to speak in this place.

2.* The first use of language, is the expression of our conceptions, that is, the begetting in another the same conceptions that we have in ourselves; and this is called TEACHING; wherein if the conceptions of him that teacheth continually accompany his words, beginning at something from experience, then it begetteth the like evidence in the hearer that understandeth them, and maketh him know something, which he is therefore said to LEARN. But if there be not such evidence, then such teaching is called PERSUASION, and begetteth no more in the hearer, than what is in the speaker, bare opinion. And the signs of two opinions contradictory one to another, namely, affirmation and negation of the same thing, is called a CONTROVERSY; but both affirmations, or both negations, CONSENT in opinion.

3. The infallible sign of teaching exactly, and without

error, is this: that no man hath ever taught the contrary; not that few, how few soever, if any. For commonly truth is on the side of the few, rather than of the multitude; but when in opinions and questions considered and discussed by many, it happeneth that not any one of the men that so discuss them differ from another, then it may be justly inferred, they know what they teach, and that otherwise they do not. And this appeareth most manifestly to them that have considered the divers subjects wherein men have exercised their pens, and the divers ways in which they have proceeded; together with the diversity of the success thereof. For those men who have taken in hand to consider nothing else but the comparison of magnitudes, numbers, times, and motions, and their proportions one to another, have thereby been the authors of all those excellences, wherein we differ from such savage people as are now the inhabitants of divers places in America; and as have been the inhabitants heretofore of those countries where at this day arts and sciences do most flourish. For from the studies of these men hath proceeded, whatsoever cometh to us for ornament by navigation; and whatsoever we have beneficial to human society by the division, distinction, and portraying of the face of the earth; whatsoever also we have by the account of times, and foresight of the course of heaven; whatsoever by measuring distances, planes, and solids of all sorts; and whatsoever either elegant or defensible in building: all which supposed away, what do we differ from the wildest of the Indians? Yet to this day was it never heard of, that there was any controversy concerning any conclusion in this subject; the science whereof hath nevertheless been continually amplified and enriched with conclusions of most difficult and profound speculation. The reason whereof is apparent to every man that looketh into their writings; for they proceed from most low and humble principles, evident even to the meanest capacity; going on slowly, and with most scrupulous ratiocination (viz.) from the imposition of names they infer the truth of their first propositions; and from two of the first, a third; and from any two of the three a fourth; and so on, according to the steps of science, mentioned chap. VI, sect. 4.

On the other side, those men who have written concerning the faculties, passions, and manners of men, that is to say, of moral philosophy, or of policy, government, and laws, whereof there be infinite volumes have been so far from removing doubt and controversy in the questions they have handled, that they have very much multiplied the same; nor doth any man at this day so much as pretend to know more than hath been delivered two thousand years ago by Aristotle. And yet every man thinks that in this subject he knoweth as much as any other; supposing there needeth thereunto no study but that it accrueth to them by natural wit; though they play, or employ their mind otherwise in the purchase of wealth or place. The reason whereof is no other, than that in their writings and discourses they take for principles those opinions which are already vulgarly received, whether true or false; being for the most part false. There is therefore a great deal of difference between teaching and persuading; the signs of this being controversy; the sign of the former, no controversy.

4. There be two sorts of men that be commonly called learned: one is that sort that proceedeth evidently from humble principles, as is described in the last section; and these men are called *mathematici*; the other are they that take up maxims from their education, and from the authority of men, or of custom, and take the habitual discourse of the tongue for ratiocination; and these are called *dogmatici*. Now seeing in the last section, those we call mathematici are absolved of the crime of breeding controversy; and they that pretend not to learning cannot be accused; the fault lieth altogether in the dogmatics, that is to say, those that are imperfectly learned, and with passion press to have their opinions pass everywhere for truth, without any evident demonstration either from experience, or from places of Scripture of uncontroverted interpretation.

5. The expression of those conceptions which cause in us the expectation of good while we deliberate, as also of those which cause our expectation of evil, is that which we call COUNSELLING. And as in the internal deliberation of the mind concerning what we ourselves are to do, or not to

do, the consequences of the action are our counsellors, by alternate succession in the mind; so in the counsel which a man taketh from other men, the counsellors alternately do make appear the consequences of the action, and do not any of them deliberate, but furnish amongst them all him that is counselled, with arguments whereupon to deliberate within himself.

6. Another use of speech is the expression of appetite, intention, and will; as the appetite of knowledge by interrogation; appetite to have a thing done by another, as request, prayer, petition; expressions of our purpose or intention, as PROMISE, which is the affirmation or negation of some action to be done in the future; THREATENING, which is the promise of evil; and COMMANDING, which is that speech by which we signify to another our appetite or desire to have any thing done, or left undone, for reason contained in the will itself: for it is not properly said, *Sic volo, sic jubeo*, without that other clause, *Stet pro ratione voluntas*:* and when the command is a sufficient reason to move us to the action, then is that command called a LAW.

7. Another use of speech is INSTIGATION and APPEASING, by which we increase or diminish one another's passions; it is the same thing with persuasion: the difference not being real. For the begetting of opinion and passion is the same act; but whereas in persuasion we aim at getting opinion from passion; here, the end is, to raise passion from opinion. And as in raising an opinion from passion, any premises are good enough to infer the desired conclusion; so, in raising passion from opinion, it is no matter whether the opinion be true or false, or the narration historical or fabulous. For not truth, but image, maketh passion; and a tragedy affecteth no less than a murder if well acted.

8. Though words be the signs we have of one another's opinions and intentions: because the equivocation of them is so frequent, according to the diversity of contexture, and of the company wherewith they go (which the presence of him that speaketh, our sight of his actions, and conjecture of his intentions, must help to discharge us of): it must be extreme hard to find out the opinions and meanings of those men

that are gone from us long ago, and have left us no other signification thereof but their books; which cannot possibly be understood without history enough to discover those aforementioned circumstances, and also without great prudence to observe them.

9. When it happeneth that a man signifieth unto us two contradictory opinions whereof the one is clearly and directly signified, and the other either drawn from that by consequence, or not known to be contradictory to it; then (when he is not present to explicate himself better) we are to take the former of his opinions; for that is clearly signified to be his, and directly, whereas the other might proceed from error in the deduction, or ignorance of the repugnancy. The like also is to be held in two contradictory expressions of a man's intention and will, for the same reason.

10. Forasmuch as whosoever speaketh to another, intendeth thereby to make him understand what he saith; if he speak unto him, either in a language which he that heareth understandeth not, or use any word in other sense than he believeth is the sense of him that heareth; he intendeth also to make him not understand what he saith; which is a contradiction of himself. It is therefore always to be supposed, that he which intendeth not to deceive, alloweth the private interpretation of his speech to him to whom it is addressed.

11. Silence in them that think it will be so taken, is a sign of consent; for so little labour being required to say No, it is to be presumed, that in this case he that saith it not, consenteth.*

CHAPTER XIV*

OF THE ESTATE AND RIGHT OF NATURE

1. In the precedent chapters* hath been set forth the whole nature of man, consisting in the powers natural of his body and mind, and may all be comprehended in these four: strength of body, experience, reason, and passion.

2. In this chapter it will be expedient to consider in what estate of security this our nature hath placed us, and what probability it hath left us of continuing and preserving ourselves against the violence of one another. And first, if we consider how little odds there is of strength or knowledge between men of mature age, and with how great facility he that is the weaker in strength or in wit, or in both, may utterly destroy the power of the stronger, since there needeth but little force to the taking away of a man's life; we may conclude that men considered in mere nature,* ought to admit amongst themselves equality; and that he that claimeth no more, may be esteemed moderate.

3. On the other side, considering the great difference there is in men, from the diversity of their passions, how some are vainly glorious, and hope for precedency and superiority above their fellows, not only when they are equal in power, but also when they are inferior; we must needs acknowledge that it must necessarily follow, that those men who are moderate, and look for no more but equality of nature, shall be obnoxious to the force of others, that will attempt to subdue them. And from hence shall proceed a general diffidence in mankind, and mutual fear one of another.

4. Farther, since men by natural passion are divers ways offensive one to another, every man thinking well of himself, and hating to see the same in others, they must needs provoke one another by words, and other signs of contempt and hatred, which are incident to all comparison: till at last they must determine the pre-eminence by strength and force of body.

5. Moreover, considering that many men's appetites carry them to one and the same end; which end sometimes can neither be enjoyed in common, nor divided, it followeth that the stronger must enjoy it alone, and that it be decided by battle who is the stronger. And thus the greatest part of men, upon no assurance of odds, do nevertheless, through vanity, or comparison, or appetite, provoke the rest, that otherwise would be contented with equality.

6. And forasmuch as necessity of nature maketh men to

will and desire *bonum sibi*, that which is good for themselves, and to avoid that which is hurtful; but most of all that terrible enemy of nature, death, from whom we expect both the loss of all power, and also the greatest of bodily pains in the losing; it is not against reason that a man doth all he can to preserve his own body and limbs, both from death and pain. And that which is not against reason, men call RIGHT, or *jus*, or blameless liberty of using our own natural power and ability. It is therefore a *right of nature*: that every man may preserve his own life and limbs, with all the power he hath.

7. And because where a man hath right to the end, and the end cannot be attained without the means, that is, without such things as are necessary to the end, it is consequent that it is not against reason, and therefore right for a man, to use all means and do whatsoever action is necessary for the preservation of his body.

8. Also every man by right of nature is judge himself of the necessity of the means, and of the greatness of the danger. For if it be against reason, that I be judge of mine own danger myself, then it is reason, that another man be judge thereof. But the same reason that maketh another man judge of those things that concern me, maketh me also judge of that that concerneth him. And therefore I have reason to judge of his sentence, whether it be for my benefit, or not.

9. As a man's judgment, in right of nature, is to be employed for his own benefit, so also the strength, knowledge, and art of every man is then rightly employed, when he useth it for himself; else must not a man have right to preserve himself.

10. Every man by nature hath right to all things, that is to say, to do whatsoever he listeth to whom he listeth, to possess, use, and enjoy all things he will and can. For seeing all things he willeth, must therefore be good unto him in his own judgment, because he willeth them; and may tend to his preservation some time or other; or he may judge so, and we have made him judge thereof, sect. 8: it followeth that all things may rightly also be done by him. And for this

cause it is rightly said: *Natura dedit omnia omnibus*, that Nature hath given all things to all men; insomuch, that *jus* and *utile*, right and profit, is the same thing. But that right of all men to all things, is in effect no better than if no man had right to any thing. For there is little use and benefit of the right a man hath, when another as strong, or stronger than himself, hath right to the same.

11. Seeing then to the offensiveness of man's nature one to another, there is added a right of every man to every thing, whereby one man invadeth with right, and another with right resisteth; and men live thereby in perpetual diffidence, and study how to preoccupate each other; the estate of men in this natural liberty is the estate of war. For WAR is nothing else but that time wherein the will and intention of contending by force is either by words or actions sufficiently declared; and the time which is not war is PEACE.

12. The estate of hostility and war being such, as thereby nature itself is destroyed, and men kill one another (as we know also that it is, both by the experience of savage nations that live at this day, and by the histories of our ancestors, the old inhabitants of Germany and other now civil countries, where we find the people few and short lived, and without the ornaments and comforts of life, which by peace and society are usually invented and procured): he therefore that desireth to live in such an estate, as is the estate of liberty and right of all to all, contradicteth himself. For every man by natural necessity desireth his own good, to which this estate is contrary, wherein we suppose contention between men by nature equal, and able to destroy one another.

13. Seeing this right of protecting ourselves by our own discretion and force, proceedeth from danger, and that danger from the equality between men's forces: much more reason is there, that a man prevent such equality before the danger cometh, and before there be necessity of battle. A man therefore that hath another man in his power to rule or govern, to do good to, or harm, hath right, by the advantage of this his present power, to take caution at his pleasure, for his security against that other in the time to come. He

therefore that hath already subdued his adversary, or gotten into his power any other that either by infancy, or weakness, is unable to resist him, by right of nature may take the best caution, that such infant, or such feeble and subdued person can give him, of being ruled and governed by him for the time to come. For seeing we intend always our own safety and preservation, we manifestly contradict that our intention, if we willingly dismiss such a one, and suffer him at once to gather strength and be our enemy. Out of which may also be collected, that irresistible might in the state of nature is right.

14. But since it is supposed from the equality of strength and other natural faculties of men, that no man is of might sufficient, to assure himself for any long time, of preserving himself thereby, whilst he remaineth in the state of hostility and war; reason therefore dictateth to every man for his own good, to seek after peace, as far forth as there is hope to attain the same; and to strengthen himself with all the help he can procure, for his own defence against those, from whom such peace cannot be obtained; and to do all those things which necessarily conduce thereunto.

CHAPTER XV

OF THE DIVESTING NATURAL RIGHT BY
GIFT AND COVENANT

1. WHAT it is we call the law of nature, is not agreed upon, by those that have hitherto written. For the most part, such writers as have occasion to affirm, that anything is against the law of nature, do allege no more than this, that it is against the consent of all nations, or the wisest and most civil nations. But it is not agreed upon, who shall judge which nations are the wisest. Others make that against the law of nature, which is contrary to the consent of all mankind; which definition cannot be allowed, because then no man could offend against the law of nature; for the nature of every man is contained under the nature of man-

kind. But forasmuch as all men, carried away by the violence of their passion, and by evil customs, do those things which are commonly said to be against the law of nature; it is not the consent of passion, or consent in some error gotten by custom, that makes the law of nature. Reason* is no less of the nature of man than passion, and is the same in all men, because all men agree in the will to be directed and governed in the way to that which they desire to attain, namely their own good, which is the work of reason. There can therefore be no other law of nature than reason, nor no other precepts of NATURAL LAW, than those which declare unto us the ways of peace, where the same may be obtained, and of defence where it may not.

2. One precept of the law of nature therefore is this, *that every man divest himself of the right he hath to all things by nature*. For when divers men have right not only to all things else, but to one another's persons, if they use the same, there ariseth thereby invasion on the one part, and resistance on the other, which is war; and therefore contrary to the law of nature, the sun whereof consisteth in making peace.

3. When a man divesteth and putteth from himself his right, he either simply relinquisheth it, or transferreth the same to another man. To RELINQUISH it, is by sufficient signs to declare, that it is his will no more to do that action, which of right he might have done before. To TRANSFER right to another, is by sufficient signs to declare to that other accepting thereof, that it is his will not to resist, or hinder him, according to that right he had thereto before he transferred it. For seeing that by nature every man hath right to every thing, it is impossible for a man to transfer unto another any right that he had not before. And therefore all that a man doth in transferring of right, is no more but a declaring of the will, to suffer him, to whom he hath so transferred his right, to make benefit of the same, without molestation. As for example, when a man giveth his land or goods to another, he taketh from himself the right to enter into, and make use of the said land or goods, or otherwise to hinder him of the use of what he hath given.

4. In transferring of right, two things therefore are re-

quired: one on the part of him that transferreth; which is, a sufficient signification of his will therein: the other, on the part of him to whom it is transferred; which is, a sufficient signification of his acceptation thereof. Either of these failing, the right remaineth where it was; nor is it to be supposed, that he which giveth his right to one that accepteth it not, doth thereby simply relinquish it, and transfer it to whomsoever will receive it; inasmuch as the cause of the transferring the same to one, rather than to another, is in that one, rather than in the rest.

5. When there appear no other signs that a man hath relinquished, or transferred his right, but only words; it behoveth that the same be done in words, that signify the present time, or the time past, and not only the time to come. For he that saith of the time to come, as for example, to-morrow: I will give, declareth evidently, that he hath not yet given. The right therefore remaineth in him to-day, and so continues till he have given actually. But he that saith: I give, presently, or have given to another any thing, to have and enjoy the same to-morrow, or any other time future, hath now actually transferred the said right, which otherwise he should have had at the time that the other is to enjoy it.

6. But because words alone are not a sufficient declaration of the mind, as hath been shewn chap. XIII, sect. 8 words spoken *de futuro*, when the will of him that speaketh them may be gathered by other signs, may be taken very often as if they were meant *de præsenti*. For when it appeareth that he that giveth would have his word so understood, by him to whom he giveth, as if he did actually transfer his right, then he must needs be understood to will all that is necessary to the same.

7. When a man transferreth any right of his to another, without consideration of reciprocal benefit, past, present, or to come; this is called FREE GIFT. And in free gift no other words can be binding, but those which are *de præsenti*, or *de præterito*: for being *de futuro** only, they transfer nothing, nor can they be understood, as if they proceeded from the will of the giver; because being a free gift, it carrieth with it no obligation greater than that which is enforced by the

words. For he that promiseth to give, without any other consideration but his own affection, so long as he hath not given, deliberateth still, according as the causes of his affections continue or diminish; and he that deliberateth hath not yet willed, because the will is the last act of his deliberation. He that promiseth therefore, is not thereby a donor, but *doson*; which name was given to that Antiochus,* that promised often, but seldom gave.

8. When a man transferreth his right, upon consideration of reciprocal benefit, this is not free gift, but mutual donation; and is called CONTRACT. And in all contracts, either both parties presently perform, and put each other into a certainty and assurance of enjoying what they contract for: as when men buy or sell, or barter; or one party performeth presently, and the other promiseth, as when one selleth upon trust; or else neither party performeth presently, but trust one another. And it is impossible there should be any kind of contract besides these three. For either both the contractors trust, or neither; or else one trusteth, and the other not.

9. In all contracts where there is trust, the promise of him that is trusted, is called a COVENANT.* And this, though it be a promise, and of the time to come, yet doth it transfer the right, when that time cometh, no less than an actual donation. For it is a manifest sign, that he which did perform, understood it was the will of him that was trusted, to perform also. Promises therefore, upon consideration of reciprocal benefit, are covenants and signs of the will, or last act of deliberation, whereby the liberty of performing, or not performing, is taken away, and consequently are obligatory. For where liberty ceaseth, there beginneth obligation.

10. Nevertheless, in contracts that consist of such mutual trust, as that nothing be by either party performed for the present, when the contract is between such as are not compellable, he that performeth first, considering the disposition of men to take advantage of every thing for their benefit, doth but betray himself thereby to the covetousness, or other passion of him with whom he contracteth. And therefore such covenants are of none effect. For there is no

reason why the one should perform first, if the other be likely not to perform afterward. And whether he be likely or not, he that doubteth, shall be judge himself (as hath been said chap. XIV, sect. 8), as long as they remain in the estate and liberty of nature. But when there shall be such power coercive over both the parties, as shall deprive them of their private judgments in this point; then may such covenants be effectual; seeing he that performeth first shall have no reasonable cause to doubt of the performance of the other, that may be compelled thereunto.

11. And forasmuch as in all covenants, and contracts, and donations, the acceptance of him to whom the right is transferred, is necessary to the essence of those covenants, donations, &c., it is impossible to make a covenant or donation to any, that by nature, or absence, are unable, or if able, do not actually declare their acceptation of the same. First of all therefore it is impossible for any man to make a covenant with God Almighty, farther than it hath pleased him to declare who shall receive and accept of the said covenant in his name. Also it is impossible to make covenant with those living creatures, of whose wills we have no sufficient sign, for want of common language.

12. A covenant to do any action at a certain time and place, is then dissolved by the covenanter, when that time cometh, either by the performance, or by the violation. For a covenant is void that is once impossible. But a covenant not to do, without time limited, which is as much as to say, a covenant never to do, is dissolved by the covenanter then only, when he violateth it, or dieth. And generally all covenants are dischargeable by the covenantee, to whose benefit, and by whose right, he that maketh the covenant is obliged. This right therefore of the covenantee relinquished, is a release of the covenant. And universally, for the same reason, all obligations are determinable at the will of the obliger.

13. It is a question often moved, whether such covenants oblige, as are extorted from men by fear. As for example: whether, if a man for fear of death, have promised to give a thief an hundred pounds the next day, and not discover him,

whether such covenant be obligatory or not. And though in some cases such covenant may be void, yet it is not therefore void, because extorted by fear. For there appeareth no reason, why that which we do upon fear, should be less firm than that which we do for covetousness. For both the one and the other maketh the action voluntary.* And if no covenant should be good, that proceedeth from fear of death, no conditions of peace between enemies, nor any laws could be of force; which are all consented to from that fear. For who would lose the liberty that nature hath given him, of governing himself by his own will and power, if they feared not death in the retaining of it? What prisoner in war might be trusted to seek his ransom, and ought not rather to be killed, if he were not tied by the grant of his life, to perform his promise? But after the introduction of policy and laws, the case may alter; for if by the law the performance of such a covenant be forbidden, then he that promiseth anything to a thief, not only may, but must refuse to perform it. But if the law forbid not the performance, but leave it to the will of the promiser, then is the performance still lawful: and the covenant of things lawful is obligatory, even towards a thief.

14. He that giveth, promiseth, or covenanteth to one, and after giveth, promiseth, or covenanteth the same to another, maketh void the latter act. For it is impossible for a man to transfer that right which he himself hath not; and that right he hath not, which he himself hath before transferred.

15. An OATH is a clause annexed to a promise, containing a renunciation of God's mercy, by him that promiseth, in case he perform not as far as is lawful and possible for him to do. And this appeareth by the words which make the essence of the oath (viz.) *so help me God*. So also was it amongst the heathen. And the form of the Romans was, *Thou Jupiter kill him that breaketh, as I kill this beast*. The intention therefore of an oath being to provoke vengeance upon the breakers of covenants; it is to no purpose to swear by men, be they never so great, because their punishment by divers accidents may be avoided, whether they will, or

no; but God's punishment not. Though it were a custom of many nations, to swear by the life of their princes; yet those princes being ambitious of divine honour, give sufficient testimony, that they believed, nothing ought to be sworn by, but the Deity.

16. And seeing men cannot be afraid of the power they believe not, and an oath is to no purpose, without fear of him they swear by; it is necessary that he that sweareth, do it in that form which himself admitteth in his own religion, and not in that form which he useth, that putteth him to the oath. For though all men may know by nature, that there is an Almighty power, nevertheless they believe not, that they swear by him, in any other form or name, than what their own (which they think the true) religion teacheth them.

17. And by the definition of an oath, it appeareth that it addeth not a greater obligation to perform the covenant sworn, than the covenant carrieth in itself, but it putteth a man into a greater danger, and of greater punishment.

18. Covenants and oaths are *de voluntariis*, that is, *de possibilibus*. Nor can the covenantee understand the covenanter to promise impossibles; for they fall not under deliberation: and consequently (by chap. XIII, sect. 10, which maketh the covenantee interpreter), no covenant is understood to bind further, than to our best endeavour, either in performance of the thing promised, or in something equivalent.

CHAPTER XVI

SOME OF THE LAWS OF NATURE

1. IT is a common saying that nature maketh nothing in vain. And it is most certain, that as the truth of a conclusion, is no more but the truth of the premises that make it; so the force of the command, or law of nature, is no more than the force of the reasons inducing thereunto. Therefore the law of nature mentioned in the former chapter, sect. 2, namely,

That every man should divest himself of the right, &c. were utterly vain, and of none effect, if this also were not a law of the same Nature, *That every man is obliged to stand to, and perform, those covenants which he maketh*. For what benefit is it to a man, that any thing be promised, or given unto him, if he that giveth, or promiseth, performeth not, or retaineth still the right of taking back what he hath given?

2. The breach or violation of covenant, is that which men call INJURY, consisting in some action or omission, which is therefore called UNJUST. For it is action or omission, without *jus*, or right; which was transferred or relinquished before. There is a great similitude between that we call injury, or injustice in the actions and conversations of men in the world, and that which is called *absurd* in the arguments and disputations of the Schools. For as he, that is driven to contradict an assertion by him before maintained, is said to be reduced to an absurdity; so he that through passion doth, or omitteth that which before by covenant he promised not to do, or not to omit, is said to commit injustice. And there is in every breach of covenant a contradiction properly so called; for he that covenanteth, willeth to do, or omit, in the time to come; and he that doth any action, willeth it in that present, which is part of the future time, contained in the covenant: and therefore he that violateth a covenant, willeth the doing and the not doing of the same thing, at the same time; which is a plain contradiction. And so injury is an absurdity of conversation, as absurdity is a kind of injustice in disputation.

3. In all violation of covenant, (to whomsoever accrueth the damage) the injury is done only to him to whom the covenant was made. For example, if a man covenant to obey his master, and the master command him to give money to a third, which he promiseth to do, and doth not; though this be to the damage of the third, yet the injury is done to the master only. For he could violate no covenant with him, with whom none was made, and therefore doth him no injury: for injury consisteth in violation of covenant, by the definition thereof.

4. The names of just, unjust, justice, injustice, are

equivocal, and signify diversely. For justice and injustice, when they be attributed to actions, signify the same thing with no injury, and injury; and denominate the action just, or unjust, but not the man so; for they denominate him guilty, or not guilty. But when justice and injustice are attributed to men, they signify proneness and affection, and inclination of nature, that is to say, passions of the mind apt to produce just and unjust actions. So that when a man is said to be just, or unjust, not the action, but the passion, and aptitude to do such action is considered. And therefore a just man may have committed an unjust act; and an unjust man may have done justly not only one, but most of his actions. For there is an *oderunt peccare** in the unjust, as well as in the just, but from different causes; for the unjust man who abstaineth from injuries for fear of punishment, declareth plainly that the justice of his actions dependeth upon civil constitution, from whence punishments proceed; which would otherwise in the estate of nature be unjust, according to the fountain from whence they spring. This distinction therefore of justice, and injustice, ought to be remembered: that when injustice is taken for guilt, the action is unjust, but not therefore the man; and when justice is taken for guiltlessness, the actions are just, and yet not always the man. Likewise when justice and injustice are taken for habits of the mind, the man may be just, or unjust, and yet not all his actions so.

5. Concerning the justice of actions, the same is usually divided into two kinds, whereof men call the one commutative, and the other distributive; and are said to consist, the one in proportion arithmetical, the other in geometrical: and commutative justice, they place in permutation, as buying, selling, and barter; distributive, in giving to every man according to their deserts. Which distinction is not well made, inasmuch as injury, which is the injustice of action, consisteth not in the inequality of things changed, or distributed, but in the inequality that men (contrary to nature and reason) assume unto themselves above their fellows; of which inequality shall be spoken hereafter. And for commutative justice placed in buying and selling, though the

thing bought be unequal to the price given for it; yet forasmuch as both the buyer and the seller are made judges of the value, and are thereby both satisfied: there can be no injury done on either side, neither party having trusted, or covenanted with the other. And for distributive justice, which consisteth in the distribution of our own benefits; seeing a thing is therefore said to be our own, because we may dispose of it at our own pleasure: it can be no injury to any man, though our liberality be further extended towards another, than towards him; unless we be thereto obliged by covenant: and then the injustice consisteth in the violation of that covenant, and not in the inequality of distribution.

6. It happeneth many times that a man benefitteth or contributeth to the power of another, without any covenant, but only upon confidence and trust of obtaining the grace and favour of that other, whereby he may procure a greater, or no less benefit or assistance to himself. For by necessity of nature every man doth in all his voluntary actions intend some good unto himself.* In this case it is a law of nature, *That no man suffer him, that thus trusteth to his charity, or good affection towards him, to be in the worse estate for his trusting.** For if he shall so do, men will not dare to confer mutually to each other's defence, nor put themselves into each other's mercy upon any terms whatsoever; but rather abide the utmost and worst event of hostility; by which general diffidence, men will not only be enforced to war, but also afraid to come so much within the danger of one another, as to make any overture of peace. But this is to be understood of those only, that confer their benefits (as I have said) upon trust only, and not for triumph or ostentation. For as when they do it upon trust, the end they aimed at, namely to be well used, is the reward; so also when they do it for ostentation, they have the reward in themselves.

7. But seeing in this case there passeth no covenant, the breach of this law of nature is not to be called injury; it hath another name (viz.) INGRATITUDE.

8. It is also a law of nature, *That every man do help and endeavour to accommodate each other, as far as may be without danger of their persons, and loss of their means, to*

maintain and defend themselves. For seeing the causes of war and desolation proceed from those passions, by which we strive to accommodate ourselves, and to leave others as far as we can behind us: it followeth that that passion by which we strive mutually to accommodate each other, must be the cause of peace. And this passion is that charity defined chap. IX, sect. 17.

9. And in this precept of nature is included and comprehended also this, *That a man forgive and pardon him that hath done him wrong, upon his repentance, and caution for the future.* FOR PARDON is peace granted to him, that (having provoked to war) demandeth it. It is not therefore charity, but fear, when a man giveth peace to him that repenteth not, nor giveth caution for maintaining thereof in the time to come. For he that repenteth not, remaineth with the affection of an enemy; as also doth he that refuseth to give caution, and consequently is presumed not to seek after peace, but advantage. And therefore to forgive him is not commanded in this law of nature, nor is charity, but may sometimes be prudence. Otherwise, not to pardon upon repentance and caution, considering men cannot abstain from provoking one another, is never to give peace; and that is against the general definition of the law of nature.

10. And seeing the law of nature commandeth pardon when there is repentance, and caution for the future; it followeth that the same law ordaineth, *That no revenge be taken upon the consideration only of the offence past, but of the benefit to come*; that is to say, that all revenge ought to tend to amendment, either of the person offending, or of others, by the example of his punishment; which is sufficiently apparent, in that the law of nature commandeth pardon, where the future time is secured. The same is also apparent by this: that revenge when it considereth the offence past, is nothing else but present triumph and glory, and directeth to no end; for end implieth some future good; and what is directed to no end, is therefore unprofitable; and consequently the triumph of revenge, is vain glory: and whatsoever is vain, is against reason; and to hurt one another without reason, is contrary to that, which by

supposition is every man's benefit, namely peace; and what is contrary to peace, is contrary to the law of nature.

11. And because all signs which we shew to one another of hatred and contempt, provoke in the highest degree to quarrel and battle (inasmuch as life itself, with the condition of enduring scorn, is not esteemed worth the enjoying, much less peace); it must necessarily be implied as a law of nature, *That no man reproach, revile, deride, or any otherwise declare his hatred, contempt, or disesteem of any other.* But this law is very little practised. For what is more ordinary than reproaches of those that are rich, towards them that are not? or of those that sit in place of judicature, towards those that are accused at the bar? although to grieve them in that manner, be no part of the punishment for their crime, nor contained in their office; but use hath prevailed, that what was lawful in the lord towards the servant whom he maintaineth, is also practised as lawful in the more mighty towards the less; though they contribute nothing towards their maintenance.

12. It is also a law of nature, *That men allow commerce and traffic indifferently to one another.* For he that alloweth that to one man, which he denieth to another, declareth his hatred to him, to whom he denieth; and to declare hatred is war. And upon this title was grounded the great war between the Athenians and the Peloponnesians.* For would the Athenians have condescended to suffer the Megareans, their neighbours, to traffic in their ports and markets, that war had not begun.

13. And this also is a law of nature, *That all messengers of peace, and such as are employed to procure and maintain amity between man and man, may safely come and go.* For seeing peace is the general law of nature, the means thereto, such as are these men, must in the same law be comprehended.

CHAPTER XVII

OTHER LAWS OF NATURE

1.* THE question, which is the better man, is determinable only in the estate of government and policy, though it be mistaken for a question of nature, not only by ignorant men, that think one man's blood better than another's by nature; but also by him, whose opinions are at this day, and in these parts of greater authority than any other human writings (Aristotle). For he putteth so much difference between the powers of men by nature, that he doubteth not to set down, as the ground of all his politics, that some men are by nature worthy to govern, and others by nature ought to serve. Which foundation hath not only weakened the whole frame of his politics, but hath also given men colour and pretences, whereby to disturb and hinder the peace of one another. For though there were such a difference of nature, that master and servant were not by consent of men, but by inherent virtue; yet who hath that eminency of virtue, above others, and who is so stupid as not to govern himself, shall never be agreed upon amongst men; who do every one naturally think himself as able, at the least, to govern another, as another to govern him. And when there was any contention between the finer and the coarser wits, (as there hath been often in times of sedition and civil war) for the most part these latter carried away the victory and as long as men arrogate to themselves more honour than they give to others, it cannot be imagined how they can possibly live in peace: and consequently we are to suppose, that for peace sake, nature hath ordained this law, *That every man acknowledge other for his equal*. And the breach of this law, is that we call PRIDE.

2. As it was necessary that a man should not retain his right to every thing, so also was it, that he should retain his right to some things: to his own body (for example) the right of defending, whereof he could not transfer; to the use of fire, water, free air, and place to live in, and to all things necessary for life. Nor doth the law of nature command any divesting of other rights, than of those only which cannot be

retained without the loss of peace. Seeing then many rights are retained, when we enter into peace one with another, reason and the law of nature dictateth, *Whatsoever right any man requireth to retain, he allow every other man to retain the same.* For he that doth not so, alloweth not the equality mentioned in the former section. For there is no acknowledgement of the equality of worth, without attribution of the equality of benefit and respect. And this allowance of *æqualia æqualibus*, is the same thing with the allowing of *proportionalia proportionalibus.* For when a man alloweth to every man alike, the allowance he maketh will be in the same proportion, in which are the numbers of men to whom they are made. And this is it men mean by distributive justice, and is properly termed EQUITY. The breach of this law is that which the Greeks call Πλεονεξία, which is commonly rendered covetousness, but seemeth to be more precisely expressed by the word ENCROACHING.*

3. If there pass no other covenant, the law of nature is, *That such things as cannot be divided, be used in common, proportionably to the numbers of them that are to use the same, or without limitation when the quantity thereof sufficeth.* For first supposing the thing to be used in common not sufficient for them that are to use it without limitation, if a few shall make more use thereof than the rest, that equality is not observed, which is required in the second section. And this is to be understood, as all the rest of the laws of nature, without any other covenant antecedent; for a man may have given away his right of common, and so the case be altered.

4. In those things which neither can be divided, nor used in common, the rule of nature must needs be one of these: lot, or alternate use; for besides these two ways, there can no other equality be imagined. And for alternate use, he that beginneth hath the advantage; and to reduce that advantage to equality, there is no other way but lot: in things, therefore, indivisible and incommunicable, it is the law of nature, *That the use be alternate, or the advantage given away by lot*; because there is no other way of equality; and equality is the law of nature.

5. There be two sorts of lots: one arbitrary, made by men, and commonly known by the names of lot, chance, hazard, and the like; and there is natural lot, such as is primogeniture, which is no more but the chance, or lot of being first born; which, it seemeth, they considered, that call inheritance by the name of *cleronomia*, which signifieth distribution by lot. Secondly, *prima occupatio*, first seizing or finding of a thing, whereof no man made use before, which for the most part also is merely chance.

6. Although men agree upon these laws of nature, and endeavour to observe the same; yet considering the passions of men, that make it difficult to understand by what actions, and circumstances of actions, those laws are broken; there must needs arise many great controversies about the interpretation thereof, by which the peace must needs be dissolved, and men return again to their former estate of hostility. For the taking away of which controversies, it is necessary that there be some common arbitrator and judge, to whose sentence both the parties to the controversy ought to stand. And therefore it is a law of nature, *That in every controversy, the parties thereto ought mutually to agree upon an arbitrator, whom they both trust; and mutually to covenant to stand to the sentence he shall give therein*. For where every man is his own judge, there properly is no judge at all; as where every man carveth out his own right, it hath the same effect, as if there were no right at all; and where is no judge, there is no end of controversy, and therefore the right of hostility remaineth.

7. AN ARBITRATOR therefore or judge is he that is trusted by the parties to any controversy, to determine the same by the declaration of his own judgment therein. Out of which followeth: first, that the judge ought not to be concerned in the controversy he endeth; for in that case he is party, and ought by the same reason to be judged by another; secondly, that he maketh no covenant with either of the parties, to pronounce sentence for the one, more than for the other. Nor doth he covenant so much, as that his sentence shall be just; for that were to make the parties judges of the sentence, whereby the controversy would remain still un-

decided. Nevertheless for the trust reposed in him, and for the equality which the law of nature requireth him to consider in the parties, he violateth that law, if for favour, or hatred to either party, he give other sentence than he thinketh right. And thirdly, that no man ought to make himself judge in any controversy between others, unless they consent and agree thereto.

8. It is also of the law of nature, *That no man obtrude or press his advice or counsel to any man that declareth himself unwilling to hear the same*. For seeing a man taketh counsel concerning what is good or hurt of himself only, and not of his counsellor; and that counsel is a voluntary action, and therefore tendeth also to the good of the counsellor: there may often be just cause to suspect the counsellor. And though there be none, yet seeing counsel unwilling heard is a needless offence to him that is not willing to hear it, and offences tend all to the breach of peace: it is therefore against the law of nature to obtrude it.

9. A man that shall see these laws of nature set down and inferred with so many words, and so much ado, may think there is yet much more difficulty and subtlety required to acknowledge and do according to the said laws in every sudden occasion, when a man hath but a little time to consider. And while we consider man in most passions, as of anger, ambition, covetousness, vain glory, and the like that tend to the excluding of natural equality, it is true; but without these passions, there is an easy rule to know upon a sudden, whether the action I be to do, be against the law of nature or not: and it is but this, *That a man imagine himself in the place of the party with whom he hath to do, and reciprocally him in his*; which is no more but a changing (as it were) of the scales. For every man's passion weigheth heavy in his own scale, but not in the scale of his neighbour. And this rule is very well known and expressed by this old dictate, *Quod tibi fieri non vis, alteri ne feceris*.*

10. These laws of nature, the sum whereof consisteth in forbidding us to be our own judges, and our own carvers, and in commanding us to accommodate one another; in case they should be observed by some, and not by others, would make the observers but a prey to them that should neglect

them; leaving the good, both without defence against the wicked, and also with a charge to assist them: which is against the scope of the said laws, that are made only for the protection and defence of them that keep them. Reason therefore, and the law of nature over and above all these particular laws, doth dictate this law in general, *That those particular laws be so far observed, as they subject us not to any incommodity, that in our own judgments may arise, by the neglect thereof in those towards whom we observe them*; and consequently requireth no more but the desire and constant intention to endeavour and be ready to observe them, unless there be cause to the contrary in other men's refusal to observe them towards us. The force therefore of the law of nature is not *in foro externo*, till there be security for men to obey it; but is always *in foro interno*, wherein the action of obedience being unsafe, the will and readiness to perform is taken for the performance.

11. Amongst the laws of nature, customs and prescriptions are not numbered. For whatsoever action is against reason, though it be reiterated never so often, or that there be never so many precedents thereof, is still against reason, and therefore not a law of nature, but contrary to it. But consent and covenant may so alter the cases, which in the law of nature may be put, by changing the circumstances, that that which was reason before, may afterwards be against it; and yet is reason still the law. For though every man be bound to allow equality to another; yet if that other shall see cause to renounce the same, and make himself inferior, then, if from thenceforth he consider him as inferior, he breaketh not thereby that law of nature that commandeth to allow equality. In sum, *a man's own consent may abridge him of the liberty which the law of nature leaveth him, but custom not*; nor can either of them abrogate either these, or any other law of nature.

12. And forasmuch as law (to speak properly) is a command, and these dictates, as they proceed from nature, are not commands; they are not therefore called laws in respect of nature, but in respect of the author of nature, God Almighty.

13. And seeing the laws of nature concern the conscience,

not he only breaketh them that doth any action contrary, but also he whose action is conformable to them, in case he think it contrary. For though the action chance to be right, yet in his judgment he despiseth the law.

14. Every man by natural passion, calleth that good which pleaseth him for the present, or so far forth as he can foresee; and in like manner that which displeaseth him evil. And therefore he that foreseeth the whole way to his preservation (which is the end that every one by nature aimeth at) must also call it good, and the contrary evil. And this is that good and evil, which not every man in passion calleth so, but all men by reason.* And therefore the fulfilling of all these laws is good in reason; and the breaking of them evil. And so also the habit, or disposition, or intention to fulfil them good; and the neglect of them evil. And from hence cometh that distinction of *malum pœnæ*, and *malum culpæ*; for *malum pœnæ* is any pain or molestation of mind whatsoever; but *malum culpæ* is that action which is contrary to reason and the law of nature; as also the habit of doing according to these and other laws of nature that tend to our preservation, is that we call VIRTUE; and the habit of doing the contrary, VICE. As for example, justice is that habit by which we stand to covenants, injustice the contrary vice; equity that habit by which we allow equality of nature, arrogance the contrary vice; gratitude the habit whereby we requite the benefit and trust of others, ingratitude the contrary vice; temperance the habit by which we abstain from all things that tend to our destruction, intemperance the contrary vice; prudence, the same with virtue in general. As for the common opinion, that virtue consisteth in mediocrity, and vice in extremes,* I see no ground for it, nor can find any such mediocrity. Courage may be virtue, when the daring is extreme, if the cause be good; and extreme fear no vice when the danger is extreme. To give a man more than his due, is no injustice, though it be to give him less; and in gifts it is not the sum that maketh liberality, but the reason. And so in all other virtues and vices. I know that this doctrine of mediocrity is Aristotle's, but his opinions concerning virtue and vice, are no other than those which were

received then, and are still by the generality of men un-studied; and therefore not very likely to be accurate.

15. The sum of virtue is to be sociable with them that will be sociable, and formidable to them that will not. And the same is the sum of the law of nature; for in being sociable, the law of nature taketh place by the way of peace and society; and to be formidable, is the law of nature in war, where to be feared is a protection a man hath from his own power; and as the former consisteth in actions of equity and justice, the latter consisteth in actions of honour. And equity, justice, and honour, contain all virtues whatsoever.

CHAPTER XVIII

A CONFIRMATION OF THE SAME OUT OF THE WORD OF GOD

1. THE laws mentioned in the former chapters, as they are called the laws of nature, for that they are the dictates of natural reason; and also moral laws, because they concern men's manners and conversation one towards another; so are they also divine laws in respect of the author thereof, God Almighty; and ought therefore to agree, or at least, not to be repugnant to the word of God revealed in Holy Scripture. In this chapter therefore I shall produce such places of Scripture as appear to be most consonant to the said laws.

2. And first the word of God seemeth to place the divine law in reason; by all such texts as ascribe the same to the heart and understanding; as Psalm 40, 8: *Thy law is in my heart.* Heb. 8, 10: *After those days, saith the Lord, I will put my laws in their mind;* and Heb. 10, 16, the same. Psalm 37, 31, speaking of the righteous man, he saith, *The law of God is in his heart.* Psalm 19, 7, 8: *The law of God is perfect, converting the soul. It giveth wisdom to the simple, and light unto the eyes.* Jer. 31, 33: *I will put my law in their inward parts, and write it in their hearts.* And John 1, the lawgiver

himself, God Almighty, is called by the name of Λόγος, which is also called: verse 4, *The light of men*: and verse 9, *The light which lighteth every man, which cometh into the world*: all which are descriptions of natural reason.

3. And that the law divine, for so much as is moral, are those precepts that tend to peace, seemeth to be much confirmed by such places of Scripture as these: Rom. 3, 17, righteousness which is the fulfilling of the law, is called *the way of peace*. And Psalm 85, 10: *Righteousness and peace shall kiss each other*. And Matth. 5, 9: *Blessed are the peace-makers*. And Heb. 7, 2, *Melchisedec king of Salem* is interpreted *king of righteousness*, and *king of peace*. And, verse 21, our Saviour Christ is said to be a priest *for ever after the order of Melchisedec*; out of which may be inferred: that the doctrine of our Saviour Christ annexeth the fulfilling of the law to peace.

4. That the law of nature is unalterable, is intimated by this, that the priesthood of Melchisedec is everlasting; and by the words of our Saviour, Matth. 5, 18: *Heaven and earth shall pass away, but one jot or tittle of the law shall not pass till all things be fulfilled*.

5. That men ought to stand to their covenants, is taught Psalm 15, where the question being asked, verse 1, *Lord who shall dwell in thy tabernacle*, &c., it is answered, verse 4, *He that sweareth to his own hindrance, and yet changeth not*. And that men ought to be grateful, where no covenant passeth, Deut. 25, 4: *Thou shalt not muzzle the ox that treadeth out the corn*, which St. Paul (1 Cor. 9, 9) interpreteth not of oxen, but of men.

6. That men content themselves with equality, as it is the foundation of natural law, so also is it of the second table of the divine law, Matth. 22, 39, 40: *Thou shalt love thy neighbour as thyself. On these two laws depend the whole law and the prophets*; which is not so to be understood, as that a man should study so much his neighbour's profit as his own, or that he should divide his goods amongst his neighbours; but that he should esteem his neighbour worthy all rights and privileges that he himself enjoyeth; and attribute unto him, whatsoever he looketh should be attributed unto himself;

which is no more but that he should be humble, meek, and contented with equality.

7. And that in distributing of right amongst equals, that distribution is to be made according to the proportions of the numbers, which is the giving of *æqualia æqualibus*, and *proportionalia proportionalibus*; we have Numb. 26, 53, 54, the commandment of God to Moses: *Thous shalt divide the land according to the number of names; to many thou shalt give more, to few thou shalt give less, to every one according to his number*. That decision by lot is a means of peace, Prov. 18, 18: *The lot causeth contention to cease, and maketh partition among the mighty*.

8. That the accommodation and forgiveness of one another, which have before been put for laws of nature, are also law divine, there is no question. For they are the essence of charity, which is the scope of the whole law. That we ought not to reproach, or reprehend each other, is the doctrine of our Saviour, Matth. 7, 1: *Judge not, that ye be not judged*; (verse 3): *Why seest thou the mote that is in thy brother's eye, and seest not the beam that is in thine own eye?* Also the law that forbiddeth us to press our counsel upon others further than they admit, is a divine law. For after our charity and desire to rectify one another is rejected, to press it further, is to reprehend him, and condemn him, which is forbidden in the text last recited; as also Rom. 14, 12, 13: *Every one of us shall give account of himself to God. Let us not therefore judge one another any more, but use your judgment rather in this, that no man put an occasion to fall, or a stumbling block before his brother*.

9. Further, the rule of men concerning the law of nature, *Quod tibi fieri non vis, alteri ne feceris*, is confirmed by the like, Matth. 7, 12: *Whatsoever therefore you would have men do unto you, that do you unto them: for this is the law and the prophets*. And Rom. 2, 1: *In that thou judgest another, thou condemnest thyself*, &c.

10. It is also manifest by the Scriptures, that these laws concern only the tribunal of our conscience; and that the actions contrary to them, shall be no farther punished by God Almighty, than as they proceed from negligence and

contempt. And first, that these laws are made to the conscience, appeareth, Matth. 5, 20: *For I say unto you, except your righteousness exceed the righteousness of the Scribes and Pharisees, ye shall not enter into the kingdom of heaven.* Now the Pharisees were the most exact amongst the Jews in the external performance; they therefore must want the sincerity of conscience; else could not our Saviour have required a greater righteousness than theirs. For the same reason our Saviour Christ saith: *The publican departed from the temple justified, rather than the Pharisee.* And Christ saith: *His yoke is easy, and his burthen light*; which proceeded from this, that Christ required no more than our best endeavour. And Rom. 14, 23: *He that doubteth, is condemned, if he eat.* And in innumerable places both in the Old and New Testament, God Almighty declareth, that he taketh the will for the deed, both in good and evil actions. By all which it plainly appears, that the divine law is dictated to the conscience. On the other side it is no less plain: that how many and how heinous actions soever a man commit through infirmity, he shall nevertheless, whensoever he shall condemn the same in his own conscience, be freed from the punishments that to such actions otherwise belong. For, *At what time soever a sinner doth repent him of his sins from the bottom of his heart, I will put all his iniquities out of my remembrance, saith the Lord.*

11. Concerning revenge which by the law of nature ought not to aim, as I have said chapter XVI, section 10, at present delight, but at future profit, there is some difficulty made, as if the same accorded not with the law divine, by such as object the continuance of punishment after the day of judgment, when there shall be no place, neither for amendment, nor for example. This objection had been of some force, if such punishment had been ordained after all sins were past; but considering the punishment was instituted before sin, it serveth to the benefit of mankind, because it keepeth men in peaceable and virtuous conversation by the terror; and therefore such revenge was directed to the future only.

12. Finally, there is no law of natural reason, that can be

against the law divine; for God Almighty hath given reason to a man to be a light unto him. And I hope it is no impiety to think, that God Almighty will require a strict account thereof, at the day of judgment, as of the instructions which we were to follow in our peregrination here; notwithstanding the opposition and affronts of supernaturalists now-a-days, to rational and moral conversation.

CHAPTER XIX

OF THE NECESSITY AND DEFINITION OF A BODY POLITIC

1. IN chap. XII, sect. 16, it hath been shewed, that the opinions men have of the rewards and punishments which are to follow their actions, are the causes that make and govern the will to those actions. In this estate of man therefore, wherein all men are equal, and every man allowed to be his own judge, the fears they have one of another are equal, and every man's hopes consist in his own sleight and strength; and consequently when any man by his natural passion, is provoked to break these laws of nature, there is no security in any other man of his own defence but anticipation. And for this cause, every man's right (howsoever he be inclined to peace) of doing whatsoever seemeth good in his own eyes, remaineth with him still, as the necessary means of his preservation. And therefore till there be security amongst men for the keeping of the law of nature one towards another, men are still in the estate of war, and nothing is unlawful to any man that tendeth to his own safety or commodity; and this safety and commodity consisteth in the mutual aid and help of one another, whereby also followeth the mutual fear of one another.

2. It is a proverbial saying, *inter arma silent leges*. There is little therefore to be said concerning the laws that men are to observe one towards another in time of war, wherein every man's being and well-being is the rule of his actions.

Yet thus much the law of nature commandeth in war: that men satiate not the cruelty of their present passions, whereby in their own conscience they foresee no benefit to come. For that betrayeth not a necessity, but a disposition of the mind to war, which is against the law of nature. And in old time we read that rapine was a trade of life, wherein nevertheless many of them that used it, did not only spare the lives of those they invaded, but left them also such things, as were necessary to preserve that life which they had given them; as namely their oxen and instruments for tillage, though they carried away all their other cattle and substance. And as the rapine itself was warranted in the law of nature, by the want of security otherwise to maintain themselves; so the exercise of cruelty was forbidden by the same law of nature, unless fear suggested anything to the contrary. For nothing but fear can justify the taking away of another's life. And because fear can hardly be made manifest, but by some action dishonourable, that bewrayeth* the conscience of one's own weakness; all men in whom the passion of courage or magnanimity have been predominated, have abstained from cruelty; insomuch that though there be in war no law, the breach whereof is injury, yet there are those laws, the breach whereof is dishonour. In one word, therefore, the only law of actions in war is honour; and the right of war providence.

3. And seeing mutual aid is necessary for defence, as mutual fear is necessary for peace; we are to consider how great aids are required for such defence, and for the causing of such mutual fear, as men may not easily adventure on one another. And first it is evident: that the mutual aid of two or three men is of very little security; for the odds on the other side, of a man or two, giveth sufficient encouragement to an assault. And therefore before men have sufficient security in the help of one another, their number must be so great, that the odds of a few which the enemy may have, be no certain and sensible advantage.

4. And supposing how great a number soever of men assembled together for their mutual defence, yet shall not the effect follow, unless they all direct their actions to one

and the same end; which direction to one and the same end is that which, chap. XII, sect. 7, is called consent. This consent (or concord) amongst so many men, though it may be made by the fear of a present invader, or by the hope of a present conquest, or booty; and endure as long as that action endureth; nevertheless, by the diversity of judgments and passions in so many men contending naturally for honour and advantage one above another: it is impossible, not only that their consent to aid each other against an enemy, but also that the peace should last between themselves, without some mutual and common fear to rule them.

5. But contrary hereunto may be objected, the experience we have of certain living creatures irrational, that nevertheless continually live in such good order and government, for their common benefit, and are so free from sedition and war amongst themselves, that for peace, profit, and defence, nothing more can be imaginable. And the experience we have in this, is in that little creature the bee, which is therefore reckoned amongst *animalia politica*. Why therefore may not men, that foresee the benefit of concord, continually maintain the same without compulsion, as well as they? To which I answer, that amongst other living creatures, there is no question of precedence in their own species, nor strife about honour or acknowledgment of one another's wisdom, as there is amongst men; from whence arise envy and hatred of one towards another, and from thence sedition and war. Secondly, those living creatures aim every one at peace and food common to them all; men aim at dominion, superiority, and private wealth, which are distinct in every man, and breed contention. Thirdly, those living creatures that are without reason, have not learning enough to espy, or to think they espy, any defect in the government; and therefore are contented therewith; but in a multitude of men, there are always some that think themselves wiser than the rest, and strive to alter what they think amiss; and divers of them strive to alter divers ways; and that causeth war. Fourthly, they want speech, and are therefore unable to instigate one another to faction, which men want not. Fifthly, they have no conception of right and

wrong, but only of pleasure and pain, and therefore also no censure of one another, nor of their commander, as long as they are themselves at ease; whereas men that make themselves judges of right and wrong, are then least at quiet, when they are most at ease. Lastly, natural concord, such as is amongst those creatures, is the work of God by the way of nature; but concord amongst men is artificial, and by way of covenant. And therefore no wonder if such irrational creatures, as govern themselves in multitude, do it much more firmly than mankind, that do it by arbitrary institution.

6. It remaineth therefore still that consent (by which I understand the concurrence of many men's wills to one action) is not sufficient security for their common peace, without the erection of some common power, by the fear whereof they may be compelled both to keep the peace amongst themselves, and to join their strengths together, against a common enemy. And that this may be done, there is no way imaginable, but only union; which is defined chap. XII, sect. 8 to be the involving or including the wills of many in the will of one man, or in the will of the greatest part of any one number of men, that is to say, in the will of one man, or of one COUNCIL; for a council is nothing else but an assembly of men deliberating concerning something common to them all.

7. The making of union consisteth in this, that every man by covenant oblige himself to some one and the same man, or to some one and the same council, by them all named and determined, to do those actions, which the said man or council shall command them to do; and to do no action which he or they shall forbid, or command them not to do.* And farther: in case it be a council whose commands they covenant to obey, that then also they covenant, that every man shall hold that for the command of the whole council, which is the command of the greater part of those men, whereof such council consisteth. And though the will of man, being not voluntary, but the beginning of voluntary actions, is not subject to deliberation and covenant; yet when a man covenanteth to subject his will to the command of another, he obligeth himself to this, that he resign his

strength and means to him, whom he covenanteth to obey; and hereby, he that is to command may by the use of all their means and strength, be able by the terror thereof, to frame the will of them all to unity and concord amongst themselves.

8. This union so made, is that which men call now-a-days a BODY POLITIC or civil society; and the Greeks call it πόλις, that is to say, a city; which may be defined to be a multitude of men, united as one person by a common power, for their common peace, defence, and benefit.

9. And as this union into a city or body politic, is instituted with common power over all the particular persons, or members thereof, to the common good of them all; so also may there be amongst a multitude of those members, instituted a subordinate union of certain men, for certain common actions to be done by those men for some common benefit of theirs, or of the whole city; as for subordinate government, for counsel, for trade, and the like. And these subordinate bodies politic are usually called CORPORATIONS; and their power such over the particulars of their own society, as the whole city whereof they are members have allowed them.

10. In all cities or bodies politic not subordinate, but independent, that one man or one council, to whom the particular members have given that common power, is called their SOVEREIGN, and his power the sovereign power; which consisteth in the power and the strength that every of the members have transferred to him from themselves, by covenant. And because it is impossible for any man really to transfer his own strength to another, or for that other to receive it; it is to be understood: that to transfer a man's power and strength, is no more but to lay by or relinquish his own right of resisting him to whom he so transferreth it. And every member of the body politic, is called a SUBJECT, (viz.) to the sovereign.

11. The cause in general which moveth a man to become subject to another, is (as I have said already) the fear of not otherwise preserving himself, and a man may subject himself, to him that invadeth, or may invade him for fear of

him; or men may join amongst themselves to subject themselves to such as they shall agree upon for fear of others. And when many men subject themselves the former way, there ariseth thence a body politic, as it were naturally; from whence proceedeth dominion, paternal, and despotic and when they subject themselves the other way, by mutual agreement amongst many, the body politic they make, is for the most part called a commonwealth in distinction from the former, though the name be the general name for them both and I shall speak in the first place of commonwealths, and afterward of bodies politic, patrimonial and despotical.

PART II
DE CORPORE POLITICO

CHAPTER XX

OF THE REQUISITES TO THE CONSTITUTION
OF A COMMONWEALTH

1. THAT part of this treatise which is already past,* hath been wholly spent, in the consideration of the natural power, and the natural estate of man; namely of his cognition and passions in the first eleven chapters; and how from thence proceed his actions in the twelfth; how men know one another's minds in the thirteenth; in what estate men's passions set them in the fourteenth; what estate they are directed unto by the dictates of reason, that is to say, what be the principal articles of the law of nature, in the fifteenth, sixteenth, seventeenth, eighteenth, and lastly how a multitude of persons natural are united by covenants into one person civil or body politic. In this part therefore shall be considered, the nature of a body politic, and the laws thereof, otherwise called civil laws. And whereas it hath been said in the last chapter, and last section of the former part, that there be two ways of erecting a body politic; one by arbitrary institution of many men assembled together, which is like a creation out of nothing by human wit; the other by compulsion, which is as it were a generation thereof out of natural force; I shall first speak of such erection of a body politic, as proceedeth from the assembly and consent of a multitude.

2. Having in this place to consider a multitude of men about to unite themselves into a body politic, for their security, both against one another, and against common enemies; and that by covenants, the knowledge of what covenants, they must needs make, dependeth on the knowl-

edge of the persons, and the knowledge of their end. First, for their persons they are many, and (as yet) not one; nor can any action done in a multitude of people met together, be attributed to the multitude, or truly called the action of the multitude, unless every man's hand, and every man's will, (not so much as one excepted) have concurred thereto. For multitude, though in their persons they run together, yet they concur not always in their designs. For even at that time when men are in tumult, though they agree a number of them to one mischief, and a number of them to another; yet, in the whole, they are amongst themselves in the state of hostility, and not of peace; like the seditious Jews besieged in Jerusalem, that could join against their enemies, and yet fight amongst themselves; whensoever therefore any man saith, that a number of men hath done any act: it is to be understood, that every particular man in that number hath consented thereunto, and not the greatest part only. Secondly, though thus assembled with intention to unite themselves, they are yet in that estate in which every man hath right to everything, and consequently, as hath been said, chap. XIV, sect. 10, in an estate of enjoying nothing: and therefore *meum* and *tuum* hath no place amongst them.

3. The first thing therefore they are to do, is expressly every man to consent to something by which they may come nearer to their ends; which can be nothing else imaginable but this: that they allow the wills of the major part of their whole number, or the wills of the major part of some certain number of men by them determined and named; or lastly the will of some one man, to involve and be taken for the wills of every man. And this done they are united, and a body politic. And if the major part of their whole number be supposed to involve the wills of all the particulars, then are they said to be a DEMOCRACY, that is to say a government wherein the whole number, or so many of them as please, being assembled together, are the sovereign, and every particular man a subject. If the major part of a certain number of men named or distinguished from the rest, be supposed to involve the wills of every one of the particulars, then are they said to be an OLIGARCHY, or ARISTOCRACY;

which two words signify the same thing, together with the divers passions of those that use them; for when the men that be in that office please, they are called an aristocracy, otherwise an oligarchy; wherein those, the major part of which declare the wills of the whole multitude, being assembled, are the sovereign, and every man severally a subject. Lastly if their consent be such, that the will of one man, whom they name, shall stand for the wills of them all, then is their government or union called a MONARCHY; and that one man the sovereign, and every of the rest a subject.

4. And those several sorts of unions, governments, and subjections of man's will, may be understood to be made, either absolutely, that is to say, for all future time, or for a time limited only. But forasmuch as we speak here of a body politic, instituted for the perpetual benefit and defence of them that make it; which therefore men desire should last for ever, I will omit to speak of those that be temporary, and consider those that be for ever.

5. The end for which one man giveth up, and relinquisheth to another, or others, the right of protecting and defending himself by his own power, is the security which he expecteth thereby, of protection and defence from those to whom he doth so relinquish it. And a man may then account himself in the estate of security,* when he can foresee no violence to be done unto him, from which the doer may not be deterred by the power of that sovereign, to whom they have every one subjected themselves; and without that security there is no reason for a man to deprive himself of his own advantages, and make himself a prey to others. And therefore when there is not such a sovereign power erected, as may afford this security; it is to be understood that every man's right of doing whatsoever seemeth good in his own eyes, remaineth still with him. And contrariwise, where any subject hath right by his own judgment and discretion, to make use of his force; it is to be understood that every man hath the like, and consequently that there is no commonwealth at all established. How far therefore in the making of a commonwealth, a man subjecteth his will to the power of

others, must appear from the end, namely security. For whatsoever is necessary to be by covenant transferred for the attaining thereof, so much is transferred, or else every man is in his natural liberty to secure himself.

6. Covenants agreed upon by every man assembled for the making of a commonwealth, and put in writing without erecting of a power of coercion, are no reasonable security for any of them that so covenant, nor are to be called laws; and leave men still in the estate of nature and hostility. For seeing the wills of most men are governed only by fear, and where there is no power of coercion, there is no fear;* the wills of most men will follow their passions of covetousness, lust, anger, and the like, to the breaking of those covenants, whereby the rest, also, who otherwise would keep them, are set at liberty, and have no law but from themselves.

7. This power of coercion, as hath been said chap. XV, sect. 3, of the former part, consisteth in the transferring of every man's right of resistance against him to whom he hath transferred the power of coercion. It followeth therefore, that no man in any commonwealth whatsoever hath right to resist him, or them, on whom they have conferred this power coercive, or (as men use to call it) the sword of justice; supposing the not-resistance possible. For (Part I. chapter XV, sect. 18) covenants bind but to the utmost of our endeavour.

8. And forasmuch as they who are amongst themselves in security, by the means of this sword of justice that keeps them all in awe, are nevertheless in danger of enemies from without; if there be not some means found, to unite their strengths and natural forces in the resistance of such enemies, their peace amongst themselves is but in vain. And therefore it is to be understood as a covenant of every member to contribute their several forces for the defence of the whole; whereby to make one power as sufficient, as is possible, for their defence. Now seeing that every man hath already transferred the use of his strength to him or them, that have the sword of justice; it followeth that the power of defence, that is to say the sword of war, be in the same hands wherein is the sword of justice: and consequently

those two swords are but one, and that inseparably and essentially annexed to the sovereign power.

9. Moreover seeing to have the right of the sword, is nothing else but to have the use thereof depending only on the judgment and discretion of him or them that have it; it followeth that the power of judicature (in all controversies, wherein the sword of justice is to be used) and (in all deliberations concerning war, wherein the use of that sword is required), the right of resolving and determining what is to be done, belong to the same sovereign.

10.* Farther: considering it is no less, but much more necessary to prevent violence and rapine, than to punish the same when it is committed; and all violence proceedeth from controversies that arise between men concerning *meum* and *tuum*, right and wrong, good and bad, and the like, which men use every one to measure by their own judgments; it belongeth also to the judgment of the same sovereign power, to set forth and make known the common measure by which every man is to know what is his, and what another's; what is good, and what bad; and what he ought to do, and what not; and to command the same to be observed. And these measures of the actions of the subjects are those which men call LAWS POLITIC, or civil. The making whereof must of right belong to him that hath the power of the sword, by which men are compelled to observe them; for otherwise they should be made in vain.

11. Farthermore: seeing it is impossible that any one man that hath such sovereign power, can be able in person to hear and determine all controversies, to be present at all deliberations concerning common good, and to execute and perform all those common actions that belong thereunto, whereby there will be necessity of magistrates and ministers of public affairs; it is consequent, that the appointment, nomination, and limitation of the same, be understood as an inseparable part of the same sovereignty, to which the sum of all judicature and execution hath been already annexed.

12. And: forasmuch as the right to use the forces of every particular member, is transferred from themselves, to their sovereign; a man will easily fall upon this conclusion of

himself: that to sovereign power (whatsoever it doth) there belongeth impunity.*

13. The sum of these rights of sovereignty, namely the absolute use of the sword in peace and war, the making and abrogating of laws, supreme judicature and decision in all debates judicial and deliberative, the nomination of all magistrates and ministers, with other rights contained in the same, make the sovereign power no less absolute in the commonwealth, than before commonwealth every man was absolute in himself to do, or not to do, what he thought good; which men that have not had the experience of that miserable estate, to which men are reduced by long war, think so hard a condition that they cannot easily acknowledge, such covenants and subjection, on their parts, as are here set down, to have been ever necessary to their peace. And therefore some have imagined that a commonwealth may be constituted in such manner, as the sovereign power may be so limited, and moderated, as they shall think fit themselves. For example: they suppose a multitude of men to have agreed upon certain articles (which they presently call laws), declaring how they will be governed; and that done to agree farther upon some man, or number of men to see the same articles performed, and put in execution. And to enable him, or them thereunto, they allot unto them a provision limited, as of certain lands, taxes, penalties, and the like, than which (if mis-spent), they shall have no more, without a new consent of the same men that allowed the former. And thus they think they have made a commonwealth, in which it is unlawful for any private man to make use of his own sword for his security; wherein they deceive themselves.

14. For first, if to the revenue, it did necessarily follow that there might be forces raised, and procured at the will of him that hath such revenue; yet since the revenue is limited, so must also be the forces; but limited forces, against the power of an enemy, which we cannot limit, are unsufficient. Whensoever therefore there happeneth an invasion greater than those forces are able to resist, and there be no other right to levy more, then is every man, by necessity of nature,

allowed to make the best provision he can for himself; and thus is the private sword, and the estate of war again reduced. But seeing revenue, without the right of commanding men, is of not use, neither in peace, nor war; it is necessary to be supposed, that he that hath the administration of those articles, which are in the former section supposed, must have also right to make use of the strengths of particular men; and what reason soever giveth him that right over any one, giveth him the same over them all. And then is his right absolute; for he that hath right to all their forces, hath right to dispose of the same. Again: supposing those limited forces and revenue, either by the necessary, or negligent use of them, to fail; and that for a supply, the same multitude be again to be assembled, who shall have power to assemble them, that is to compel them to come together? If he that demandeth the supply hath that right (viz.) the right to compel them all; then is his sovereignty absolute: if not, then is every particular man at liberty to come or not; to frame a new commonwealth or not; and so the right of the private sword returneth. But suppose them willingly and of their own accord assembled, to consider of this supply; if now it be still in their choice, whether they shall give it or not, it is also in their choice whether the commonwealth shall stand or not. And therefore there lieth not upon any of them any civil obligation that may hinder them from using force, in case they think it tend to their defence. This device therefore of them that will make civil laws first, and then a civil body afterwards, (as if policy made a body politic, and not a body politic made policy) is of no effect.

15. Others to avoid the hard condition, as they take it, of absolute subjection, (which in hatred thereto they also call slavery) have devised a government as they think mixed of the three sorts of sovereignty. As for example: they suppose the power of making laws given to some great assembly democratical, the power of judicature to some other assembly; and the administration of the laws to a third, or to some one man; and this policy they call mixed monarchy, or mixed aristocracy, or mixed democracy, according as any of

these three sorts do most visibly predominate. And in this
estate of government they think the use of the private sword
excluded.

16. And supposing it were so: how were this condition
which they call slavery eased thereby? For in this estate they
would have no man allowed, either to be his own judge, or
own carver, or to make any laws unto himself; and as long
as these three agree, they are as absolutely subject to them,
as is a child to the father, or a slave to the master in the
state of nature. The ease therefore of this subjection, must
consist in the disagreement of those, amongst whom they
have distributed the rights of sovereign power. But the
same disagreement is war. The division therefore of the
sovereignty, either worketh no effect, to the taking away of
simple subjection, or introduceth war; wherein the private
sword hath place again. But the truth is, as hath been
already shewed in 7, 8, 9, 10, 11, 12 precedent sections:
the sovereignty is indivisible; and that seeming mixture
of several kinds of government, not mixture of the things
themselves, but confusion in our understandings, that cannot
find out readily to whom we have subjected ourselves.

17. But though the sovereignty be not mixed, but be
always either simple democracy, or simple aristocracy, or
pure monarchy; nevertheless in the administration thereof,
all those sorts of government may have place subordinate.
For suppose the sovereign power be democracy, as it was
sometimes in Rome, yet at the same time they may have a
council aristocratical, such as was the senate; and at the
same time they may have a subordinate monarch, such as
was their dictator, who had for a time the exercise of the
whole sovereignty, and such as are all generals in war. So
also in a monarchy there may be a council aristocratical of
men chosen by the monarch; or democratical of men chosen
by the consent (the monarch permitting) of all the particular
men of the commonwealth. And this mixture is it that im-
poseth; as if it were the mixture of sovereignty. As if a
man should think, because the great council of Venice doth
nothing ordinarily but choose magistrates, ministers of state,
captains, and governors of towns, ambassadors, counsellors,

and the like; that therefore their part of the sovereignty is only choosing of magistrates; and that the making of war, and peace, and laws, were not theirs, but the part of such councillors as they appointed thereto; whereas it is the part of these to do it but subordinately, the supreme authority thereof being in the great council that choose them.

18. And as reason teacheth us, that a man considered out of subjection to laws, and out of all covenants obligatory to others, is free to do, and undo, and deliberate as long as he listeth; every member being obedient to the will of the whole man; that liberty being nothing else but his natural power, without which he is no better than an inanimate creature, not able to help himself; so also it teacheth us: that a body politic of what kind soever, not subject to another, nor obliged by covenants, ought to be free, and in all actions to be assisted by the members, every one in their place, or at the least not resisted by them. For otherwise, the power of a body politic (the essence whereof is the not-resistance of the members) is none, nor a body politic of any benefit. And the same is confirmed by the use of all nations and commonwealths in the world. For what nation is there or commonwealth wherein that man or council, which is virtually the whole, hath not absolute power over every particular member? or what nation or commonwealth is there, that hath not power and right to constitute a general in their wars? But the power of a general is absolute; and consequently there was absolute power in the commonwealth, from whom it was derived. For no person, natural or civil, can transfer unto another more power than himself hath.

19. In every commonwealth where particular men are deprived of their right to protect themselves, there resideth an absolute sovereignty, as I have already shewed. But in what man or in what assembly of men the same is placed, is not so manifest, as not to need some marks whereby it may be discerned. And first it is an infallible mark of absolute sovereignty in a man, or in an assembly of men, if there be no right in any other person natural or civil to punish that man, or to dissolve that assembly. For he that cannot of

right be punished, cannot of right be resisted; and he that cannot of right be resisted, hath coercive power over all the rest, and thereby can frame and govern their actions at his pleasure; which is absolute sovereignty. Contrariwise he that in a commonwealth is punishable by any, or that assembly that is dissolvable, is not sovereign. For a greater power is always required to punish and dissolve, than theirs who are punished or dissolved; and that power cannot be called sovereign, than which there is a greater. Secondly, that man or assembly, that by their own right not derived from the present right of any other, may make laws, or abrogate them, at his, or their pleasure, have the sovereignty absolute. For seeing the laws they make, are supposed to be made by right, the members of the commonwealth to whom they are made, are obliged to obey them; and consequently not to resist the execution of them; which not-resistance maketh the power absolute of him that ordaineth them. It is likewise a mark of this sovereignty, to have the right original of appointing magistrates, judges, counsellors, and ministers of state. For without that power no act of sovereignty, or government, can be performed. Lastly, and generally: whosoever by his own authority independent can do any act, which another of the same commonwealth may not, must needs be understood to have the sovereign power. For by nature men have equal right; this inequality therefore must proceed from the power of the commonwealth. He therefore that doth any act lawfully by his own authority, which another may not, doth it by the power of the commonwealth in himself; which is absolute sovereignty.

CHAPTER XXI

OF THE THREE SORTS OF COMMONWEALTH

1. HAVING spoken in general concerning instituted policy in the former chapter, I come in this to speak of the sorts thereof in special, how every one of them is instituted. The first in order of time of these three sorts is democracy, and

it must be so of necessity, because an aristocracy and a monarchy, require nomination of persons agreed upon; which agreement in a great multitude of men must consist in the consent of the major part; and where the votes of the major part involve the votes of the rest, there is actually a democracy.

2. In the making of a democracy, there passeth no covenant, between the sovereign and any subject. For while the democracy is a making, there is no sovereign with whom to contract. For it cannot be imagined, that the multitude should contract with itself, or with any one man, or number of men, parcel of itself, to make itself sovereign; nor that a multitude, considered as one aggregate, can give itself anything which before it had not. Seeing then that sovereignty democratical is not conferred by the covenant of any multitude (which supposeth union and sovereignty already made), it resteth, that the same be conferred by the particular covenants of every several man; that is to say, every man with every man, for and in consideration of the benefit of his own peace and defence, covenanteth to stand to and obey, whatsoever the major part of their whole number, or the major part of such a number of them, as shall be pleased to assemble at a certain time and place, shall determine and command. And this is that which giveth being to a democracy; wherein the sovereign assembly was called of the Greeks by the name of *Demus* (*id est*, the people), from whence cometh democracy. So that where, to the supreme and independent court, every man may come that will and give his vote, there the sovereign is called the people.

3. Out of this that hath been already said, may readily be drawn: that whatsoever the people doth to any one particular member or subject of the commonwealth, the same by him ought not to be styled injury. For first, injury (by the definition, Part I. chap. XVI, sect. 2) is breach of covenant; but covenants (as hath been said in the precedent section) there passed none from the people to any private man; and consequently it (viz. the people) can do him no injury. Secondly, how unjust soever the action be, that this sovereign *demus* shall do, is done by the will of every

particular man subject to him, who are therefore guilty of the same. If therefore they style it injury, they but accuse themselves. And it is against reason for the same man, both to do and complain; implying this contradiction, that whereas he first ratified the people's acts in general, he now disalloweth some of them in particular. It is therefore said truly, *volenti non fit injuria.** Nevertheless nothing doth hinder, but that divers actions done by the people, may be unjust before God Almighty, as breaches of some of the laws of nature.

4. And when it happeneth, that the people by plurality of voices shall decree or command any thing contrary to the law of God or nature, though the decree and command be the act of every man, not only present in the assembly, but also absent from it; yet is not the injustice of the decree, the injustice of every particular man, but only of those men by whose express suffrages, the decree or command was passed. For a body politic, as it is a fictitious body, so are the faculties and will thereof fictitious also. But to make a particular man unjust, which consisteth of a body and soul natural, there is required a natural and very will.

5.* In all democracies, though the right of sovereignty be in the assembly, which is virtually the whole body; yet the use thereof is always in one, or a few particular men. For in such great assemblies as those must be, whereinto every man may enter at his pleasure, there is no means any ways to deliberate and give counsel what to do, but by long and set orations; whereby to every man there is more or less hope given, to incline and sway the assembly to their own ends. In a multitude of speakers therefore, where always, either one is eminent alone, or a few being equal amongst themselves, are eminent above the rest, that one or few must of necessity sway the whole; insomuch, that a democracy, in effect, is no more than an aristocracy of orators, interrupted sometimes with the temporary monarchy of one orator.

6. And seeing a democracy is by institution the beginning both of aristocracy and monarchy, we are to consider next how aristocracy is derived from it. When the particular

members of the commonwealth growing weary of attendance at public courts, as dwelling far off, or being attentive to their private businesses, and withal displeased with the government of the people, assemble themselves to make an aristocracy; there is no more required to the making thereof but putting to the question one by one, the names of such men as it shall consist of, and assenting to their election; and by plurality of vote, to transfer that power which before the people had, to the number of men so named and chosen.

7. And from this manner of erecting an aristocracy it is manifest that the few or optimates,* have entered into no covenant, with any of the particular members of the commonwealth whereof they are sovereign; and consequently cannot do any thing to any private man that can be called injury to him, howsoever their act be wicked before Almighty God, according to that which hath been said before, section 3. Farther it is impossible that the people, as one body politic should covenant with the aristocracy or optimates, on whom they intend to transfer their sovereignty; for no sooner is the aristocracy erected, but the democracy is annihilated, and the covenants made unto them void.

8. In all aristocracies, the admission of such as are from time to time to have vote in the sovereign assembly, dependeth on the will and decree of the present optimates; for they being the sovereign, have the nomination (by the eleventh section of the former chapter) of all magistrates, ministers, and counsellors of state whatsoever, and may therefore choose either to make them elective, or hereditary, at their pleasure.

9. Out of the same democracy, the institution of a political monarch proceedeth in the same manner, as did the institution of the aristocracy (viz.) by a decree of the sovereign people, to pass the sovereignty to one man named, and approved by plurality of suffrage. And if this sovereignty be truly and indeed transferred, the estate or commonwealth is an absolute monarchy, wherein the monarch is at liberty, to dispose as well of the succession, as of the possession;

and not an elective kingdom. For suppose a decree be made, first in this manner: that such a one shall have the sovereignty for his life; and that afterward they will choose a new; in this case, the power of the people is dissolved, or not. If dissolved, then after the death of him that is chosen, there is no man bound to stand to the decrees of them that shall, as private men, run together to make a new election: and consequently, if there be any man, who by the advantage of the reign of him that is dead, hath strength enough to hold the multitude in peace and obedience, he may lawfully, or rather is by the law of nature obliged so to do. If this power of the people were not dissolved, at the choosing of their king for life; then is the people sovereign still, and the king a minister thereof only, but so, as to put the whole sovereignty in execution; a great minister, but no otherwise for his time, than a dictator was in Rome. In this case, at the death of him that was chosen, they that meet for a new election, have no new, but their old authority for the same. For they were the sovereign all the time, as appeareth by the acts of those elective kings, that have procured from the people, that their children might succeed them. For it is to be understood, when a man receiveth any thing from the authority of the people, he receiveth it not from the people his subjects, but from the people his sovereign. And farther, though in the election of a king for his life, the people grant him the exercise of their sovereignty for that time; yet if they see cause, they may recall the same before the time. As a prince that conferreth an office for life, may nevertheless, upon suspicion of abuse thereof, recall it at his pleasure; inasmuch as offices that require labour and care, are understood to pass from him that giveth them as *onera*, burthens to them that have them; the recalling whereof are therefore not injury, but favour. Nevertheless, if in making an elective king with intention to reserve the sovereignty, they reserve not a power at certain known and determined times and places to assemble themselves; the reservation of their sovereignty is of no effect, inasmuch as no man is bound to stand to the decrees and determinations of those that assemble themselves without the sovereign authority.

10. In the former section is showed that elective kings, that exercise their sovereignty for a time, which determines with their life, either are subjects and not sovereigns; and that is, when the people in election of them reserve unto themselves the right of assembling at certain times and places limited and made known; or else absolute sovereigns, to dispose of the succession at their pleasure; and that is, when the people in their election hath declared no time nor place of their meeting, or have left it to the power of the elected king to assemble and dissolve them at such times, as he himself shall think good. There is another kind of limitation of time, to him that shall be elected to use the sovereign power (which whether it hath been practised anywhere or not, I know not, but it may be imagined, and hath been objected against the rigour of sovereign power), and it is this: that the people transfer their sovereignty upon condition. As for example: for so long as he shall observe such and such laws, as they then prescribe him. And here as before in elected kings, the question is to be made, whether in the electing of such a sovereign, they reserved to themselves a right of assembling at times and places limited and known, or not; if not, then is the sovereignty of the people dissolved, and they have neither power to judge of the breach of the conditions given him, nor to command any forces for the deposing of him, whom on that condition they had set up; but are in the estate of war amongst themselves, as they were before they made themselves a democracy; and consequently: if he that is elected, by the advantage of the possession he hath of the public means, be able to compel them to unity and obedience, he hath not only the right of nature to warrant him, but also the law of nature to oblige him thereunto. But if in electing him, they reserved to themselves a right of assembling, and appointed certain times and places to that purpose, then are they sovereign still, and may call their conditional king to account, at their pleasure, and deprive him of his government, if they judge he deserve it, either by breach of the condition set him, or otherwise. For the sovereign power can by no covenant with a subject, be bound to continue him in the charge he under-

goeth by their command, as a burden imposed not particularly for his good, but for the good of the sovereign people.

11. The controversies that arise concerning the right of the people, proceed from the equivocation of the word. For the word people hath a double signification. In one sense it signifieth only a number of men, distinguished by the place of their habitation; as the people of England, or the people of France; which is no more, but the multitude of those particular persons that inhabit those regions, without consideration of any contracts or covenants amongst them, by which any one of them is obliged to the rest. In another sense, it signifieth a person civil, that is to say, either one man, or one council, in the will whereof is included and involved the will of every one in particular; as for example: in this latter sense the lower house of parliament is all the commons, as long as they sit there with authority and right thereto; but after they be dissolved, though they remain, they be no more the people, nor the commons, but only the aggregate, or multitude of the particular men there sitting; how well soever they agree, or concur, in opinions amongst themselves; whereupon they that do not distinguish between these two significations, do usually attribute such rights to a dissolved multitude, as belong only to the people virtually contained in the body of the commonwealth or sovereignty. And when a great number of their own authority flock together in any nation, they usually give them the name of the whole nation. In which sense they say the people rebelleth, or the people demandeth, when it is no more than a dissolved multitude, of which though any one man may be said to demand or have right to something, yet the heap, or multitude, cannot he said to demand or have right to any thing. For where every man hath his right distinct, there is nothing left for the multitude to have right unto; and when the particulars say: *this is mine*, *this is thine*, and *this is his*, and have shared all amongst them, there can be nothing whereof the multitude can say: *this is mine*; nor are they one body, as behoveth them to be, that demand anything under the name of *mine* or *his*; and when they say *ours*, every man is understood to pretend in several, and not the multitude.

On the other side, when the multitude is united into a body politic, and thereby are a people in the other signification, and their wills virtually in the sovereign, there the rights and demands of the particulars do cease; and he or they that have the sovereign power, doth for them all demand and vindicate under the name of *his*, that which before they called in the plural, *theirs*.

12. We have seen how particular men enter into subjection, by transferring their rights; it followeth to consider how such subjection may be discharged. And first, if he or they have the sovereign power, shall relinquish the same voluntarily, there is no doubt but every man is again at liberty, to obey or not; likewise if he or they retaining the sovereignty over the rest, do nevertheless exempt some one or more from their subjection, every man so exempted is discharged. For he or they to whom any man is obliged, hath the power to release him.

13. And here it is to be understood: that when he or they that have the sovereign power, give such exemption or privilege to a subject, as is not separable from the sovereignty, and nevertheless directly retain the sovereign power, not knowing the consequence of the privilege they grant, the person or persons exempted or privileged are not thereby released. For in contradictory significations of the will (Part I. chap. XIII, sect. 9), that which is directly signified, is to be understood for the will, before that which is drawn from it by consequence.

14. Also exile perpetual, is a release of subjection, forasmuch as being out of the protection of the sovereignty that expelled him, he hath no means of subsisting but from himself. Now every man may lawfully defend himself, that hath no other defence; else there had been no necessity that any man should enter into voluntary subjection, as they do in commonwealths.

15. Likewise a man is released of his subjection by conquest; for when it cometh to pass, that the power of a commonwealth is overthrown, and any particular man thereby, lying under the sword of his enemy yieldeth himself captive, he is thereby bound to serve him that taketh him,

and consequently discharged of his obligation to the former. For no man can serve two masters.

16. Lastly, ignorance of the succession dischargeth obedience; for no man can be understood to be obliged to obey he knoweth not whom.

CHAPTER XXII*

OF THE POWER OF MASTERS

1. HAVING set forth, in the two preceding chapters, the nature of a commonwealth institutive, by the consent of many men together; I come now to speak of dominion, or a body politic by acquisition, which is commonly called a patrimonial kingdom. But before I enter thereinto: it is necessary to make known, upon what title one man may acquire right, that is to say, property or dominion, over the person of another. For when one man hath dominion over another, there is a little kingdom; and to be a king by acquisition, is nothing else, but to have acquired a right or dominion over many.

2. Considering men therefore again in the state of nature, without covenants or subjection one to another, as if they were but even now all at once created male and female; there be three titles only, by which one man may have right and dominion over another; whereof two may take place presently, and those are: voluntary offer of subjection, and yielding by compulsion; the third is to take place, upon the supposition of children begotten amongst them. Concerning the first of these three titles, it is handled before in the two last chapters; for from thence cometh the right of sovereigns* over their subjects in a commonwealth institutive. Concerning the second title (which is when a man submitteth to an assailant for fear of death), thereby accrueth a right of dominion. For where every man (as it happeneth in this case) hath right to all things, there needs no more for the making of the said right effectual, but a covenant from him

that is overcome, not to resist him that overcometh. And thus cometh the victor to have a right of absolute dominion over the conquered. By which there is presently constituted a little body politic, which consisteth of two persons, the one sovereign, which is called the MASTER, or lord; the other subject, which is called the SERVANT. And when a man hath acquired right over a number of servants so considerable, as they cannot by their neighbours be securely invaded, this body politic is a kingdom despotical.

3. And it is to be understood: that when a servant taken in the wars, is kept bound in natural bonds, as chains, and the like, or in prison; there hath passed no covenant from the servant to his master; for those natural bonds have no need of strengthening by the verbal bonds of covenant; and they shew the servant is not trusted. But covenant (Part I. chap. XV, sect. 9) supposeth trust. There remaineth therefore in the servant thus kept bound, or in prison, a right of delivering himself, if he can, by what means soever. This kind of servant is that which ordinarily and without passion, is called a SLAVE. The Romans had no such distinct name, but comprehended all under the name of *servus*; whereof such as they loved and durst trust, were suffered to go at liberty, and admitted to places of office, both near to their persons, and in their affairs abroad; the rest were kept chained, or otherwise restrained with natural impediments to their resistance. And as it was amongst the Romans, so it was amongst other nations; the former sort having no other bond but a supposed covenant, without which the master had no reason to trust them; the latter being without covenant, and no otherwise tied to obedience, but by chains, or other like forcible custody.

4. A master therefore is to be supposed to have no less right over those, whose bodies he leaveth at liberty, than over those he keepeth in bonds and imprisonment; and hath absolute dominion over both; and may say of his servant, that he is *his*, as he may of any other thing. And whatsoever the servant had, and might call *his*, is now the master's; for he that disposeth of the person, disposeth of all the person could dispose of; insomuch as though there be *meum* and

tuum amongst servants distinct from one another by the dispensation, and for the benefit of their master; yet there is no *meum* and *tuum* belonging to any of them against the master himself, whom they are not to resist, but to obey all his commands as law.

5. And seeing both the servant and all that is committed to him, is the property of the master, and every man may dispose of his own, and transfer the same at his pleasure, the master may therefore alienate his dominion over them, or give the same, by his last will, to whom he list.

6. And if it happen, that the master himself by captivity or voluntary subjection, become servant to another, then is that other master paramount; and those servants of him that becometh servant, are no further obliged, than their master paramount shall think good; forasmuch as he disposing of the master subordinate, disposeth of all he hath, and consequently of his servants; so that the restriction of absolute power in masters proceedeth not from the law of nature, but from the political law of him that is their master supreme or sovereign.

7. Servants immediate to the supreme master, are discharged of their servitude or subjection in the same manner that subjects are released of their allegiance in a commonwealth institutive. As first, by release; for he that captiveth (which is done by accepting what the captive transferreth to him) setteth again at liberty, by transferring back the same. And this kind of release is called MANUMISSION. Secondly, by exile; for that is no more but manumission given to a servant, not in the way of benefit, but punishment. Thirdly, by new captivity, where the servant having done his endeavour to defend himself, hath thereby performed his covenant to his former master, and for the safety of his life, entering into new covenant with the conqueror, is bound to do his best endeavour to keep that likewise. Fourthly, ignorance of who is successor to his deceased master, dischargeth him of obedience; for no covenant holdeth longer than a man knoweth to whom he is to perform it. And lastly, that servant that is no longer trusted, but committed to his chains and custody, is thereby discharged of the

obligation *in foro interno*, and therefore if he can get loose, may lawfully go his way.

8. But servants subordinate, though manumitted by their immediate lord, are not thereby discharged of subjection to their lord paramount; for the immediate master hath no property in them, having transferred his right before to another, namely to his own and supreme master. Nor if the chief lord should manumit his immediate servant, doth he thereby release the servants of their obligation to him that is so manumitted. For by this manumission, he recovereth again the absolute dominion he had over them before. For after a release (which is the discharge of a covenant) the right standeth as it did before the covenant was made.

9. This right of conquest, as it maketh one man master over another, so also maketh it a man to be master of the irrational creatures. For if a man in the state of nature, be in hostility with men, and thereby have lawful title to subdue or kill, according as his own conscience and discretion shall suggest unto him for his safety and benefit; much more may he do the same to beasts; that is to say, save and preserve for his own service, according to his discretion, such as are of nature apt to obey, and commodious for use; and to kill and destroy, with perpetual war, all other, as fierce, and noisome to him. And this dominion is therefore of the law of nature, and not of the divine law positive. For if there had been no such right before the revealing of God's will in the Scripture, then should no man, to whom the Scripture hath not come, have right to make use of those creatures, either for his food or sustenance. And it were a hard condition of mankind, that a fierce and savage beast should with more right kill a man, than the man a beast.

CHAPTER XXIII*

OF THE POWER OF FATHERS,
AND OF PATRIMONIAL KINGDOM

1. OF three ways by which a man becometh subject to another, mentioned section 2. chap. ult., namely voluntary offer, captivity and birth, the former two have been spoken of, under the name of subjects and servants. In the next place, we are to set down the third way of subjection, under the name of children; and by what title one man cometh to have propriety in a child, that proceedeth from the common generation of two, (viz.) of male and female. And considering men again dissolved from all covenants one with another, and that (Part I. chap. XVII, sect. 2) every man by the law of nature, hath right or propriety to his own body, the child ought rather to be the propriety of the mother (of whose body it is part, till the time of separation) than of the father. For the understanding therefore of the right that a man or woman hath to his or their child, two things are to be considered: first what title the mother or any other originally hath to a child new born; secondly, how the father, or any other man, pretendeth by the mother.

2. For the first: they that have written of this subject have made generation to be a title of dominion over persons, as well as the consent of the persons themselves. And because generation giveth title to two, namely, father and mother, whereas dominion is indivisible, they therefore ascribe dominion over the child to the father only, *ob præstantiam sexūs*;* but they shew not, neither can I find out by what coherence, either generation inferreth dominion, or advantage of so much strength, which, for the most part, a man hath more than a woman, should generally and universally entitle the father to a propriety in the child, and take it away from the mother.

3. The title to dominion over a child, proceedeth not from the generation, but from the preservation of it; and therefore in the estate of nature, the mother in whose power it is to save or destroy it, hath right thereto by that

power, according to that which hath been said Part I. chap. XIV, sect. 13. And if the mother shall think fit to abandon, or expose her child to death, whatsoever man or woman shall find the child so exposed, shall have the same right which the mother had before; and for the same reason, namely for the power not of generating, but preserving. And though the child thus preserved, do in time acquire strength, whereby he might pretend equality with him or her that hath preserved him, yet shall that pretence be thought unreasonable, both because his strength was the gift of him, against whom he pretendeth; and also because it is to be presumed, that he which giveth sustenance to another, whereby to strengthen him, hath received a promise of obedience in consideration thereof. For else it would be wisdom in men, rather to let their children perish, while they are infants, than to live in their danger or subjection, when they are grown.

4. For the pretences which a man may have to dominion over a child by the right of the mother, they be of divers kinds. One by the absolute subjection of the mother: another, by some particular covenant from her, which is less than a covenant of such subjection. By absolute subjection, the master of the mother, hath right to her child, according to section 6, chap. XXII whether he be the father thereof, or not. And thus the children of the servant are the goods of the master in *perpetuum*.

5. Of covenants that amount not to subjection between a man and woman, there be some which are made for a time and some for life; and where they are for a time, they are covenants of cohabitation, or else of copulation only. And in this latter case, the children pass by covenants particular. And thus in the copulation of the Amazons with their neighbours, the fathers by covenant had the male children only, the mothers retaining the females.

6. And covenants of cohabitation are either for society of bed, or for society of all things; if for society of bed only, then is the woman called a CONCUBINE. And here also the child shall be his or hers, as they shall agree particularly by covenant; for although for the most part a concubine is

supposed to yield up the right of her children to the father, yet doth not concubinate enforce so much.

7. But if the covenants of cohabitation be for society of all things, it is necessary that but one of them govern and dispose of all that is common to them both; without which (as hath been often said before) society cannot last. And therefore the man, to whom for the most part the woman yieldeth the government, hath for the most part also the sole right and dominion over the children. And the man is called the HUSBAND, and the woman the WIFE; but because sometimes the government may belong to the wife only, sometimes also the dominion over the children shall be in her only; as in the case of a sovereign queen, there is no reason that her marriage should take from her the dominion over her children.

8. Children therefore, whether they be brought up and preserved by the father, or by the mother, or by whomsoever, are in most absolute subjection to him or her, that so bringeth them up, or preserveth them. And they may alienate them, that is, assign his or her dominion, by selling or giving them in adoption or servitude to others; or may pawn them for hostages, kill them for rebellion, or sacrifice them for peace, by the law of nature, when he or she, in his or her conscience, think it to be necessary.

9. The subjection of them who institute a commonwealth amongst themselves, is no less absolute, than the subjection of servants. And therein they are in equal estate; but the hope of those is greater than the hope of these. For he that subjecteth himself uncompelled, thinketh there is reason he should be better used, than he that doth it upon compulsion; and coming in freely, calleth himself, though in subjection, a FREEMAN; whereby it appeareth, that liberty is not any exemption from subjection and obedience to the sovereign power, but a state of better hope than theirs, that have been subjected by force and conquest. And this was the reason, that the name that signifieth children, in the Latin tongue is *liberi*, which also signifieth freemen. And yet in Rome, nothing at that time was so obnoxious to the power of others, as children in the family of their fathers. For both

the state had power over their life without consent of their fathers; and the father might kill his son by his own authority, without any warrant from the state. Freedom therefore in commonwealths is nothing but the honour of equality of favour with other subjects, and servitude the estate of the rest. A freeman therefore may expect employ-ments of honour, rather than a servant. And this is all that can be understood by the liberty of the subject. For in all other senses, liberty is the state of him that is not subject.

10. Now when a father that hath children, hath servants also, the children (not by the right of the child, but by the natural indulgence of the parents) are such freemen. And the whole consisting of the father or mother, or both, and of the children, and of the servants, is called a FAMILY; wherein the father or master of the family is sovereign of the same; and the rest (both children and servants equally) subjects. The same family if it grow by multiplication of children, either by generation or adoption; or of servants, either by generation, conquest, or voluntary submission, to be so great and numerous, as in probability it may protect itself, then is that family called a PATRIMONIAL KINGDOM, or monarchy by acquisition; wherein the sovereignty is in one man, as it is in a monarch made by political institution. So that whatsoever rights be in the one, the same also be in the other. And therefore I shall no more speak of them, as distinct, but as of monarchy in general.

11. Having shewed by what right the several sorts of commonwealths, democracy, aristocracy, and monarchy, are erected; it followeth to shew by what right they are continued. The right by which they are continued, is called the right of succession to the sovereign power; whereof there is nothing to be said in a democracy, because the sovereign dieth not, as long as there be subjects alive; nor in an aristocracy, because it cannot easily fall out, that the optimates should every one fail at once; and if it should so fall out, there is no question, but the commonwealth is thereby dissolved. It is therefore in a monarchy only, that there can happen a question concerning the succession. And first: forasmuch as a monarch, which is absolute sovereign,

hath the dominion in his own right, he may dispose thereof at his own will. If therefore, by his last will, he shall name his successor, the right passeth by that will.

12. Nor if the monarch die without any will concerning the succession declared, is it therefore to be presumed that it was his will, his subjects which are to him as his children and servants, should return again to the state of anarchy, that is, to war and hostility; for that were expressly against the law of nature, which commandeth to procure peace, and to maintain the same. It is therefore to be conjectured with reason, that it was his intention to bequeath them peace, that is to say, a power coercive, whereby to keep them from sedition amongst themselves; and rather in the form of monarchy, than any other government; forasmuch as he, by the exercise thereof in his own person, hath declared that he approveth of the same.

13. Further, it is to be supposed his intention was, that his own children should be preferred in the succession, (when nothing to the contrary is expressly declared) before any other. For men naturally seek their own honour, and that consisteth in the honour of their children after them.

14. Again, seeing every monarch is supposed to desire to continue the government in his successors, as long as he may; and that generally men are endued with greater parts of wisdom and courage, by which all monarchies are kept from dissolution, than women are; it is to be presumed, where no express will is extant to the contrary, he preferreth his male children before the female. Not but that women may govern, and have in divers ages and places governed wisely, but are not so apt thereto in general as men.

15. Because the sovereign power is indivisible, it cannot be supposed, that he intended the same should be divided, but that it should descend entirely upon one of them, which is to be presumed should be the eldest, assigned thereto by the lot of nature; because he appointed no other lot for the decision thereof. Besides, what difference of ability soever there may be amongst the brethren, the odds shall be adjudged to the elder, because no subject hath authority otherwise to judge thereof.

16. And for want of issue in the possessor, the brother shall be the presumed successor. For by the judgment of nature, next in blood is next in love; and next in love is next to preferment.

17. And as the succession followeth the first monarch, so also it followeth him or her that is in possession; and consequently, the children of him in possession shall be preferred before the children of his father or predecessor.

CHAPTER XXIV

THE INCOMMODITIES OF SEVERAL SORTS OF GOVERNMENT COMPARED

1. HAVING set forth the nature of a person politic, and the three sorts thereof, democracy, aristocracy, and monarchy; in this chapter shall be declared, the conveniences, and inconveniences, that arise from the same, both in general, and of the said several sorts in particular. And first, seeing a body politic is erected only for the ruling and governing of particular men, the benefit and damage thereof consisteth in the benefit or damage of being ruled. The benefit is that for which a body politic was instituted, namely, the peace and preservation of every particular man, than which it is not possible there can be a greater, as hath been touched before, Part I. chap. XIV, sect. 12. And this benefit extendeth equally both to the sovereign, and to the subjects. For he or they that have the sovereign power, have but the defence of their persons, by the assistance of the particulars; and every particular man hath his defence by their union in the sovereign. As for other benefits which pertain not to their safety and sufficiency, but to their well and delightful being, such as are superfluous riches, they so belong to the sovereign, as they must also be in the subject; and so to the subject, as they must also be in the sovereign. For the riches and treasure of the sovereign, is the dominion he hath over the riches of his subjects. If therefore the sovereign provide

not so as that particular men may have means, both to preserve themselves, and also to preserve the public; the common or sovereign treasure can be none. And on the other side, if it were not for a common and public treasure belonging to the sovereign power, men's private riches would sooner serve to put them into confusion and war, than to secure or maintain them. Insomuch, as the profit of the sovereign and subject goeth always together. That distinction therefore of government, that *there is one government for the good of him that governeth, and another for the good of them that be governed; whereof the former is despotical (that is lordly); the other, a government of freemen*, is not right; no more is the opinion of them that hold it to be no city, which consisteth of a master and his servants. They might as well say, it were no city, that consisted in a father and his own issue, how numerous soever they were. For to a master that hath no children, the servants have in them all those respects, for which men love their children; for they are his strength and his honour; and his power is no greater over them, than over his children.

2. The inconvenience arising from government in general to him that governeth, consisteth partly in the continual care and trouble about the business of other men, that are his subjects; and partly, in the danger of his person. For the head always is that part, not only where the care resideth, but also against which the stroke of an enemy most commonly is directed. To balance this incommodity, the sovereignty, together with the necessity of this care and danger, comprehendeth so much honour, riches, and means whereby to delight the mind, as no private man's wealth can attain unto. The inconveniences of government in general to a subject are none at all, if well considered; but in appearance there be two things that may trouble his mind, or two general grievances. The one is loss of liberty; the other the uncertainty of *meum* and *tuum*. For the first, it consisteth in this, that a subject may no more govern his own actions according to his own discretion and judgment, or, (which is all one) conscience, as the present occasions from time to time shall dictate to him; but must be tied to do according to

that will only, which once for all he had long ago laid up, and involved in the wills of the major part of an assembly, or in the will of some one man. But this is really no inconvenience. For, as it hath been shewed before, it is the only means by which we have any possibility of preserving ourselves; for if every man were allowed this liberty of following his conscience,* in such difference of consciences, they would not live together in peace an hour. But it appeareth a great inconvenience to every man in particular, to be debarred of this liberty, because every one apart considereth it as in himself, and not as in the rest; by which means, liberty appeareth in the likeness of rule and government over others; for where one man is at liberty, and the rest bound, there that one hath government. Which honour, he that understandeth not so much, demanding by the name simply of liberty, thinketh it a great grievance and injury to be denied it. For the second grievance concerning *meum* and *tuum*, it is also none, but in appearance only. It consisteth in this, that the sovereign power taketh from him that which he used to enjoy, knowing no other propriety, but use and custom. But without such sovereign power, the right of men is not propriety to any thing, but a community; no better than to have no right at all, as hath been shewed Part I. chap. XIV, sect. 10. Propriety therefore being derived from the sovereign power, is not to be pretended against the same; especially when by it every subject hath his propriety against every other subject, which when sovereignty ceaseth, he hath not, because in that case they return to war amongst themselves. Those levies therefore which are made upon men's estates, by the sovereign authority, are no more but the price of that peace and defence which the sovereignty maintaineth for them.* If this were not so, no money nor forces for the wars or any other public occasion, could justly be levied in the world; for neither king, nor democracy, nor aristocracy, nor the estates of any land, could do it, if the sovereignty could not. For in all those cases, it is levied by virtue of the sovereignty; nay more, by the three estates here, the land of one man may be transferred to another, without crime of him from whom it was taken, and without pretence of public benefit; as hath been done. And this without injury, because done by the sovereign power; for the power whereby it is done, is no less than sovereign, and cannot be greater. Therefore this grievance for *meum* and *tuum* is not real; unless more be exacted than is necessary. But it seemeth a grievance, because to them that either know not the right of sovereignty, or to whom that right belongeth, it seemeth an injury; and injury, how light soever the damage, is always grievous, as putting us in mind of our disability to help ourselves; and into envy of the power to do us wrong.

3. Having spoken of the inconveniences of the subject, by government in general, let us consider the same in the three several sorts thereof, namely, democracy, aristocracy, and monarchy; whereof the two former are in effect but one. For (as I have shewed before) democracy is but the government of a few orators. The comparison therefore will be between monarchy and aristocracy; and to omit that the world, as it was created, so also it is governed by one God Almighty; and that all the ancients have preferred monarchy before other governments, both in opinion, because they feigned a monarchical government amongst their gods; and also by their custom, for that in the most ancient times all people were so governed; and that paternal government, which is monarchy, was instituted in the beginning from the creation; and that other governments have proceeded from the dissolution thereof, caused by the rebellious nature of mankind, and be but pieces of broken monarchies cemented by human wit; I will insist only in this comparison upon the inconveniences that may happen to the subjects, in consequence to each of these governments.

4. And first it seemeth inconvenient, there should be committed so great a power to one man, as that it might be lawful to no other man or men to resist the same; and some think it inconvenient *eo nomine*,* because he hath the power. But this reason we may not by any means admit, for it maketh it inconvenient to be ruled by Almighty God, who without question hath more power over every man, than can be conferred upon any monarch. This inconvenience there-

fore must be derived, not from the power, but from the affections and passions which reign in every one, as well monarch as subject; by which the monarch may be swayed to use that power amiss. And because an aristocracy consisteth of men, if the passions of many men be more violent when they are assembled together, than the passions of one man alone, it will follow, that the inconvenience arising from passion will be greater in an aristocracy, than a monarchy. But there is no doubt, when things are debated in great assemblies, but every man delivering his opinion at large, without interruption, endeavoureth to make whatsoever he is to set forth for good, better; and what he would have apprehended as evil, worse, as much as is possible; to the end his counsel may take place; which counsel also is never without aim at his own benefit, or honour: every man's end being some good to himself.* Now this cannot be done without working upon the passions of the rest. And thus the passions of those that are singly moderate, are altogether vehement; even as a great many coals, though but warm asunder, being put together inflame one another.

5. Another inconvenience of monarchy is this: that the monarch, besides the riches necessary for the defence of the commonwealth, may take so much more from the subjects, as may enrich his children, kindred and favourites, to what degree he pleaseth; which though it be indeed an inconvenience, if he should so do; yet is the same both greater in an aristocracy, and also more likely to come to pass; for there not one only, but many have children, kindred, and friends to raise; and in that point they are as twenty monarchs for one, and likely to set forward one another's designs mutually, to the oppression of all the rest. The same also happeneth in a democracy, if they all do agree; otherwise they bring in a worse inconvenience, (viz.) sedition.

6. Another inconvenience of monarchy, is the power of dispensing with the execution of justice;* whereby the family and friends of the monarch, may with impunity, commit outrages upon the people, or oppress them with extortion. But in aristocracies, not only one, but many have power of taking men out of the hands of justice; and no man is willing

his kindred or friends should be punished according to their demerits. And therefore they understand amongst themselves without farther speaking, as a tacit covenant: *Hodie mihi, cras tibi.**

7. Another inconvenience of monarchy, is the power of altering laws; concerning which, it is necessary that such a power be, that the laws may be altered, according as men's manners change, or as the conjuncture of all circumstances within and without the commonwealth shall require; the change of law being then inconvenient, when it proceedeth from the change, not of the occasion, but of the minds of him or them, by whose authority the laws are made. Now it is manifest enough of itself, that the mind of one man is not so variable in that point, as are the decrees of an assembly. For not only they have all their natural changes, but the change of any one man be enough, with eloquence and reputation, or by solicitation and faction, to make that law to-day, which another by the very same means, shall abrogate to-morrow.

8. Lastly, the greatest inconvenience that can happen to a commonwealth, is the aptitude to dissolve into civil war; and to this are monarchies much less subject, than any other governments. For where the union, or band of a commonwealth, is one man, there is no distraction; whereas in assemblies, those that are of different opinions, and give different counsel, are apt to fall out amongst themselves, and to cross the designs of commonwealth for one another's sake: and when they cannot have the honour of making good their own devices, they yet seek the honour to make the counsels of their adversaries to prove vain. And in this contention, when the opposite factions happen to be anything equal in strength, they presently fall to war. Wherein necessity teacheth both sides, that an absolute monarch, (viz.) a general, is necessary both for their defence against one another, and also for the peace of each faction within itself. But this aptitude to dissolution, is to be understood for an inconvenience in such aristocracies only where the affairs of state are debated in great and numerous assemblies, as they were anciently in Athens, and in Rome;

and not in such as do nothing else in great assemblies, but choose magistrates and counsellors, and commit the handling of state affairs to a few; such as is the aristocracy of Venice at this day. For these are no more apt to dissolve from this occasion, than monarchies, the counsel of state being both in the one and the other alike.

CHAPTER XXV

THAT SUBJECTS ARE NOT BOUND TO FOLLOW THEIR PRIVATE JUDGMENTS IN CONTROVERSIES OF RELIGION

1. HAVING showed that in all commonwealths whatsoever, the necessity of peace and government requireth, that there be existent some power, either in one man, or in one assembly of men, by the name of the power sovereign, to which it is not lawful for any member of the same commonwealth to disobey; there occurreth now a difficulty, which, if it be not removed, maketh it unlawful for any man to procure his own peace and preservation, because it maketh it unlawful for a man to put himself under the command of such absolute sovereignty as is required thereto. And the difficulty is this: we have amongst us the Word of God for the rule of our actions; now if we shall subject ourselves to men also, obliging ourselves to do such actions as shall be by them commanded; when the commands of God and man shall differ, we are to obey God, rather than man: and consequently the covenant of general obedience to man is unlawful.

2. This difficulty hath not been of very great antiquity in the world. There was no such dilemma amongst the Jews; for their civil law, and divine law, was one and the same law of Moses: the interpreters whereof were the priests, whose power was subordinate to the power of the king; as was the power of Aaron to the power of Moses. Nor is it a controversy that was ever taken notice of amongst the Grecians,

Romans, or other Gentiles; for amongst these their several civil laws were the rules whereby not only righteousness and virtue, but also religion and the external worship of God, was ordered and approved; that being esteemed the true worship of God, which was κατὰ τὰ νόμιμα, (i.e.) according to the laws civil. Also those Christians that dwell under the temporal dominion of the bishop of Rome, are free from this question; for that they allow unto him (their sovereign) to interpret the Scriptures, which are the law of God, as he in his own judgment shall think right. This difficulty therefore remaineth amongst, and troubleth those Christians only, to whom it is allowed to take for the sense of the Scripture that which they make thereof, either by their own private interpretation, or by the interpretation of such as are not called thereunto by public authority: they that follow their own interpretation, continually demanding liberty of conscience; and those that follow the interpretation of others not ordained thereunto by the sovereign of the commonwealth, requiring a power in matters of religion either above the power civil, or at least not depending on it.

3. To take away this scruple of conscience concerning obedience to human laws, amongst those that interpret to themselves the word of God in the Holy Scriptures; I propound to their consideration, first: that no human law is intended to oblige the conscience of a man,* but the actions only. For seeing no man (but God alone) knoweth the heart or conscience of a man, unless it break out into action, either of the tongue, or other part of the body; the law made thereupon would be of none effect, because no man is able to discern, but by word or other action whether such law be kept or broken. Nor did the apostles themselves pretend dominion over men's consciences concerning the faith they preached, but only persuasion and instruction. And therefore St. Paul saith 2 Cor. 1, 24, writing to the Corinthians, concerning their controversies, that he and the rest of the apostles, *had no dominion over their faith, but were helpers of their joy*.

4. And for the actions of men which proceed from their consciences, the regulating of which actions is the only

means of peace; if they might not stand with justice, it were impossible that justice towards God, and peace amongst men should stand together in that religion that teacheth us, *that justice and peace should kiss each other*, and in which we have so many precepts of absolute obedience to human authority; as Matth. 23, 2, 3, we have this precept: *The Scribes and Pharisees sit in Moses' seat; all therefore whatsoever they bid you observe, that observe and do.* And yet were the Scribes and Pharisees not priests, but men of temporal authority. Again Luke 11, 17: *Every kingdom divided against itself shall be desolate*; and is not that kingdom divided against itself, where the actions of every one shall be ruled by his private opinion, or conscience; and yet those actions such as give occasion of offence and breach of peace? Again Rom. 13, 5, *Wherefore you must be subject, not because of wrath only, but also for conscience sake.* Titus 3, 1: *Put them in remembrance, that they be subject to principalities and powers.* 1 Peter 2, 3, 13–14: *Submit yourselves unto all manner of ordinance of man, for the Lord's sake, whether it be unto the king, as unto the superior, or unto governors, as unto them that are sent of him for the punishment of evil-doers.* Jude, verse 8: *These dreamers also that defile the flesh, and despise government, and speak evil of them that are in authority.* And forasmuch as all subjects in commonwealths are in the nature of children and servants, that which is a command to them, is a command to all subjects. But to these St. Paul saith, Colos. 3, 20, 22: *Children, obey your parents in all things; servants, be obedient to your masters according to the flesh, in all things.* And verse 23: *Do it heartily as to the Lord.* These places considered, it seemeth strange to me, that any man in a Christian commonwealth should have any occasion to deny his obedience to public authority, upon this ground, that *it is better to obey God than man.* For though St. Peter and the apostles did so answer the council of the Jews that forbad them to preach Christ, there appeareth no reason that Christians should allege the same against their Christian governors, that command to preach Christ. To reconcile this seeming contradiction of simple obedience to God and simple obedience to man, we are to consider a Christian subject, as under a Christian sovereign, or under an infidel.

5. And under a Christian sovereign we are to consider, what actions we are forbidden by God Almighty to obey them in, and what not. The actions we are forbidden to obey them in, are such only as imply a denial of that faith which is necessary to our salvation; for otherwise there can be no pretence of disobedience. For why should a man incur the danger of a temporal death, by displeasing of his superior, if it were not for fear of eternal death hereafter? It must therefore be enquired, what those propositions and articles they be, the belief whereof our Saviour or his apostles have declared to be such, as without believing them a man cannot be saved; and then all other points that are now controverted, and make distinction of sects, Papists, Lutherans, Calvinists, Arminians, &c., as in old time the like made Paulists, Apollonians, and Cephasians, must needs be such, as a man needeth not for the holding thereof deny obedience to his superiors. And for the points of faith necessary to salvation, I shall call them FUNDAMENTAL, and every other point a SUPERSTRUCTION.

6. And without all controversy, there is not any more necessary point to be believed for man's salvation than this, that Jesus is the Messiah, that is, the Christ; which proposition is explicated in sundry sorts, but still the same in effect; as, *that he is God's anointed*; for that is signified by the word Christ; *that he was the true and lawful king of Israel, the son of David; and Saviour of the world, the redeemer of Israel; the salvation of God; he that should come into the world, the son of God*, and (which I desire by the way to have noted, against the new sect of Arians), *the begotten Son of God*, Acts 3, 13; Heb. 1, 5; 5, 5: *the only begotten Son of God*, John 1, 14, 18; John 3, 16, 18; 1 John 4, 9: *that he was God*, John 1, 1; John 20, 28: *that the fulness of the Godhead dwelt in him bodily*. Moreover, *the Holy One, the Holy One of God, the forgiver of sins, that he is risen from the dead*: these are explications, and parts of that general article, *that Jesus is the Christ*. This point therefore, and all the explications thereof are fundamental; as also all such as be evidently

inferred from thence; as, belief in God the Father: John 12, 44: *He that believeth in me, believeth not in me, but in him that sent me*; 1 John 2, 23: *He that denieth the Son, hath not the Father*: belief in God the Holy Ghost, of Whom Christ saith, John 14, 26: *But the Comforter, which is the Holy Ghost, whom the Father will send in my name*; and John 15, 26: *But when the Comforter shall come, whom I will send unto you from the Father, even the Spirit of truth*: belief of the Scriptures, by which we believe those points, and of the immortality of the soul, without which we cannot believe he is a Saviour.

7. And as these are the fundamental points of faith, necessary to salvation; so also are they only necessary as matter of faith, and only essential to the calling of a Christian; as may appear by many evident places of Holy Scripture: John 5, 39: *Search the Scriptures, for in them you think to have eternal life, and they are they which testify of me*. Now, forasmuch as by the Scripture is meant there the Old Testament (the New being then not written), the belief of that which was written concerning our Saviour in the Old Testament, was sufficient belief for the obtaining of eternal life; but in the Old Testament, there is nothing revealed concerning Christ, but that he is the Messiah, and such things as belong to the fundamental points thereupon depending; and therefore those fundamental points are sufficient to salvation, as of faith. And John 6, 28, 29: *Then said they unto him, What shall we do, that we might work the works of God? Jesus answered and said unto them, This is the work of God, that ye believe in him, whom he hath sent*. So that the point to be believed is, *That Jesus Christ came forth from God, and he which believeth it, worketh the works of God*. John 11, 26, 27: *Whosoever liveth and believeth in me, shall never die. Believest thou this? She said unto him, Yea, Lord, I believe that thou art the Christ, the Son of God, which should come into the world*. Hence followeth that he that believeth this shall never die. John 20, 31: *But these things are written, that ye might believe, that Jesus is the Christ, the Son of God; and that believing, ye might have life through his name*. By which appeareth that this fundamental point is

all that is required, as of faith to our salvation. 1 John 4, 2: *Every spirit that confesseth that Jesus Christ is come in the flesh, is of God*: 1 John 5, 1: *Whosoever believeth that Jesus is the Christ, is born of God*; and verse 4; *Who is it that overcometh the world, but he that believeth, that Jesus is the Son of God?* and verse 13: *These things have I written unto you that believe in the name of the Son of God, that ye may know that ye have eternal life.* Acts 8, 36, 37: *The eunuch said, Here is water, what doth let me to be baptized? And Philip said unto him, If thou believest with all thy heart, thou mayest. He answered and said, I believe that Jesus Christ is the Son of God.* This point therefore was sufficient for the reception of a man to baptism, that is to say to Christianity. And Acts 16, 30: *The keeper of the prison fell down before Paul and Silas, and said, Sirs, what shall I do to be saved? And they said, Believe in the Lord Jesus Christ.* And the sermon of St. Peter, upon the day of Pentecost, was nothing else but an explication, that Jesus was the Christ. And when they that heard him, asked him, What shall we do? he said unto them, Acts 2, 38: *Amend your lives, and be baptized every one of you in the name of Jesus Christ, for the remission of sins.* Rom. 10, 9: *If thou shalt confess with thy mouth the Lord Jesus, and shalt believe in thy heart, that God raised him up from the dead, thou shalt be saved.* To these places may be added: that wheresoever our Saviour Christ doth approve the faith of any man, the proposition believed (if the same be to be collected out of the text) is always some of these fundamental points before mentioned, or something equivalent; as the faith of the centurion, Matth. 8, 8: *Speak the word only, and my servant shall be healed*; believing he was omnipotent; the faith of the woman, which had an issue of blood, Matth. 9, 21: *If I may but touch the hem of his garment*; implying, he was the Messiah; the faith required of the blind men, Matth. 9, 28: *Believe you that I am able to do this?* the faith of the Canaanitish woman, Matth. 15, 22, that he was the *Son of David*, implying the same. And so it is in every one of those places (none excepted) where our Saviour commendeth any man's faith; which because they are too many to insert here, I omit, and refer them to his inquisition that is not otherwise satisfied. And as there is no other faith required, so there was no other preaching; for the prophets of the Old Testament preached no other; and John the Baptist preached only the approach of the kingdom of heaven, that is to say, of the kingdom of Christ. The same was the commission of the apostles, Matth. 10, 7: *Go preach, saying, The kingdom of heaven is at hand*. And Paul preaching amongst the Jews, Acts 18, 5, did but testify unto the Jews, *that Jesus was the Christ*. And the heathens took notice of Christians no otherwise, but by this name that they believed *Jesus to be a king*, crying out, Acts 17, 6: *These are they that have subverted the state of the world, and here they are, whom Jason hath received. And these all do against the decrees of Cæsar, saying, that there is another king, one Jesus*. And this was the sum of the predictions, the sum of the confessions of them that believed, as well men as devils. This was the title of his cross, *Jesus of Nazareth, king of the Jews*; this the occasion of the crown of thorns, sceptre of reed, and a man to carry his cross; this was the subject of the *Hosannas*; and this the title, by which our Saviour, commanding to take another man's goods, bade them say, *The Lord hath need*; and by this title he purged the temple of the profane market kept there. Nor did the apostles themselves believe any more than that *Jesus was the Messiah* nor understand so much; for they understood the Messiah to be no more than a temporal king, till after our Saviour's resurrection. Farthermore, this point that *Christ is the Messiah*, is particularly set forth for fundamental by that word, or some other equivalent thereunto in divers places. Upon the confession of Peter, Matth. 16, 16: *Thou art the Christ, the son of the living God*, our Saviour, verse 18, saith, *Upon this rock will I build my Church*. This point therefore is the whole foundation of Christ's church. Rom. 15, 20, St. Paul saith, *So I enforced myself to preach the Gospel, not where Christ was named, lest I should have built upon another man's foundation*. 1 Cor. 3, 10, St. Paul when he had reprehended the Corinthians for their sects, and curious doctrines and questions, he distinguisheth between fundamental points, and superstruction; and saith, *I have laid the foundation, and another buildeth thereupon; but let every man take heed how he buildeth upon it. For other foundation can no man lay than that which is laid, which is Jesus the Christ.* Colos. 2, 6: *As you have received Christ Jesus the Lord, so walk in him, rooted and builded in him, and stablished in the faith.*

8. Having showed this proposition, Jesus is the Christ, to be the only fundamental and necessary point of faith; I shall set down a few places more to show that other points, though they may be true, are not so necessary to be believed, as that a man may not be saved though he believe them not. And first, if a man could not be saved without assent of the heart to the truth of all controversies, which are now in agitation concerning religion, I cannot see how any man living can be saved; so full of subtilty, and curious knowledge it is, to be so great a divine. Why therefore should a man think that our Saviour, who Matth. 11, 30, saith, *that his yoke is easy*, should require a matter of that difficulty? or how are little children said to believe? Matth. 18, 6; or how could the good thief be thought sufficiently catechised upon the cross? or St. Paul so perfect a Christian presently upon his conversion? and though there may be more obedience required in him that hath the fundamental points explicated upon him, than in him, that hath received the same but implicitly; yet there is no more faith required for salvation in one man than in another. For if it be true, that *whosoever shall confess with his mouth the Lord Jesus, and believe in his heart that God raised him from the dead, shall be saved*; as it is, Rom. 10, 9; and that *whosoever believeth that Jesus is the Christ, is born of God*; the belief of that point is sufficient for the salvation of any man whosoever he be, forasmuch as concerneth faith. And seeing he that believeth not, *that Jesus is the Christ*, whatsoever he believe else, cannot be saved; it followeth that there is no more required to the salvation of one man, than of another, in matter of faith.

9. About these points fundamental there is little controversy amongst Christians, though otherwise of different sects amongst themselves. And therefore the controversies

of religion, are altogether about points unnecessary to salvation; whereof some are doctrines raised by human ratiocination, from the points fundamental. As for example: such doctrines as concern the manner of the real presence, wherein are mingled tenets of faith concerning the omnipotency and divinity of Christ, with the tenets of Aristotle and the Peripatetics concerning substance and accidents, species, hypostasis and the subsistence and migration of accidents from place to place; words some of them without meaning, and nothing but the canting of Grecian sophisters; and these doctrines are condemned expressly Col. 2, 8, where after St. Paul had exhorted them *to be rooted and builded in Christ*, he giveth them this further caveat: *Beware lest there be any man that spoil you through philosophy and vain deceits, through the traditions of men, according to the rudiments of the world.* And such are such doctrines, as are raised out of such places of the Scriptures, as concern not the foundation, by men's natural reason; as about the concatenation of causes, and the manner of God's predestination; which are also mingled with philosophy; as if it were possible for men that know not in what manner God seeth, heareth, or speaketh, to know nevertheless the manner how he intendeth, and predestinateth. A man therefore ought not to examine by reason any point, or draw any consequence out of Scripture by reason, concerning the nature of God Almighty, of which reason is not capable. And therefore St. Paul, Rom. 12, 3, giveth a good rule, *That no man presume to understand above that which is meet to understand, but that he understand according to sobriety*; which they do not who presume out of Scripture, by their own interpretation to raise any doctrine to the understanding, concerning those things which are incomprehensible. And this whole controversy concerning the predestination of God, and the free-will of man, is not peculiar to Christian men. For we have huge volumes* of this subject, under the name of fate and contingency, disputed between the Epicureans and the Stoics, and consequently it is not matter of faith, but of philosophy; and so are also all the questions concerning any other point, but the foundation before named; and God receiveth a man, which part of the question soever he holdeth. It was a controversy in St. Paul's time, whether a Christian Gentile might eat freely of any thing which the Christian Jews did not; and the Jew condemned the Gentile that he did eat; to whom St. Paul saith, Rom. 14, 3: *Let not him that eateth not, judge him that eateth; for God hath received him.* And verse 6, in the question concerning the observing of holy days, wherein the Gentiles and the Jews differed, he saith unto them, *He that observeth the day, observeth it to the Lord; and he that observeth not the day, observeth it not, to the Lord.* And they who strive concerning such questions, and divide themselves into sects, are not therefore to be accounted zealous of the faith, their strife being but carnal, which is confirmed by St. Paul, 1 Cor. 3, 4: *When one saith, I am of Paul, and another, I am of Apollos, are ye not carnal?* For they are not questions of faith, but of wit, wherein, carnally, men are inclined to seek the mastery one of another. For nothing is truly a point of faith, but that Jesus is the Christ; as St. Paul testifieth, 1 Cor. 2, 2: *For I esteemed not the knowledge of any thing amongst you, save Jesus Christ, and him crucified.* And 1 Tim. 6, 20, 21: *O Timotheus, keep that which is committed unto thee, and avoid profane and vain babblings, and opposition of science falsely so called, which while some profess, they have erred, concerning the faith.* 2 Tim. 2, 16: *Stay profane and vain babblings,* &c. Verse 17: *Of which sort is Hymenæus and Philetus, which as concerning the truth, have erred, saying that the resurrection is past already.* Whereby St. Paul sheweth that the raising of questions by human ratiocination, though it be from the fundamental points themselves, is not only not necessary, but most dangerous to the faith of a Christian. Out of all these places I draw only this conclusion in general, that neither the points now in controversy amongst Christians of different sects, or in any point that ever shall be in controversy, excepting only those that are contained in this article, *Jesus is the Christ*, are necessary to salvation, as of faith; though as matter of obedience, a man may be bound not to oppose the same.

10. Although to the obtaining of salvation, there be re-

quired no more, as hath been already declared out of the Holy Scriptures, as matter of faith, but the belief of those fundamental articles before set forth; nevertheless, there are required other things, as matter of obedience. For, as it is not enough in temporal kingdoms (to avoid the punishment which kings may inflict) to acknowledge the right and title of the king, without obedience also to his laws; so also it is not enough to acknowledge our Saviour Christ to be the king of heaven, in which consisteth Christian faith, unless also we endeavour to obey his laws, which are the laws of the kingdom of heaven, in which consisteth Christian obedience. And forasmuch as the laws of the kingdom of heaven, are the laws of nature, as hath been shewed Part I. chap. XVIII, not only faith, but also the observation of the law of nature, which is that for which a man is called just or righteous (in that sense in which justice is taken not for the absence of all guilt, but for the endeavour, and constant will to do that which is just), not only faith, but this justice, which also from the effect thereof, is called repentance, and sometimes works, is necessary to salvation. So that faith and justice do both concur thereto; and in the several acceptation of this word justification, are properly said both of them to justify; and the want of either of them is properly said to condemn. For not only he that resisteth a king upon doubt of his title, but also he that doth it upon the inordinateness of his passions, deserveth punishment. And when faith and works are separated, not only the faith is called dead, without works, but also works are called dead works, without faith. And therefore St. James, chap. 2, 17, saith, *Even so the faith, if it have no works, is dead in itself*; and verse 26: *For as the body without the spirit is dead, even so faith without works is dead*. And St. Paul, Heb. 6, 1, calleth works without faith, dead works, where he saith, *Not laying again the foundation of repentance from dead works*. And by these dead works, is understood not the obedience and justice of the inward man, but the *opus operatum*, or external action, proceeding from fear of punishment, or from vain glory, and desire to be honoured of men; and these may be separated from faith, and conduce no way to a man's justification. And for that cause St. Paul, Rom. 4, excludeth the righteousness of the law, from having part in the justification of a sinner. For by the law of Moses, which is applied to men's actions, and requireth the absence of guilt, all men living are liable to damnation; and therefore no man is justified by works, but by faith only. But if works be taken for the endeavour to do them, that is, if the will be taken for the deed, or internal for external righteousness, then do works contribute to salvation. And then taketh place that of St. James, chap. 2, 24: *Ye see then, how that of works a man is justified, and not of faith only.* And both of these are joined to salvation, as in St. Mark 1, 15: *Repent and believe the Gospel.* And Luke 18, 18, when a certain ruler asked our Saviour, what he ought to do to inherit eternal life, he propounded to him the keeping of the commandments; which when the ruler said he had kept, he propounded to him the faith, *Sell all that thou hast, and follow me.* And John 3, 36: *He that believeth in the Son, hath everlasting life.* And *He that obeyeth not the Son, shall not see life.* Where he manifestly joineth obedience and faith together. And Rom. 1, 17: *The just shall live by faith;* not every one, but the just. For also *the devils believe and tremble.* But though both faith and justice (meaning still by justice, not absence of guilt, but the good intentions of the mind, which is called righteousness by God, that taketh the will for the deed) be both of them said to justify, yet are their parts in the act of justification to be distinguished. For justice is said to justify, not because it absolveth, but because it denominates him just, and setteth him in an estate or capacity of salvation, whensoever he shall have faith. But faith is said to justify, that is, to absolve; because by it a just man is absolved of, and forgiven his unjust actions. And thus are reconciled the places of St. Paul and St. James, *that faith only justifieth,* and *a man is not justified by faith only;* and shewed how faith and repentance must concur to salvation.

11. These things considered it will easily appear: that under the sovereign power of a Christian commonwealth, there is no danger of damnation from simple obedience to human laws; for in that the sovereign alloweth Christianity,

no man is compelled to renounce that faith which is enough for his salvation; that is to say, the fundamental points. And for other points, seeing they are not necessary to salvation, if we conform our actions to the laws, we do not only what we are allowed, but also what we are commanded, by the law of nature, which is the moral law taught by our Saviour himself. And it is part of that obedience which must concur to our salvation.

12. And though it be true, whatsoever a man doth contrary to his conscience, is sin; yet the obedience in these cases, is neither sin, nor against the conscience. For the conscience being nothing else but a man's settled judgment and opinion, when he hath once transferred his right of judging to another, that which shall be commanded, is no less his judgment, than the judgment of that other; so that in obedience to laws, a man doth still according to his conscience, but not his private conscience. And whatsoever is done contrary to private conscience, is then a sin, when the laws have left him to his own liberty, and never else. And then whatsoever a man doth, not only believing it is ill done, but doubting whether it be ill or not, is done ill; in case he may lawfully omit the doing.

13. And as it hath been proved, that a man must submit his opinions, in matters of controversy, to the authority of the commonwealth; so also is the same confessed by the practice of every one of them that otherwise deny it. For who is there differing in opinion from another, and thinking himself to be in the right, and the other in the wrong, that would not think it reasonable, if he be of the same opinion that the whole state alloweth, that the other should submit his opinion also thereunto? or that would not be content, if not that one or a few men, yet that all the divines of a whole nation, or at least an assembly of all those he liketh, should have the power to determine of all the controversies of religion? or, who is there that would not be content, to submit his opinions, either to the pope, or to a general council, or to a provincial council, or to a presbytery of his own nation? And yet in all these cases he submitteth himself to no greater than human authority. Nor can a man be said

to submit himself to Holy Scripture, that doth not submit himself to some or other for the interpretation thereof; or why should there be any church government at all instituted, if the Scripture itself could do the office of a judge in controversies of faith? But the truth is apparent, by continual experience, that men seek not only liberty of conscience, but of their actions; nor that only, but a farther liberty of persuading others to their opinions; nor that only for every man desireth, that the sovereign authority should admit no other opinions to be maintained but such as he himself holdeth.

14. The difficulty therefore of obeying both God and man, in a Christian commonwealth is none: all the difficulty resteth in this point, whether he that hath received the faith of Christ, having before subjected himself to the authority of an infidel, be discharged of his obedience thereby, or not, in matters of religion. In which case it seemeth reasonable to think, that since all covenants of obedience are entered into for the preservation of a man's life, if a man be content, without resistance to lay down his life, rather than to obey the commands of an infidel; in so hard a case he hath sufficiently discharged himself thereof. For no covenant bindeth farther than to endeavour; and if a man cannot assure himself to perform a just duty, when thereby he is assured of present death, much less can it be expected that a man should perform that, for which he believeth in his heart he shall be damned eternally. And thus much concerning the scruple of conscience that may arise concerning obedience to human laws, in them that interpret the law of God to themselves. It remaineth, to remove the same scruple from them that submit their controversies to others, not ordained thereunto by the sovereign authority. And this I refer to the chapter following.

CHAPTER XXVI

THAT SUBJECTS ARE NOT BOUND TO FOLLOW THE JUDGMENT OF ANY AUTHORITIES IN CONTROVERSIES OF RELIGION WHICH IS NOT DEPENDENT ON THE SOVEREIGN POWER

1. In the former chapter have been removed those difficulties opposing our obedience to human authority, which arise from misunderstanding of our Saviour's title and laws; in the former whereof, namely his title, consisteth our faith; and in the latter, our justice. Now they who differ not amongst themselves concerning his title and laws, may nevertheless have different opinions concerning his magistrates, and the authority he hath given them. And this is the cause why many Christians have denied obedience to their princes; pretending that our Saviour Christ hath not given this magistracy to them, but to others. As for example: some say, to the pope universally; some, to a synod aristocratical; some, to a synod democratical in every several commonwealth; and the magistrates of Christ being they by whom he speaketh: the question is, whether he speak unto us by the pope, or by convocations of bishops and ministers, or by them that have the sovereign power in every commonwealth.

2. This controversy was the cause of those two mutinies that happened against Moses in the wilderness. The first by Aaron and his sister Miriam, who took upon them to censure Moses, for marrying an Ethiopian woman. And the state of the question between them and Moses they set forth Numbers 12, 2, in these words: *What hath the Lord spoken but only by Moses? hath he not spoken also by us? And the Lord heard this*, &c., and punished the same in Miriam, forgiving Aaron upon his repentance. And this is the case of all them that set up the priesthood against the sovereignty. The other was of Corah, Dathan, and Abiram, who with two hundred and fifty captains gathered themselves together against Moses, and against Aaron. The state of their controversy was this: *Whether God were not with the multitude,*

as well as with Moses, and every man as holy as he. For, Numb. 16, 3, thus they say, *You take too much upon you, seeing all the congregation is holy; every one of them, and the Lord is amongst them: wherefore then lift ye yourselves above the congregation of the Lord?* And this is the case of them that set up their private consciences, and unite themselves to take the government of religion out of the hands of him or them, that have the sovereign power of the commonwealth; which how well it pleaseth God, may appear by the hideous punishment of Corah and his accomplices.

3. In the government therefore of Moses, there was no power neither civil nor spiritual, that was not derived from him; nor in the state of Israel under kings, was there any earthly power, by which those kings were compellable to any thing, or any subject allowed to resist them, in any case whatsoever. For though the prophets by extraordinary calling, did often admonish and threaten them, yet had they no authority over them. And therefore amongst the Jews, the power spiritual and temporal, was always in the same hand.

4. Our Saviour Christ, as he was the rightful king of the Jews in particular, as well as king of the kingdom of Heaven, in the ordaining of magistrates, revived that form of policy which was used by Moses. According to the number of the children of Jacob, Moses took unto him by the appointment of God, Numb. 1, 4, twelve men, every one of the chief of their tribe, which were to assist him in the muster of Israel. And these twelve, verse 24, are called the *princes of Israel, twelve men, every one for the house of their fathers*; which are said also Numb. 7, 2, *to be heads over the houses of their fathers, and princes of the tribes, and over them that were numbered*. And these were every one equal amongst themselves. In like manner our Saviour took unto him twelve apostles, to be next unto him in authority; of whom he saith Matth. 19, 28, *When the Son of Man shall sit in the throne of his majesty, ye which follow me in the regeneration, shall sit also upon twelve thrones, and judge the twelve tribes of Israel*. And concerning the equality of the twelve apostles amongst themselves our Saviour saith,

Matth. 20, 25: *Ye know that the Lords of the Gentiles have domination over them*, &c. Verse 26: *But it shall not be so amongst you; but whosoever will be greatest among you, let him be your servant*. And Matth. 23, 11: *He that is greatest among you, let him be your servant*. And a little before, verse 8, *Be not called Rabbi; for one is your doctor, Christ; and all ye are brethren*. And Acts 1, in choosing of Matthias to be an apostle, though St. Peter used the part of a *prolocutor*, yet did no man take upon him the authority of election, but referred the same to lot.

5. Again, Moses had the command of God, Numb. 11, 16: *Gather to me seventy men of the elders of Israel, whom thou knowest that they are the elders of the people, and governors over them, and bring them into the tabernacle*, &c. And Moses did accordingly, verse 24. And these were chosen to help Moses in bearing the burthen of the government, as appeareth verse 17 of the same chapter. And as the twelve princes of the tribes were according to the number of Jacob's children; so were the seventy elders according to the number of the persons that went down with Jacob into Egypt. In like manner our Saviour in his kingdom of Heaven, the church, out of the whole number of those that believed in him, ordained seventy persons, which peculiarly were called the seventy disciples, to whom he gave power to preach the Gospel and baptize.

6. In our Saviour's time therefore, the hierarchy of the church consisted, besides himself that was the head, of twelve apostles, who were equal amongst themselves, but ordained over others, as were the twelve heads of the tribes; and seventy disciples, who had every one of them power to baptize and teach, and help to govern the whole flock.

7. And whereas in the commonwealth instituted by Moses, there was not only a high-priest for the present, but also a succession and order of priests; it may be demanded why our Saviour Christ did not ordain the like? To which may be answered, that the high-priesthood, forasmuch as concerneth the authority thereof, was in the person of Christ, as he was Christ-King. So also was it in Moses, Aaron having the ministerial part only. For notwithstanding

that Aaron was the high-priest, yet the consecration of him belonged to Moses, Exod. 29, 1. All the utensils of sacrifice, and other holy things, were ordered by Moses; and in sum: the whole Levitical law was delivered by God by the hand of Moses, who was to Aaron a God, and Aaron to him a mouth. And for the ministerial part, there could no high-priest be ordained but himself; for seeing our Saviour was himself the sacrifice, who but himself could offer him up? And for the celebration of that sacrifice for ever after, our Saviour annexed the priesthood to those whom he had appointed to govern in the church.

8. After the ascension of our Saviour, the apostles dispersed themselves for the spreading of the Gospel; and continually as they converted any number of men, in any city or region, to the faith, they chose out such as they thought fittest, to direct them in matter of conversation and life, according to Christ's law, and to explicate unto them that mystery of Christ come in the flesh; that is to say, to unfold unto them at large the office of the Messiah. And of those elders some were subordinate to others, according as the apostles, who ordained them, thought meet. So St. Paul gave power to Titus, to ordain elders in Crete, and to redress things that were amiss. So that Titus was both an elder, and ordained elders, Tit. 1. 5: *For this cause I left thee in Crete, that thou shouldest continue to redress the things that remain, and ordain elders in every city*; where the word is καταστήσῃς, that is constitute; whereby it appeareth that in the apostles' times, one elder had authority over another, to ordain and rule them. For 1 Tim. 5, 19, Timothy an elder, is made judge of accusations against other elders. And Acts 14, 23, the disciples are said to ordain elders for all the congregations of the cities they had preached in; and though the word there be χειροτονήσαντες, yet it signifieth not election by holding up of hands, but simply and absolutely ordination. For the ordinary choosing of magistrates amongst the Grecians, which were all either popularly governed, or else by *oligarchy*, being performed by holding up of hands, made that word be taken simply for an election or ordination howsoever made. And thus in the primitive

church, the hierarchy of the church was: apostles; elders that governed other elders; and elders that ruled not, but their office was to preach, to administer the sacraments, to offer up prayers and thanksgiving in the name of the people. But at that time there appeared no distinction between the names of bishop and elder. But immediately after the apostles' time, the word bishop was taken to signify such an elder as had the government of elders, and other elders were called by the name of priests, which signifieth the same that elder doth. And thus the government of bishops hath a divine pattern in the twelve rulers, and seventy elders of Israel, in the twelve apostles and seventy disciples of our Saviour; in the ruling elders, and not ruling elders, in the time of the apostles.

9. And thus much of the magistrates over Christ's flock in the primitive church; for the office of a minister, or ministress, was to be subject to the flock, and to serve them in those things which appertain to their temporal business. The next thing to be considered is the authority which our Saviour gave to them, either over those whom they had converted, or those whom they were about to convert. And for these latter, which as yet were without the church, the authority which our Saviour gave to his apostles was no more but this: to preach unto them that Jesus was the Christ, to explicate the same in all points that concern the kingdom of heaven, and to persuade men to embrace our Saviour's doctrine, but by no means to compel any man to be subject to them. For seeing the laws of the kingdom of heaven, as hath been showed, Part I. chap. XVIII, sect. 10, are dictated to the conscience only, which is not subject to compulsion and constraint; it was not congruent to the style of the King of Heaven to constrain men to submit their actions to him, but to advise them only; nor for him that professeth the sum of his law to be love, to extort any duty from us with fear of temporal punishment. And therefore as the mighty men in the world, that hold others in subjection by force, are called in Scripture by the name of hunters; so our Saviour calleth those whom he appointed to draw the world unto him, by subduing their affections, *fishers*; and

therefore he saith to Peter and Andrew, Matth. 4, 19: *Follow me, and I will make ye fishers of men*. And Luke 10, 3: *Behold*, saith Christ, *I send ye forth as lambs amongst wolves*. And it were to no end to give them the right of compelling, without strengthening the same with greater power than of lambs amongst wolves. Moreover, Matth. 10, where our Saviour giveth a commission to his twelve apostles to go forth and convert the nations to the faith, he giveth them no authority of coercion and punishment, but only saith, verse 14: *Whosoever shall not receive you, nor hear your words, when ye depart out of that house, or that city, shake off the dust of your feet. Truly I say unto you, it shall be easier for the land of Sodom and Gomorrah in the day of judgment, than for that city*. Whereby it is manifest, that all that the apostles could do by their authority, was no more than to renounce communion with them, and leave their punishment to God Almighty, in the day of judgment. Likewise the comparisons of the kingdom of heaven to the seed, Matth. 13, 3, and to the leaven, Matth. 13, 33, doth intimate unto us that the increase thereof ought to proceed from internal operation of God's word preached, and not from any law or compulsion of them that preach it. Moreover our Saviour himself saith, John 28, 36, that *his kingdom is not of this world*; and consequently his magistrates derive not from him any authority of punishing men in this world. And therefore also, Matth. 26, 52, after St. Peter had drawn his sword in his defence, our Saviour saith, *Put up thy sword into his place. For all that take the sword shall perish by the sword*. And, verse 54, *How then shall the Scriptures be fulfilled, which say, that it must be so?* showing out of the Scriptures, that the kingdom of Christ was not to be defended by the sword.

10. But concerning the authority of the apostles or bishops over those who were already converted and within the church, there be that think it greater than over them without. For some have said (Bellarmin.* *Lib. de Rom. Pont.* cap. 29): *Though the law of Christ deprive no prince of his dominion, and Paul did rightly appeal to Cæsar, whilst kings were infidels and out of the church; yet when they became*

*Christians, and of their own accord underwent the laws
of the gospel, presently as sheep to a shepherd, and as members to the head, they became subject to the prelate of the
ecclesiastical hierarchy.* Which, whether it be true or not, is
to be considered by that light which we have from the Holy
Scripture, concerning the power of our Saviour and his
apostles, over such as they had converted. But our Saviour,
as he imitated the commonwealth of the Jews in his magistrates, the twelve and the seventy; so did he also in the
censure of the church, which was excommunication; but
amongst the Jews, the church did put the excommunicated
persons from the congregation, which they might do by their
power temporal; but our Saviour and his apostles, who took
upon them no such power, could not forbid the excommunicated person to enter into any place and congregation,
into which he was permitted to enter by the prince, or
sovereign of the place; for that had been to deprive the
sovereign of his authority; and therefore the excommunication of a person subject to an earthly power, was but a
declaration of the church, which did excommunicate, that
the person so excommunicated was to be reputed still as an
infidel, but not to be driven by their authority out of any
company he might otherwise lawfully come into. And this is
it our Saviour saith, Matth. 18, 17: *If he refuseth to hear
the church, let him be unto thee as an heathen man and a
publican.* So that the whole effect of excommunicating a
Christian prince, is no more than he or they that so excommunicate him, depart, and banish themselves out of his
dominion.* Nor can they thereupon discharge any of his
subjects of their obedience to him; for that were to deprive
him of his dominion, which they may not do; for being out
of the church, it is confessed by them that make this objection, and proved in the former section, that our Saviour
gave no authority to his apostles to be judges over them.
And therefore in no case can the sovereign power of a
commonwealth be subject to any authority ecclesiastical,
besides that of Christ himself. And though he be informed
concerning the kingdom of heaven, and subject himself
thereto at the persuasions of persons ecclesiastical, yet is not

he thereby subject to their government and rule. For if it were by their authority he took that yoke upon him, and not by their persuasion, then by the same authority he might cast it off; but this is unlawful. For if all the churches in the world should renounce the Christian faith, yet is not this sufficient authority for any of the members to do the same. It is manifest therefore that they who have sovereign power, are immediate rulers of the church under Christ, and all others but subordinate to them. If that were not, but kings should command one thing upon pain of death, and priests another upon pain of damnation, it would be impossible that peace and religion should stand together.

11. And therefore there is no just cause for any man to withdraw his obedience from the sovereign state, upon pretence that Christ hath ordained any state ecclesiastical above it. And though kings take not upon them the ministerial priesthood (as they might if it pleased them) yet are they not so merely laic, as not to have sacerdotal jurisdiction. To conclude this chapter: since God speaketh not in these days to any man by his private interpretation of the Scriptures, nor by the interpretation of any power, above, or not depending on the sovereign power of every commonwealth; it remaineth that he speaketh by his vice-gods, or lieutenants here on earth, that is to say, by sovereign kings, or such as have sovereign authority as well as they.

CHAPTER XXVII

OF THE CAUSES OF REBELLION

1. HITHERTO of the causes why, and the manner how, men have made commonwealths. In this chapter I shall show briefly, by what causes, and in what manner, they be again destroyed; not meaning to say anything concerning the dissolution of a commonwealth from foreign invasions, which is as it were the violent death thereof, I shall speak only of sedition, which is also the death of the commonwealth, but

like to that which happeneth to a man from sickness and distemper. To dispose men to sedition three things concur. The first is discontent; for as long as a man thinketh himself well, and that the present government standeth not in his way to hinder his proceeding from well to better; it is impossible for him to desire the change thereof. The second is pretence of right; for though a man be discontent, yet if in his own opinion there be no just cause of stirring against, or resisting the government established, nor any pretence to justify his resistance, and to procure aid, he will never show it. The third is hope of success; for it were madness to attempt without hope, when to fail is to die the death of a traitor. Without these three: discontent, pretence, and hope, there can be no rebellion; and when the same are all together, there wanteth nothing thereto, but a man of credit to set up the standard, and to blow the trumpet.

2. And as for discontent, it is of two sorts: for it consisteth either in bodily pain present or expected, or else in trouble of the mind (which is the general division of pleasure and pain, Part I. chap. VII, sect. 9). The presence of bodily pain disposeth not to sedition; the fear of it doth. As for example: when a great multitude, or heap of people, have concurred to a crime worthy of death, they join together, and take arms to defend themselves for fear thereof. So also the fear of want, or in present want the fear of arrests and imprisonment, dispose to sedition. And therefore great exactions, though the right thereof be acknowledged, have caused great seditions. As in the time of Henry VII. the seditions of the Cornish men that refused to pay a subsidy, and, under the conduct of the Lord Audley, gave the King battle upon Blackheath; and that of the northern people, who in the same king's time, for demanding a subsidy granted in parliament, murdered the Earl of Northumberland in his house.

3. Thirdly, the other sort of discontent which troubleth the mind of them who otherwise live at ease, without fear of want, or danger of violence, ariseth only from a sense of their want of that power, and that honour and testimony thereof, which they think is due unto them. For all joy and grief of mind consisting (as hath been said, Part I. chap. IX,

sect. 21) in a contention for precedence to them with whom they compare themselves; such men must needs take it ill, and be grieved with the state, as find themselves postponed to those in honour, whom they think they excel in virtue and ability to govern. And this is it for which they think themselves regarded but as slaves. Now seeing freedom cannot stand together with subjection, liberty in a commonwealth is nothing but government and rule, which because it cannot be divided, men must expect in common; and that can be no where but in the popular state, or democracy. And Aristotle saith well* (lib. 6, cap. 2 of his *Politics*), *The ground or intention of a democracy, is liberty*; which he confirmeth in these words: *For men ordinarily say this: that no man can partake of liberty, but only in a popular commonwealth.* Whosoever therefore in a monarchical estate, where the sovereign power is absolutely in one man, claimeth liberty, claimeth (if the hardest construction should be made thereof) either to have the sovereignty in his turn, or to be colleague with him that hath it, or to have the monarchy changed into a democracy. But if the same be construed (with pardon of that unskilful expression) according to the intention of him that claimeth, then doth he thereby claim no more but this, that the sovereign should take notice of his ability and deserving, and put him into employment and place of subordinate government, rather than others that deserve less. And as one claimeth, so doth another, every man esteeming his own desert greatest. Amongst all those that pretend to, or are ambitious of such honour, a few only can be served, unless it be in a democracy; the rest therefore must be discontent. And so much of the first thing that disposeth to rebellion, namely, discontent, consisting in fear and ambition.

4. The second thing that disposeth to rebellion, is pretence of right. And that is when men have an opinion, or pretend to have an opinion: that in certain cases they may lawfully resist him or them that have the sovereign power, or deprive him or them of the means to execute the same. Of which pretences there be six special cases. One is, when the command is against their conscience, and they believe it

is unlawful for a subject at the command of the sovereign power to do any action, which he thinketh in his own conscience not lawful for him to do, or to omit any action, which he thinketh not lawful for him to omit. Another is, when the command is against the laws, and they think the sovereign power in such sort obliged to his own laws, as the subject is; and that when he performeth not his duty, they may resist his power. A third is, when they receive commands from some man or men, and a *supersedeas** to the same from others, and think the authority is equal, as if the sovereign power were divided. A fourth is, when they are commanded to contribute their persons or money to the public service, and think they have a propriety in the same distinct from the dominion of the sovereign power; and that therefore they are not bound to contribute their goods and persons, no more than every man shall of himself think fit. A fifth, when the commands seem hurtful to the people; and they think, every one of them, that the opinion and sense of the people is the same with the opinion of himself, and those that consent with him; calling by the name of people, any multitude of his own faction. The sixth is, when the commands are grievous; and they account him that commandeth grievous things, a tyrant; and tyrannicide, that is, the killing of a tyrant, not only lawful, but also laudable.

5. All these opinions are maintained in the books of the dogmatics, and divers of them taught in public chairs, and nevertheless are most incompatible with peace and government, and contradictory to the necessary and demonstrable rules of the same. And for the first, namely, that a man may lawfully do or omit any thing against his conscience, and from whence arise all seditions concerning religion and ecclesiastical government, it hath been plainly declared in the two last chapters, that such opinion is erroneous. For those two chapters have been wholly spent, to prove, that Christian religion not only forbiddeth not, but also commandeth, that in every commonwealth, every subject should in all things to the uttermost of his power obey the commands of him or them that is the sovereign thereof; and that a man in so obeying, doth according to his conscience and

judgment, as having deposited his judgment in all controversies in the hands of the sovereign power; and that this error proceedeth from the ignorance of what and by whom God Almighty speaketh.

6. As for the second opinion which is: that the sovereign is in such sort obliged to his own laws, as the subject is; the contrary thereof hath been showed, Part II. chap. XX sections 7–12, by which it appeareth that the sovereign power is not to be resisted; that it carrieth the sword both of war and justice; that it hath the right of deciding all controversies, both judicial and deliberative; that it hath the making of all the laws civil; that it appointeth magistrates and public ministers, and that it implieth a universal impunity. How can he or they be said to be subject to the laws which they may abrogate at their pleasure, or break without fear of punishment? And this error seemeth to proceed from this, that men ordinarily understand not aright, what is meant by this word law, confounding law and covenant, as if they signified the same thing. But law implieth a command; covenant is but a promise. And not every command is a law, but only (Part I. chap. XIII, sect. 6) when the command is the reason we have of doing the action commanded. And then only is the reason of our actions in the command, when the omitting is therefore hurtful, because the action was commanded, not because it was hurtful of itself; and doing contrary to a command, were not at all hurtful, if there were not a right in him that commandeth to punish him that so doth. He or they that have all punishments in their own disposing, cannot be so commanded, as to receive hurt for disobeying, and consequently no command can be a law unto them. It is an error therefore to think: that the power which is virtually the whole power of the commonwealth, and which in whomsoever it resideth, is usually called supreme or sovereign, can be subject to any law but that of God Almighty.

7. The third opinion: that the sovereign power may be divided, is no less an error than the former, as hath been proved, Part II. chap. XX, sect. 15. And if there were a commonwealth, wherein the rights of sovereignty were divided,

we must confess with Bodin, Lib. II. chap. I. *De Republica*,*
that they are not rightly to be called commonwealths, but
the corruption of commonwealths. For if one part should
have power to make the laws for all, they would by their
laws, at their pleasure, forbid others to make peace or war,
to levy taxes, or to yield fealty and homage without their
leave; and they that had the right to make peace and war,
and command the militia, would forbid the making of other
laws, than what themselves liked. And though monarchies
stand long, wherein the right of sovereignty hath seemed so
divided, because monarchy of itself is a durable kind of
government; yet monarchs have been thereby divers times
thrust out of their possession. But the truth is, that the right
of sovereignty is such, as he or they that have it, cannot,
though they would, give away any part thereof, and retain
the rest. As for example: if we should suppose the people of
Rome to have had the absolute sovereignty of the Roman
state, and to have chosen them a council by the name of the
senate, and that to this senate they had given the supreme
power of making laws, reserving nevertheless to themselves,
in direct and express terms, the whole right and title of the
sovereignty (which may easily happen amongst them that
see not the inseparable connexion between the sovereign
power and the power of making laws), I say, this grant of
the people to the senate is of no effect, and the power of
making laws is in the people still. For the senate understanding it to be the will and intention of the people, to
retain the sovereignty, ought not to take that for granted,
which was contradictory thereto, and passed by error. For,
Part I. chap. XIII, sect. 9, in contradictory promises, that
which is directly promised, is preferred before that which is
opposite thereunto by consequence; because the consequence of a thing is not always observed, as is the thing
itself. The error concerning mixed government hath proceeded from want of understanding of what is meant by this
word *body politic*, and how it signifieth not the concord, but
the union of many men. And though in the charters of
subordinate corporations, a corporation be declared to be
one person in law, yet the same hath not been taken notice

of in the body of a commonwealth or city, nor have any of those innumerable writers of politics observed any such union.

8. The fourth opinion (viz.): that subjects have their *meum*, *tuum*, and *suum*, in property, not only by virtue of the sovereign power over them all, distinct from one another, but also against the sovereign himself, by which they would pretend to contribute nothing to the public, but what they please, hath been already confuted, by proving the absoluteness of the sovereignty; and more particularly, Part II. chap. XXIV, sect. 2; and ariseth from this: that they understand not ordinarily, that before the institution of sovereign power *meum* and *tuum* implied no propriety, but a community, where every man had right to every thing, and was in state of war with every man.

9. The fifth opinion: that the people is a distinct body from him or them that have the sovereignty over them, is an error already confuted, Part II. chap. XXI, sect. 11, where it is showed, that when men say: the people rebelleth, it is to be understood of those particular persons only, and not of the whole nation. And when the people claimeth any thing otherwise than by the voice of the sovereign power, it is not the claim of the people, but only of those particular men, that claim in their own persons; and this error ariseth from the equivocation of the word people.

10. Lastly, for the opinion, that tyrannicide is lawful, meaning by a tyrant any man in whom resideth the right of sovereignty, it is no less false and pernicious to human society, than frequent in the writings of those moral philosophers, Seneca* and others, so greatly esteemed amongst us. For when a man hath the right of sovereignty, he cannot justly be punished, as hath been often showed already, and therefore much less deposed, or put to death. And howsoever he might deserve punishment, yet punishment is unjust without judgment preceding, and judgment unjust without power of judicature, which a subject hath not over his sovereign. But this doctrine proceedeth from the Schools of Greece, and from those that writ in the Roman state, in

which not only the name of a tyrant, but of a king, was hateful.

11. Besides discontent, to the disposing of a man to rebellion, and pretence, there is required, in the third place, hope of success, which consisteth in four points: 1. That the discontented have mutual intelligence; 2. that they have sufficient number; 3. that they have arms; 4. that they agree upon a head. For these four must concur to the making of one body of rebellion, in which intelligence is the life, number the limbs, arms the strength, and a head the unity, by which they are directed to one and the same action.

12. The authors of rebellion, that is, the men that breed these dispositions to rebel in others, of necessity must have in them these three qualities: 1. To be discontented themselves; 2. to be men of mean judgment and capacity; and 3. to be eloquent men or good orators. And as for their discontent, from whence it may proceed, hath been already declared. And for the second and third, I am to show now, first, how they may stand together; for it seemeth a contradiction, to place small judgment and great eloquence, or, as they call it, powerful speaking, in the same man: and then in what manner they both concur to dispose other men to sedition.

13. It was noted by Sallust,* that in Catiline (who was author of the greatest sedition that ever was in Rome) there was *Eloquentiæ satis, sapientiæ parum*; eloquence sufficient, but little wisdom. And perhaps this was said of Catiline, as he was Catiline: but it was true of him as an author of sedition. For the conjunction of these two qualities made him not Catiline, but seditious. And that it may be understood, how want of wisdom, and store of eloquence, may stand together, we are to consider, what it is we call wisdom, and what eloquence. And therefore I shall here again remember some things that have been said already, Part I. chap. V, VI. It is manifest that wisdom consisteth in knowledge. Now of knowledge there are two kinds; whereof the one is the remembrance of such things, as we have conceived by our senses, and of the order in which they follow one

another. And this knowledge is called experience; and the wisdom that proceedeth from it, is that ability to conjecture by the present, of what is past, and to come, which men call prudence. This being so, it is manifest presently, that the author of sedition, whosoever he be, must not be prudent. For if he consider and take his experiences aright, concerning the success which they have had, who have been the movers and authors of sedition, either in this or any other state, he shall find that of one man that hath thereby advanced himself to honour, twenty have come to a reproachful end. The other kind of knowledge is the remembrance of the names or appellations of things, and how every thing is called, which is, in matters of common conversation, a remembrance of pacts and covenants of men made amongst themselves, concerning how to be understood of one another. And this kind of knowledge is generally called science,* and the conclusions thereof truth. But when men remember not how things are named, by general agreement, but either mistake and misname things, or name them aright by chance, they are not said to have science, but opinion; and the conclusions thence proceeding are uncertain, and for the most part erroneous. Now that science in particular from which proceed the true and evident conclusions of what is right and wrong, and what is good and hurtful to the being and well-being of mankind, the Latins call *sapientia*, and we by the general name of wisdom. For generally, not he that hath skill in geometry, or any other science speculative, but only he that understandeth what conduceth to the good and government of the people, is called a wise man. Now that no author of sedition can be wise in this acceptation of the word, is sufficiently proved, in that it hath been already demonstrated, that no pretence of sedition can be right or just; and therefore the authors of sedition must be ignorant of the right of state, that is to say, unwise. It remaineth therefore, that they be such, as name things not according to their true and generally agreed-upon names; but call right and wrong, good and bad, according to their passions, or according to the authorities of such as they admire, as Aristotle, Cicero, Seneca, and others of like authority, who have given the names of right and wrong, as their passions have dictated; or have followed the authority of other men, as we do theirs. It is required therefore in an author of sedition, that he think right, that which is wrong; and profitable, that which is pernicious; and consequently that there be in him *sapientiæ parum*, little wisdom.

14. Eloquence is nothing else but the power of winning belief of what we say; and to that end we must have aid from the passions of the hearer. Now to demonstration and teaching of the truth, there are required long deductions, and great attention, which is unpleasant to the hearer; therefore they which seek not truth, but belief, must take another way, and not only derive what they would have to be believed, from somewhat believed already, but also by aggravations and extenuations make good and bad, right and wrong, appear great or less, according as it shall serve their turns. And such is the power of eloquence, as many times a man is made to believe thereby, that he sensibly feeleth smart and damage, when he feeleth none, and to enter into rage and indignation, without any other cause, than what is in the words and passion of the speaker. This considered, together with the business that he hath to do, who is the author of rebellion, (viz.) to make men believe that their rebellion is just, their discontents grounded upon great injuries, and their hopes great; there needeth no more to prove, there can be no author of rebellion, that is not an eloquent and powerful speaker, and withal (as hath been said before) a man of little wisdom. For the faculty of speaking powerfully, consisteth in a habit gotten of putting together passionate words, and applying them to the present passions of the hearer.

15. Seeing then eloquence and want of discretion concur to the stirring of rebellion, it may be demanded, what part each of these acteth therein? The daughters of Pelias, king of Thessaly, desiring to restore their old decrepit father to the vigour of his youth, by the counsel of Medea chopped him in pieces, and set him a boiling with I know not what herbs in a cauldron, but could not make him revive again.* So when eloquence and want of judgment go together,

want of judgment, like the daughters of Pelias, consenteth, through eloquence, which is as the witchcraft of Medea, to cut the commonwealth in pieces, upon pretence or hope of reformation, which when things are in combustion, they are not able to effect.

CHAPTER XXVIII

OF THE DUTY OF THEM THAT HAVE SOVEREIGN POWER

1. HAVING hitherto set forth how a body politic is made, and how it may be destroyed, this place requireth to say something concerning the preservation of the same. Not purposing to enter into the particulars of the art of government, but to sum up the general heads, wherein such art is to be employed, and in which consisteth the duty of him or them that have the sovereign power. For the duty of a sovereign consisteth in the good government of the people; and although the acts of sovereign power be no injuries to the subjects who have consented to the same by their implicit wills, yet when they tend to the hurt of the people in general, they be breaches of the law of nature, and of the divine law; and consequently, the contrary acts are the duties of sovereigns, and required at their hands to the utmost of their endeavour, by God Almighty, under the pain of eternal death. And as the art and duty of sovereigns consist in the same acts, so also doth their profit. For the end of art is profit; and governing to the profit of the subjects, is governing to the profit of the sovereign, as hath been showed Part II. chapter XXIV, section 1. And these three: 1. the law over them that have sovereign power; 2. their duty; 3. their profit: are one and the same thing contained in this sentence, *Salus populi suprema lex*; by which must be understood, not the mere preservation of their lives, but generally their benefit and good. So that this is the general law for sovereigns: that they procure, to the uttermost of their endeavour, the good of the people.

2. And forasmuch as eternal is better than temporal good, it is evident, that they who are in sovereign authority, are by the law of nature obliged to further the establishing of all such doctrines and rules, and the commanding of all such actions, as in their conscience they believe to be the true way thereunto. For unless they do so, it cannot be said truly, that they have done the uttermost of their endeavour.

3. For the temporal good of people, it consisteth in four points: 1. Multitude. 2. Commodity of living. 3. Peace amongst ourselves. 4. Defence against foreign power. Concerning multitude, it is the duty of them that are in sovereign authority, to increase the people, in as much as they are governors of mankind under God Almighty, who having created but one man, and one woman, declared that it was his will they should be multiplied and increased afterwards. And seeing this is to be done by ordinances concerning copulation: they are by the law of nature bound to make such ordinances concerning the same, as may tend to the increase of mankind. And hence it cometh, that in them who have sovereign authority: not to forbid such copulations as are against the use of nature; not to forbid the promiscuous use of women; not to forbid one woman to have many husbands; not to forbid marriages within certain degrees of kindred and affinity: are against the law of nature.* For though it be not evident, that a private man living under the law of natural reason only, doth break the same, by doing any of these things aforesaid; yet it is manifestly apparent, that being so prejudicial as they are to the improvement of mankind, that not to forbid the same, is against the law of natural reason, in him that hath taken into his hands any portion of mankind to improve.

4. The commodity of living consisteth in liberty and wealth. By liberty I mean, that there be no prohibition without necessity of any thing to any man, which was lawful to him in the law of nature; that is to say, that there be no restraint of natural liberty, but what is necessary for the good of the commonwealth; and that well-meaning men may not fall into the danger of laws, as into snares, before

they be aware. It appertaineth also to this liberty, that a man may have commodious passage from place to place, and not be imprisoned or confined with the difficulty of ways, and want of means for transportation of things necessary. And for the wealth of people, it consisteth in three things: the well ordering of trade, procuring of labour, and forbidding the superfluous consuming of food and apparel. All those therefore that are in sovereign authority, and have taken upon them the government of people, are bound by the law of nature to make ordinances consisting in the points aforenamed; as being contrary to the law of nature, unnecessarily, either for one's own fancy, to enthral, or tie men so, as they cannot move without danger; or to suffer them whose maintenance is our benefit, to want anything necessary for them, by our negligence.

5. For maintaining of peace at home, there be so many things necessarily to be considered, and taken order in, as there be several causes concurring to sedition. And first, it is necessary to set out to every subject his propriety, and distinct lands and goods, upon which he may exercise and have the benefit of his own industry, and without which men would fall out amongst themselves, as did the herdsmen of Abraham and Lot, every man encroaching and usurping as much of the common benefit as he can, which tendeth to quarrel and sedition. Secondly, to divide the burthens, and charge of the commonwealth proportionably. Now there is a proportionably to every man's ability, and there is a proportionably to his benefit by commonwealth: and this latter is it, which is according to the law of nature. For the burdens of the commonwealth being the price that we pay for the benefit thereof, they ought to be measured thereby. And there is no reason, when two men equally enjoying, by the benefit of the commonwealth, their peace and liberty, to use their industry to get their livings, whereof one spareth, and layeth up somewhat, the other spendeth all he gets, why they should not equally contribute to the common charge. That seemeth therefore to be the most equal way of dividing the burden of public charge, when every man shall contribute according to what he spendeth,* and not according to

what he gets; and this is then done, when men pay the commonwealth's part in the payments they make for their own provision. And this seemeth not only most equal, but also least sensible, and least to trouble the mind of them that pay it. For there is nothing so aggravateth the grief of parting with money, to the public, as to think they are over-rated, and that their neighbours whom they envy, do there-upon insult over them; and this disposeth them to resistance, and (after that such resistance hath produced a mischief) to rebellion.

6. Another thing necessary for the maintaining of peace, is the due execution of justice; which consisteth principally in the right performance of their duties, on the parts of those, who are the magistrates ordained for the same by and under the authority of the sovereign power; which being private men in respect of the sovereign, and consequently such as may have private ends, whereby they may be cor-rupted by gifts, or intercession of friends, ought to be kept in awe, by a higher power, lest people, grieved by their injustice, should take upon them to make their own re-venges, to the disturbance of the common peace; which can by no way be avoided in the principal and immediate magis-trates, without the judicature of the sovereign himself, or some extraordinary power delegated by him. It is therefore necessary, that there be a power extraordinary, as there shall be occasion from time to time, for the syndication of judges and other magistrates, that shall abuse their auth-ority, to the wrong and discontent of the people; and a free and open way for the presenting of grievances to him or them that have the sovereign authority.

7. Besides those considerations by which are prevented the discontents that arise from oppression, there ought to be some means for the keeping under of those, that are dis-posed to rebellion by ambition; which consist principally in the constancy of him that hath the sovereign power, who ought therefore constantly to grace and encourage such, as being able to serve the commonwealth, do nevertheless contain themselves within the bounds of modesty, without repining at the authority of such as are employed, and

without aggravating the errors, which (as men) they may commit; especially when they suffer not in their own particular; and constantly to show displeasure and dislike of the contrary. And not only so, but also to ordain severe punishments, for such as shall by reprehension of public actions, affect popularity and applause amongst the multitude, by which they may be enabled to have a faction in the commonwealth at their devotion.

8.* Another thing necessary, is the rooting out from the consciences of men all those opinions which seem to justify, and give pretence of right to rebellious actions; such as are: the opinion, that a man can do nothing lawfully against his private conscience; that they who have the sovereignty, are subject to the civil laws; that there is any authority of subjects, whose negative may hinder the affirmative of the sovereign power; that any subject hath a propriety distinct from the dominion of the commonwealth; that there is a body of the people without him or them that have the sovereign power; and that any lawful sovereign may be resisted under the name of a tyrant; which opinions are they, which, Part II. chap. XXVII, sect. 5–10, have been declared to dispose men to rebellion. And because opinions which are gotten by education, and in length of time are made habitual, cannot be taken away by force, and upon the sudden: they must therefore be taken away also, by time and education. And seeing the said opinions have proceeded from private and public teaching, and those teachers have-received them from grounds and principles, which they have learned in the Universities, from the doctrine of Aristotle, and others (who have delivered nothing concerning morality and policy demonstratively; but being passionately addicted to popular government, have insinuated their opinions, by eloquent sophistry): there is no doubt, if the true doctrine concerning the law of nature, and the properties of a body politic, and the nature of law in general, were perspicuously set down, and taught in the Universities, but that young men, who come thither void of prejudice, and whose minds are yet as white paper, capable of any instruction, would more easily receive the same, and afterward teach it to the people, both in books and otherwise, than now they do the contrary.

9. The last thing contained in that supreme law, *salus populi*, is their defence; and consisteth partly in the obedience and unity of the subjects, of which hath been already spoken, and in which consisteth the means of levying soldiers, and of having money, arms, ships, and fortified places in readiness of defence; and partly, in the avoiding of unnecessary wars. For such commonwealths, or such monarchs, as affect war for itself, that is to say, out of ambition, or of vain-glory, or that make account to revenge every little injury, or disgrace done by their neighbours, if they ruin not themselves, their fortune must be better than they have reason to expect.

CHAPTER XXIX

OF THE NATURE AND KINDS OF LAWS

1. THUS far concerning the Nature of Man, and the constitution and properties of a Body Politic. There remaineth only for the last chapter, to speak of the nature and sorts of law. And first it is manifest, that all laws are declarations of the mind, concerning some action future to be done, or omitted. And all declarations and expressions of the mind concerning future actions and omissions, are either promissive, as I will do, or not do; or provisive, as for example, If this be done or not done, this will follow; or imperative, as Do this, or do it not. In the first sort of these expressions, consisteth the nature of a covenant; in the second, consisteth counsel; in the third, command.

2. It is evident, when a man doth, or forbeareth to do any action, if he be moved thereto by this only consideration, that the same is good or evil in itself; and that there be no reason why the will or pleasure of another should be of any weight in his deliberation, that then neither to do nor omit the action deliberated, is any breach of law. And consequently, whatsoever is a law to a man, respecteth the will of

another, and the declaration thereof. But a covenant is the declaration of a man's own will. And therefore a law and a covenant differ; and though they be both obligatory, and a law obligeth no otherwise than by virtue of some covenant made by him who is subject thereunto, yet they oblige by several sorts of promises. For a covenant obligeth by promise of an action, or omission, especially named and limited; but a law bindeth by a promise of obedience in general, whereby the action to be done, or left undone, is referred to the determination of him, to whom the covenant is made. So that the difference between a covenant and a law, standeth thus: in simple covenants the action to be done, or not done, is first limited and made known, and then followeth the promise to do or not do; but in a law, the obligation to do or not to do, precedeth, and the declaration what is to be done, or not done, followeth after.

3. And from this may be deduced, that which to some may seem a paradox: that the command of him, whose command is a law in one thing, is a law in every thing. For seeing a man is obliged to obedience before what he is to do be known, he is obliged to obey in general, that is to say, in every thing.

4. That the counsel of a man is no law to him that is counselled, and that he who alloweth another to give him counsel, doth not thereby oblige himself to follow the same, is manifest enough; and yet men usually call counselling by the name of governing; not that they are not able to distinguish between them, but because they envy many times those men that are called to counsel, and are therefore angry with them that are counselled. But if to counsellors there should be given a right to have their counsel followed, then are they no more counsellors, but masters of them whom they counsel; and their counsels no more counsels, but laws. For the difference between a law and a counsel being no more but this, that in counsel the expression is, Do, because it is best; in a law, Do, because I have right to compel you; or Do, because I say, do: when counsel which should give the reason of the action it adviseth to, becometh the reason thereof itself, it is no more counsel, but a law.

5. The names *lex*, and *jus*, that is to say, law and right, are often confounded; and yet scarce are there any two words of more contrary signification. For right is that liberty which law leaveth us; and laws those restraints by which we agree mutually to abridge one another's liberty. Law and right therefore are no less different than restraint and liberty, which are contrary; and whatsoever a man doth that liveth in a commonwealth, *jure*, he doth it *jure civili*, *jure naturæ*, and *jure divino*. For whatsoever is against any of these laws, cannot be said to be *jure*. For the civil law cannot make that to be done *jure*, which is against the law divine, or of nature. And therefore whatsoever any subject doth, if it be not contrary to the civil law, and whatsoever a sovereign doth, if it be not against the law of nature, he doth it *jure divino*, by divine right. But to say, *lege divinâ*, by divine law, is another thing. For the laws of God and nature allowing greater liberty than is allowed by the law civil (for subordinate laws do still bind more than the superior laws, the essence of law being not to loose, but to bind): a man may be commanded that by a law civil, which is not commanded by the law of nature, nor by the law divine. So that of things done *lege*, that is to say, by command of the law, there is some place for a distinction between *lege divinâ* and *lege civili*. As when a man giveth an alms, or helpeth him that is in need, he doth it not *lege civili*, but *lege divinâ*, by the divine law, the precept whereof is charity. But of things that are done *jure*, nothing can be said done *jure divino*, that is not also *jure civili*, unless it be done by them that having sovereign power, are not subject to the civil law.

6. The differences of laws are according to the differences, either of the authors and lawmakers, or of the promulgation, or of those that are subject to them. From the difference of the authors, or lawmakers, cometh the division of law into divine, natural, and civil. From the difference of promulgation, proceedeth the division of laws into written and unwritten. And from the difference of the persons to whom the law appertaineth, it proceedeth, that some laws are called simply laws, and some penal. As for example:

thou shalt not steal, is simply a law; but this: he that stealeth an ox, shall restore four-fold, is a penal, or as others call it, a judicial law. Now in those laws, which are simply laws, the commandment is addressed to every man; but in penal laws the commandment is addressed to the magistrate, who is only guilty of the breach of it, when the penalties ordained are not inflicted; to the rest appertaineth nothing, but to take notice of their danger.

7. As for the first division of law into divine, natural, and civil, the first two branches are one and the same law. For the law of nature, which is also the moral law, is the law of the author of nature, God Almighty; and the law of God, taught by our Saviour Christ, is the moral law. For the sum of God's law is: Thou shalt love God above all, and thy neighbour as thyself; and the same is the sum of the law of nature, as hath been showed, Part I. chap. XVIII. And although the doctrine of our Saviour be of three parts moral, theological, and ecclesiastical; the former part only, which is the moral, is of the nature of a law universal; the latter part is a branch of the law civil; and the theological which containeth those articles concerning the divinity and kingdom of our Saviour, without which there is no salvation, is not delivered in the nature of laws, but of counsel and direction, how to avoid the punishment, which by the violation of the moral law, men are subject to. For it is not infidelity that condemneth (though it be faith that saveth), but the breach of the law and commandments of God, written first in man's heart, and afterwards in tables, and delivered to the Jews by the hands of Moses.

8.* In the state of nature, where every man is his own judge, and differeth from other concerning the names and appellations of things, and from those differences arise quarrels, and breach of peace; it was necessary there should be a common measure of all things that might fall in controversy; as for example: of what is to be called right, what good, what virtue, what much, what little, what *meum* and *tuum*, what a pound, what a quart, &c. For in these things private judgments may differ, and beget controversy. This common measure, some say, is right reason: with whom I should consent, if there were any such thing to be found or known *in rerum naturâ*. But commonly they that call for right reason to decide any controversy, do mean their own. But this is certain, seeing right reason is not existent, the reason of some man, or men, must supply the place thereof; and that man, or men, is he or they, that have the sovereign power, as hath been already proved; and consequently the civil laws are to all subjects the measures of their actions, whereby to determine, whether they be right or wrong, profitable or unprofitable, virtuous or vicious; and by them the use and definition of all names not agreed upon, and tending to controversy, shall be established. As for example, upon the occasion of some strange and deformed birth, it shall not be decided by Aristotle, or the philosophers, whether the same be a man or no, but by the laws. The civil law containeth in it the ecclesiastical, as a part thereof, proceeding from the power of ecclesiastical government, given by our Saviour to all Christian sovereigns, as his immediate vicars, as hath been said Part II. chap. XXVI, sect. 10.

9. But seeing it hath been said, that all laws are either natural or civil; it may be demanded, to which of these shall be referred that law, which is called martial law, and by the Romans *disciplina militaris*? And it may seem to be the same with the law of nature; because the laws by which a multitude of soldiers are governed in an army, are not constant, but continually changing with the occasion; and that is still a law, which is reason for the present, and reason is the law of nature. It is nevertheless true that martial law is civil law; because an army is a body politic, the whole power whereof is in the General, and the laws thereof made by him; and though they still follow and change as reason requireth, yet it is not, as the reason of every private man (as in the law of nature), but as the reason of the General requireth.

10. When he, or they, in whom is the sovereign power of a commonwealth, are to ordain laws for the government and good order of the people, it is not possible they should comprehend all cases of controversy that may fall out, nor

perhaps any considerable diversity of them; but as time shall instruct them by the rising of new occasions, so are also laws from time to time to be ordained: and in such cases where no special law is made, the law of nature keepeth its place, and the magistrates ought to give sentence according thereunto, that is to say, according to natural reason. The constitutions therefore of the sovereign power, by which the liberty of nature is abridged, are written, because there is no other way to take notice of them; whereas the laws of nature are supposed to be written in men's hearts. Written laws therefore are the constitutions of a commonwealth expressed; and unwritten, are the laws of natural reason. Custom of itself maketh no law. Nevertheless when a sentence hath been once given, by them that judge by their natural reason; whether the same be right or wrong, it may attain to the vigour of a law; not because the like sentence hath of custom been given in the like case; but because the sovereign power is supposed tacitly to have approved such sentence for right; and thereby it cometh to be a law, and numbered amongst the written laws of the commonwealth. For if custom were sufficient to introduce a law, then it would be in the power of every one that is deputed to hear a cause, to make his errors laws. In like manner, those laws that go under the title of *responsa prudentum*, that is to say, the opinions of lawyers, are not therefore laws, because *responsa prudentum*, but because they are admitted by the sovereign. And from this may be collected, that when there is a case of private contract between the sovereign and the subject, a precedent against reason shall not prejudice the cause of the sovereign; no precedent being made a law, but upon supposition that the same was reasonable from the beginning.

And thus much concerning the Elements and general grounds of Laws Natural and Politic. As for the law of nations, it is the same with the law of nature. For that which is the law of nature between man and man, before the constitution of commonwealth, is the law of nations between sovereign and sovereign, after.

DE CORPORE

DE CORPORE

CHAPTER I

OF PHILOSOPHY

1. PHILOSOPHY seems to me to be amongst men now, in the same manner as corn and wine are said to have been in the world in ancient time. For from the beginning there were vines and ears of corn growing here and there in the fields; but no care was taken for the planting and sowing of them. Men lived therefore upon acorns; or if any were so bold as to venture upon the eating of those unknown and doubtful fruits, they did it with danger of their health. In like manner, every man brought Philosophy, that is, Natural Reason, into the world with him; for all men can reason to some degree, and concerning some things: but where there is need of a long series of reasons, there most men wander out of the way, and fall into error for want of method, as it were for want of sowing and planting, that is, of improving their reason. And from hence it comes to pass, that they who content themselves with daily experience, which may be likened to feeding upon acorns, and either reject, or not much regard philosophy, are commonly esteemed, and are, indeed, men of sounder judgment than those who, from opinions, though not vulgar, yet full of uncertainty, and carelessly received, do nothing but dispute and wrangle, like men that are not well in their wits. I confess, indeed, that that part of philosophy by which magnitudes and figures are computed, is highly improved. But because I have not observed the like advancement in the other parts of it, my purpose is, as far forth as I am able, to lay open the few and first Elements of Philosophy in general, as so many seeds

from which pure and true Philosophy may hereafter spring up by little and little.

I am not ignorant how hard a thing it is to weed out of men's minds such inveterate opinions as have taken root there, and been confirmed in them by the authority of most eloquent writers; especially seeing true (that is, accurate) Philosophy professedly rejects not only the paint and false colours of language, but even the very ornaments and graces of the same; and the first grounds of all science are not only not beautiful, but poor, arid, and, in appearance, deformed. Nevertheless, there being certainly some men, though but few, who are delighted with truth and strength of reason in all things, I thought I might do well to take this pains for the sake even of those few. I proceed therefore to the matter, and take my beginning from the very definition of philosophy, which is this.

2. PHILOSOPHY* *is such knowledge of effects or appearances, as we acquire by true ratiocination from the knowledge we have first of their causes or generation: And again, of such causes or generations as may be from knowing first their effects.*

For the better understanding of which definition, we must consider, first, that although Sense and Memory of things, which are common to man and all living creatures, be knowledge, yet because they are given us immediately by nature, and not gotten by ratiocination, they are not philosophy.

Secondly, seeing Experience is nothing but memory; and Prudence, or prospect into the future time, nothing but expectation of such things as we have already had experience of, Prudence also is not to be esteemed philosophy.

By RATIOCINATION, I mean *computation*. Now to compute, is either to collect the sum of many things that are added together, or to know what remains when one thing is taken out of another. *Ratiocination*, therefore, is the same with *addition* and *substraction*; and if any man add *multiplication* and *division*, I will not be against it, seeing multiplication is nothing but addition of equals one to another, and division nothing but a substraction of equals one from another, as often as is possible. So that all ratiocination is comprehended in these two operations of the mind, addition and substraction.

3. But how by the *ratiocination* of our mind, we add and substract in our silent thoughts, without the use of words, it will be necessary for me to make intelligible by an example or two. If therefore a man see something afar off and obscurely, although no appellation had yet been given to anything, he will, notwithstanding, have the same idea of that thing for which now, by imposing a name on it, we call it *body*. Again, when, by coming nearer, he sees the same thing thus and thus, now in one place and now in another, he will have a new idea thereof, namely, that for which we now call such a thing *animated*. Thirdly, when standing nearer, he perceives the figure, hears the voice, and sees other things which are signs of a rational mind, he has a third idea, though it have yet no appellation, namely, that for which we now call anything *rational*. Lastly, when, by looking fully and distinctly upon it, he conceives all that he has seen as one thing, the idea he has now is compounded of his former ideas, which are put together in the mind in the same order in which these three single names, *body*, *animated*, *rational*, are in speech compounded into this one name, *body-animated-rational*, or *man*. In like manner, of the several conceptions of *four sides*, *equality of sides, and right angles*, is compounded the conception of a *square*. For the mind may conceive a figure of four sides without any conception of their equality, and of that equality without conceiving a right angle; and may join together all these single conceptions into one conception or one idea of a square. And thus we see how the conceptions of the mind are compounded. Again, whosoever sees a man standing near him, conceives the whole idea of that man; and if as he goes away, he follow him with his eyes only, he will lose the idea of those things which were signs of his being rational, whilst, nevertheless, the idea of a body-animated remains still before his eyes, so that the idea of rational is substracted from the whole idea of man, that is to say, of body-animated-rational, and there remains that of body-animated; and a

while after, at a greater distance, the idea of animated will be lost, and that of body only will remain; so that at last, when nothing at all can be seen, the whole idea will vanish out of sight. By which examples, I think, it is manifest enough what is the internal ratiocination of the mind without words.

We must not therefore think that computation, that is, ratiocination, has place only in numbers, as if man were distinguished from other living creatures (which is said to have been the opinion of *Pythagoras*) by nothing but the faculty of numbering; for *magnitude, body, motion, time, degrees of quality, action, conception, proportion, speech and names* (in which all the kinds of philosophy consist) are capable of addition and substraction. Now such things as we add or substract, that is, which we put into an account, we are said to *consider*, in Greek λογίζεσθαι, in which language also συλλογίζεσθαι signifies to *compute, reason*, or *reckon*.

4. But *effects* and the *appearances* of things to sense, are faculties or powers of bodies, which make us distinguish them from one another; that is to say, conceive one body to be equal or unequal, like or unlike to another body; as in the example above, when by coming near enough to any body, we perceive the motion and going of the same, we distinguish it thereby from a tree, a column, and other fixed bodies; and so that motion or going is the *property* thereof, as being proper to living creatures, and a faculty by which they make us distinguish them from other bodies.

5. How the knowledge of any effect may be gotten from the knowledge of the generation thereof, may easily be understood by the example of a circle: for if there be set before us a plain figure, having, as near as may be, the figure of a circle, we cannot possibly perceive by sense whether it be a true circle or no; than which, nevertheless, nothing is more easy to be known to him that knows first the generation of the propounded figure. For let it be known that the figure was made by the circumduction of a body whereof one end remained unmoved, and we may reason thus; a body carried about, retaining always the same length, applies itself first to one *radius*, then to another, to a third,

a fourth, and successively to all; and, therefore, the same length, from the same point, toucheth the circumference in every part thereof, which is as much as to say, as all the *radii* are equal. We know, therefore, that from such generation proceeds a figure, from whose one middle point all the extreme points are reached unto by equal *radii*. And in like manner, by knowing first what figure is set before us, we may come by ratiocination to some generation of the same, though perhaps not that by which it was made, yet that by which it might have been made; for he that knows that a circle has the property above declared, will easily know whether a body carried about, as is said, will generate a circle or no.

6. The *end* or *scope* of philosophy is, that we may make use to our benefit of effects formerly seen; or that, by application of bodies to one another, we may produce the like effects of those we conceive in our mind, as far forth as matter, strength, and industry, will permit, for the commodity of human life. For the inward glory and triumph of mind that a man may have for the mastering of some difficult and doubtful matter, or for the discovery of some hidden truth, is not worth so much pains as the study of Philosophy requires; nor need any man care much to teach another what he knows himself, if he think that will be the only benefit of his labour. The end of knowledge is power; and the use of theorems (which, among geometricians, serve for the finding out of properties) is for the construction of problems; and, lastly, the scope of all speculation is the performing of some action, or thing to be done.

7. But what the *utility* of philosophy is, especially of natural philosophy and geometry, will be best understood by reckoning up the chief commodities of which mankind is capable, and by comparing the manner of life of such as enjoy them, with that of others which want the same. Now, the greatest commodities of mankind are the arts; namely, of measuring matter and motion; of moving ponderous bodies; of architecture; of navigation; of making instruments for all uses; of calculating the celestial motions, the aspects of the stars, and the parts of time; of geography, &c.

By which sciences, how great benefits men receive is more easily understood than expressed. These benefits are enjoyed by almost all the people of Europe, by most of those of Asia, and by some of Africa: but the Americans, and they that live near the Poles, do totally want them. But why? Have they sharper wits than these? Have not all men one kind of soul, and the same faculties of mind? What, then, makes this difference, except philosophy? Philosophy, therefore, is the cause of all these benefits. But the utility of moral and civil philosophy is to be estimated, not so much by the commodities we have by knowing these sciences, as by the calamities we receive from not knowing them. Now, all such calamities as may be avoided by human industry, arise from war, but chiefly from civil war; for from this proceed slaughter, solitude, and the want of all things. But the cause of war is not that men are willing to have it; for the will has nothing for object but good, at least that which seemeth good. Nor is it from this, that men know not that the effects of war are evil; for who is there that thinks not poverty and loss of life to be great evils? The cause, therefore, of civil war is, that men know not the causes neither of war nor peace, there being but few in the world that have learned those duties which unite and keep men in peace, that is to say, that have learned the rules of civil life sufficiently. Now, the knowledge of these rules is moral philosophy. But why have they not learned them, unless for this reason, that none hitherto have taught them in a clear and exact method? For what shall we say? Could the ancient masters of Greece, Egypt, Rome, and others, persuade the unskilful multitude to their innumerable opinions concerning the nature of their gods, which they themselves knew not whether they were true or false, and which were indeed manifestly false and absurd; and could they not persuade the same multitude to civil duty, if they themselves had understood it? Or shall those few writings of geometricians which are extant, be thought sufficient for the taking away of all controversy in the matters they treat of, and shall those innumerable and huge volumes of *ethics* be thought unsufficient, if what they teach had been certain and well demonstrated? What, then, can be imagined to be the cause that the writings of those men have increased science, and the writings of these have increased nothing but words, saving that the former were written by men that knew, and the latter by such as knew not, the doctrine they taught only for ostentation of their wit and eloquence? Nevertheless, I deny not but the reading of some such books is very delightful; for they are most eloquently written, and contain many clear, wholesome and choice sentences, which yet are not universally true, though by them universally pronounced. From whence it comes to pass, that the circumstances of times, places, and persons being changed, they are no less frequently made use of to confirm wicked men in their purposes, than to make them understand the precepts of civil duties. Now that which is chiefly wanting in them, is a true and certain rule of our actions, by which we might know whether that we undertake be just or unjust. For it is to no purpose to be bidden in every thing to do right, before there be a certain rule and measure of right established, which no man hitherto hath established. Seeing, therefore, from the not knowing of civil duties, that is, from the want of moral science, proceed civil wars, and the greatest calamities of mankind, we may very well attribute to such science the production of the contrary commodities. And thus much is sufficient, to say nothing of the praises and other contentment proceeding from philosophy, to let you see the utility of the same in every kind thereof.

8. The *subject* of Philosophy, or the matter it treats of, is every body of which we can conceive any generation, and which we may, by any consideration thereof, compare with other bodies, or which is capable of composition and resolution; that is to say, every body of whose generation or properties we can have any knowledge. And this may be deduced from the definition of philosophy, whose profession it is to search out the properties of bodies from their generation, or their generation from their properties; and, therefore, where there is no generation or property, there is no philosophy. Therefore it excludes *Theology*, I mean the doctrine of God, eternal, ingenerable, incomprehensible,

and in whom there is nothing neither to divide nor compound, nor any generation to be conceived.

It excludes the doctrine of *angels*, and all such things as are thought to be neither bodies nor properties of bodies; there being in them no place neither for composition nor division, nor any capacity of more and less, that is to say, no place for ratiocination.

It excludes *history*, as well *natural* as *political*, though most useful (nay necessary) to philosophy; because such knowledge is but experience, or authority, and not ratiocination.

It excludes all such knowledge as is acquired by Divine inspiration, or revelation, as not derived to us by reason, but by Divine grace in an instant, and, as it were, by some sense supernatural.

It excludes not only all doctrines which are false, but such also as are not well-grounded; for whatsoever we know by right ratiocination, can neither be false nor doubtful; and, therefore, *astrology*, as it is now held forth, and all such divinations rather than sciences, are excluded.

Lastly, the doctrine of *God's worship* is excluded from philosophy, as being not to be known by natural reason, but by the authority of the Church; and as being the object of faith, and not of knowledge.

9. The principal parts of philosophy are two. For two chief kinds of bodies, and very different from one another, offer themselves to such as search after their generation and properties; one whereof being the work of nature, is called a *natural body*, the other is called a *commonwealth*, and is made by the wills and agreement of men. And from these spring the two parts of philosophy, called *natural* and *civil*. But seeing that, for the knowledge of the properties of a commonwealth, it is necessary first to know the dispositions, affections, and manners of men, civil philosophy is again commonly divided into two parts, whereof one, which treats of men's dispositions and manners, is called *ethics*; and the other, which takes cognizance of their civil duties, is called *politics*, or simply *civil philosophy*. In the first place, therefore (after I have set down such premises as appertain to the nature of philosophy in general), I will discourse of *bodies*

natural; in the second, of the *dispositions and manners of men*; and in the third, of the *civil duties of subjects*.

10. To conclude; seeing there may be many who will not like this my definition of philosophy, and will say, that, from the liberty which a man may take of so defining as seems best to himself, he may conclude any thing from any thing (though I think it no hard matter to demonstrate that this definition of mine agrees with the sense of all men); yet, lest in this point there should be any cause of dispute betwixt me and them, I here undertake no more than to deliver the elements of that science by which the effects of anything may be found out from the known generation of the same, or contrarily, the generation from the effects; to the end that they who search after other philosophy, may be admonished to seek it from other principles.

CHAPTER VI

OF METHOD

1. Method and science defined.—2. It is more easily known concerning singular, than universal things, that they are; and contrarily, it is more easily known concerning universal, than singular things, why they are, or what are their causes.—3. What it is philosophers seek to know.—4. The first part, by which principles are found out, is purely analytical.—5. The highest causes, and most universal in every kind, are known by themselves.—6. Method from principles found out, tending to science simply, what it is.—7. That method of civil and natural science, which proceeds from sense to principles, is analytical; and again, that, which begins at principles, is synthetical.—8. The method of searching out, whether any thing propounded be matter or accident.—9. The method of seeking whether any accident be in this, or in that subject.—10. The method of searching after the cause of any effect propounded.—11. Words serve to invention, as marks; to demonstration, as signs.—12. The method of demonstration

1. FOR the understanding of *method*, it will be necessary for me to repeat the definition of philosophy, delivered above (Chap. I, art. 2.) in this manner, *Philosophy is the knowledge we acquire, by true ratiocination, of appearances, or apparent effects, from the knowledge we have of some possible production or generation of the same; and of such production, as has been or may be, from the knowledge we have of the effects.* METHOD, therefore, in the study of philosophy, *is the shortest way of finding out effects by their known causes, or of causes by their known effects.* But we are then said to know any effect, when we know *that there be causes of the same*, and *in what subject those causes are*, and *in what subject they produce that effect*, and *in what manner they work the same.* And this is the science of causes, or, as they call it, of the διότι. All other science, which is called the ὅτι,* is either perception by sense, or the imagination, or memory remaining after such perception.

The first beginnings, therefore, of knowledge, are the phantasms of sense and imagination; and that there be such phantasms we know well enough by nature; but to know why they be, or from what causes they proceed, is the work of ratiocination; which consists (as is said above, in the 1st Chapter, Art. 2) in *composition*, and *division* or *resolution*. There is therefore no method, by which we find out the causes of things, but is either *compositive* or *resolutive*, or *partly compositive*, and *partly resolutive*. And the resolutive is commonly called *analytical* method, as the compositive is called *synthetical*.

2. It is common to all sorts of method, to proceed from known things to unknown; and this is manifest from the cited

definition of philosophy. But in knowledge by sense, the whole object is more known, than any part thereof; as when we see a man, the conception or whole idea of that man is first or more known, than the particular ideas of his being *figurate*, *animate*, and *rational* that is, we first see the whole man, and take notice of his being, before we observe in him those other particulars. And therefore in any knowledge of the ὅτι, or that any thing *is*, the beginning of our search is from the whole idea; and contrarily, in our knowledge of the διότι, or of the causes of any thing, that is, in the sciences, we have more knowledge of the causes of the parts than of the whole. For the cause of the whole is compounded of the causes of the parts; but it is necessary that we know the things that are to be compounded, before we can know the whole compound. Now, by parts, I do not here mean parts of the thing itself, but parts of its nature; as, by the parts of man, I do not understand his head, his shoulders, his arms, &c. but his figure, quantity, motion, sense, reason, and the like; which accidents being compounded or put together, constitute the whole nature of man, but not the man himself. And this is the meaning of that common saying, namely, that some things are more known to us, others more known to nature; for I do not think that they, which so distinguish, mean that something is known to nature, which is known to no man; and therefore, by those things, that are more known to us, we are to understand things we take notice of by our senses, and, by more known to nature, those we acquire the knowledge of by reason; for in this sense it is, that the *whole*, that is, those things that have universal names, (which, for brevity's sake, I call *universal*) are more known to us than the *parts*, that is, such things as have names less universal, (which I therefore call *singular*); and the causes of the parts are more known to nature than the cause of the whole; that is, universals than singulars.

3. In the study of philosophy, men search after science either simply or indefinitely; that is, to know as much as they can, without propounding to themselves any limited question; or they enquire into the cause of some determined appearance, or endeavour to find out the certainty of some-

thing in question, as what is the cause of *light*, of *heat*, of *gravity*, of a *figure* propounded, and the like; or in what *subject* any propounded *accident* is inherent; or what may conduce most to the *generation* of some propounded *effect* from many *accidents*; or in what manner particular causes ought to be compounded for the production of some certain effect. Now, according to this variety of things in question, sometimes the *analytical method* is to be used, and sometimes the *synthetical*.

4. But to those that search after science indefinitely, which consists in the knowledge of the causes of all things, as far forth as it may be attained, (and the causes of singular things are compounded of the causes of universal or simple things) it is necessary that they know the causes of universal things, or of such accidents as are common to all bodies, that is, to all matter, before they can know the causes of singular things, that is, of those accidents by which one thing is distinguished from another. And, again, they must know what those universal things are, before they can know their causes. Moreover, seeing universal things are contained in the nature of singular things, the knowledge of them is to be acquired by reason, that is, by resolution. For example, if there be propounded a conception or *idea* of some singular thing, as of a *square*, this square is to be resolved into a *plain, terminated with a certain number of equal and straight lines and right angles*. For by this resolution we have these things universal or agreeable to all matter, namely, *line*, *plain*, (which contains *superficies*) *terminated*, *angle*, *straightness*, *rectitude*, and *equality*; and if we can find out the causes of these, we may compound them altogether into the cause of a square. Again, if any man propound to himself the conception of *gold*, he may, by resolving, come to the ideas of *solid*, *visible*, *heavy*, (that is, tending to the centre of the earth, or downwards) and many other more universal than gold itself; and these he may resolve again, till he come to such things as are most universal. And in this manner, by resolving continually, we may come to know what those things are, whose causes being first known severally, and afterwards compounded, bring us to the knowledge of singular things. I conclude,

therefore, that the method of attaining to the universal knowledge of things, is purely *analytical*.

5. But the causes of universal things (of those, at least, that have any cause) are manifest of themselves, or (as they say commonly) known to nature; so that they need no method at all; for they have all but one universal cause, which is motion. For the variety of all figures arises out of the variety of those motions by which they are made; and motion cannot be understood to have any other cause besides motion; nor has the variety of those things we perceive by sense, as of *colours*, *sounds*, *savours*, &c. any other cause than motion, residing partly in the objects that work upon our senses, and partly in ourselves, in such manner, as that it is manifestly some kind of motion, though we cannot, without ratiocination, come to know what kind. For though many cannot understand till it be in some sort demonstrated to them, that all mutation consists in motion; yet this happens not from any obscurity in the thing itself, (for it is not intelligible that anything can depart either from rest, or from the motion it has, except by motion), but either by having their natural discourse corrupted with former opinions received from their masters, or else for this, that they do not at all bend their mind to the enquiring out of truth.

6. By the knowledge therefore of universals, and of their causes (which are the first principles by which we know the διότι of things) we have in the first place their definitions, (which are nothing but the explication of our simple conceptions.) For example, he that has a true conception of *place*, cannot be ignorant of this definition, *place is that space which is possessed or filled adequately by some body*; and so, he that conceives *motion* aright, cannot but know that *motion is the privation of one place, and the acquisition of another*. In the next place, we have their generations or descriptions; as (for example) that *a line is made by the motion of a point, superficies by the motion of a line*, and *one motion by another motion*, &c. It remains, that we enquire what motion begets such and such effects; as, what motion makes a straight line, and what a circular; what motion thrusts, what draws, and by what way; what makes a thing which is seen or heard, to

be seen or heard sometimes in one manner, sometimes in another. Now the method of this kind of enquiry, is *compositive*. For first we are to observe what effect a body moved produceth, when we consider nothing in it besides its motion; and we see presently that this makes a line, or length; next, what the motion of a long body produces, which we find to be superficies; and so forwards, till we see what the effects of simple motion are; and then, in like manner, we are to observe what proceeds from the addition, multiplication, subtraction, and division, of these motions, and what effects, what figures, and what properties, they produce; from which kind of contemplation sprung that part of philosophy which is called *geometry*.

From this consideration of what is produced by simple motion, we are to pass to the consideration of what effects one body moved worketh upon another; and because there may be motion in all the several parts of a body, yet so as that the whole body remain still in the same place, we must enquire first, what motion causeth such and such motion in the whole, that is, when one body invades another body which is either at rest or in motion, what way, and with what swiftness, the invaded body shall move; and, again, what motion this second body will generate in a third, and so forwards. From which contemplation shall be drawn that part of philosophy which treats of motion.

In the third place we must proceed to the enquiry of such effects as are made by the motion of the parts of any body, as, how it comes to pass, that things when they are the same, yet seem not to be the same, but changed. And here the things we search after are sensible qualities, such as *light*, *colour*, *transparency*, *opacity*, *sound*, *odour*, *savour*, *heat*, *cold*, and the like; which because they cannot be known till we know the causes of sense itself, therefore the consideration of the causes of *seeing*, *hearing*, *smelling*, *tasting*, and *touching*, belongs to this third place; and all those qualities and changes, above mentioned, are to be referred to the fourth place; which two considerations comprehend that part of philosophy which is called *physics*. And in these four parts is contained whatsoever in natural philosophy may be explicated by demonstration, properly so called. For if a cause were to be rendered of natural appearances in special, as, what are the motions and influences of the heavenly bodies, and of their parts, the reason hereof must either be drawn from the parts of the sciences above mentioned, or no reason at all will be given, but all left to uncertain conjecture.

After *physics* we must come to *moral philosophy*; in which we are to consider the motions of the mind, namely, *appetite*, *aversion*, *love*, *benevolence*, *hope*, *fear*, *anger*, *emulation*, *envy*, &c.; what causes they have, and of what they be causes. And the reason why these are to be considered after *physics* is, that they have their causes in sense and imagination, which are the subject of *physical* contemplation. Also the reason, why all these things are to be searched after in the order above-said, is, that physics cannot be understood, except we know first what motions are in the smallest parts of bodies; nor such motion of parts, till we know what it is that makes another body move; nor this, till we know what simple motion will effect. And because all appearance of things to sense is determined, and made to be of such and such quality and quantity by compounded motions, every one of which has a certain degree of velocity, and a certain and determined way; therefore, in the first place, we are to search out the ways of motion simply (in which geometry consists); next the ways of such generated motions as are manifest; and, lastly, the ways of internal and invisible motions (which is the enquiry of natural philosophers). And, therefore, they that study natural philosophy, study in vain, except they begin at geometry; and such writers or disputers thereof, as are ignorant of geometry, do but make their readers and hearers lose their time.

7. *Civil* and *moral philosophy* do not so adhere to one another, but that they may be severed. For the causes of the motions of the mind are known, not only by ratiocination, but also by the experience of every man that takes the pains to observe those motions within himself. And, therefore, not only they that have attained the knowledge of the passions and perturbations of the mind, by the *synthetical method*, and from the very first principles of philosophy, may by pro-

ceeding in the same way, come to the causes and necessity of constituting commonwealths, and to get the knowledge of what is natural right, and what are civil duties; and, in every kind of government, what are the rights of the commonwealth, and all other knowledge appertaining to civil philosophy; for this reason, that the principles of the politics consist in the knowledge of the motions of the mind, and the knowledge of these motions from the knowledge of sense and imagination; but even they also that have not learned the first part of philosophy, namely, *geometry* and *physics*, may, notwithstanding, attain the principles of civil philosophy, by the *analytical method*. For if a question be propounded, as, *whether such an action be just or unjust*; if that *unjust* be resolved into *fact against law*, and that notion *law* into the *command* of him or them that have *coercive power*; and that *power* be derived from the *wills* of men that constitute such power, to the end they may live in peace, they may at last come to this, that the appetites of men and the passions of their minds are such, that, unless they be restrained by some power, they will always be making war upon one another; which may be known to be so by any man's experience, that will but examine his own mind. And, therefore, from hence he may proceed, by compounding, to the determination of the justice or injustice of any propounded action. So that it is manifest, by what has been said, that the method of philosophy, to such as seek science simply, without propounding to themselves the solution of any particular question, is partly analytical, and partly synthetical; namely, that which proceeds from sense to the invention of principles, analytical; and the rest synthetical.

8. To those that seek the cause of some certain and propounded appearance or effect, it happens, sometimes, that they know not whether the thing, whose cause is sought after, be matter or body,* or some accident of a body. For though in geometry, when the cause is sought of magnitude, or proportion, or figure, it be certainly known that these things, namely magnitude, proportion, and figure, are accidents; yet in natural philosophy, where all questions are concerning the causes of the phantasms of sensible things, it is

not so easy to discern between the things themselves, from which those phantasms proceed, and the appearances of those things to the sense; which have deceived many, especially when the phantasms have been made by light. For example, a man that looks upon the sun, has a certain shining idea of the magnitude of about a foot over, and this he calls the sun, though he know the sun to be truly a great deal bigger; and, in like manner, the phantasm of the same thing appears sometimes round, by being seen afar off, and sometimes square, by being nearer. Whereupon it may well be doubted, whether that phantasm be matter, or some body natural, or only some accident of a body; in the examination of which doubt we may use this method. The properties of matter and accidents already found out by us, by the synthetical method, from their definitions, are to be compared with the idea we have before us; and if it agree with the properties of matter or body, then it is a body; otherwise it is an accident. Seeing, therefore, matter cannot by any endeavour of ours be either made or destroyed, or increased, or diminished, or moved out of its place, whereas that idea appears, vanishes, is increased and diminished, and moved hither and thither at pleasure; we may certainly conclude that it is not a body, but an accident only. And this method is *synthetical*.

9. But if there be a doubt made concerning the subject of any known accident (for this may be doubted sometimes, as in the precedent example, doubt may be made in what subject that splendour and apparent magnitude of the sun is), then our enquiry must proceed in this manner. First, matter in general must be divided into parts, as, into object, medium, and the sentient itself, or such other parts as seem most conformable to the thing propounded. Next, these parts are severally to be examined how they agree with the definition of the subject; and such of them as are not capable of that accident are to be rejected. For example, if by any true ratiocination the sun be found to be greater than its apparent magnitude, then that magnitude is not in the sun; if the sun be in one determined straight line, and one determined distance, and the magnitude and splendour be seen in more lines and distances than one, as it is in reflection or refraction,

then neither that splendour nor apparent magnitude are in the sun itself, and, therefore, the body of the sun cannot be the subject of that splendour and magnitude. And for the same reasons the air and other parts will be rejected, till at last nothing remain which can be the subject of that splendour and magnitude but the sentient itself. And this method, in regard the subject is divided into parts, is analytical; and in regard the properties, both of the subject and accident, are compared with the accident concerning whose subject the enquiry is made, it is synthetical.

10. But when we seek after the cause of any propounded effect, we must in the first place get into our mind an exact notion or idea of that which we call cause, namely, that *a cause is the sum or aggregate of all such accidents, both in the agents and the patient, as concur to the producing of the effect propounded; all which existing together, it cannot be understood but that the effect existeth with them; or that it can possibly exist if any one of them be absent.* This being known, in the next place we must examine singly every accident that accompanies or precedes the effect, as far forth as it seems to conduce in any manner to the production of the same, and see whether the propounded effect may be conceived to exist, without the existence of any of those accidents; and by this means separate such accidents, as do not concur, from such as concur to produce the said effect; which being done, we are to put together the concurring accidents, and consider whether we can possibly conceive, that when these are all present, the effect propounded will not follow; and if it be evident that the effect will follow, then that aggregate of accidents is the entire cause, otherwise not; but we must still search out and put together other accidents. For example, if the cause of light be propounded to be sought out; first, we examine things without us, and find that whensoever light appears, there is some principal object, as it were the fountain of light, without which we cannot have any perception of light; and, therefore, the concurrence of that object is necessary to the generation of light. Next we consider the medium, and find, that unless it be disposed in a certain manner, namely, that it be transparent, though the object

remain the same, yet the effect will not follow; and, there-fore, the concurrence of transparency is also necessary to the generation of light. Thirdly, we observe our own body, and find that by the indisposition of the eyes, the brain, the nerves, and the heart, that is, by obstructions, stupidity, and debility, we are deprived of light, so that a fitting disposition of the organs to receive impressions from without is likewise a necessary part of the cause of light. Again, of all the accidents inherent in the object, there is none that can conduce to the effecting of light, but only action (or a cer-tain motion), which cannot be conceived to be wanting, whensoever the effect is present; for, that anything may shine, it is not requisite that it be of such or such magnitude or figure, or that the whole body of it be moved out of the place it is in (unless it may perhaps be said, that in the sun, or other body, that which causes light is the light it hath in itself; which yet is but a trifling exception, seeing nothing is meant thereby but the cause of light; as if any man should say that the cause of light is that in the sun which produceth it); it remains, therefore, that the action, by which light is gen-erated, is motion only in the parts of the object. Which being understood, we may easily conceive what it is the medium contributes, namely, the continuation of that motion to the eye;* and, lastly, what the eye and the rest of the organs of the sentient contribute, namely, the continuation of the same motion to the last organ of sense, the heart. And in this manner the cause of light may be made up of motion con-tinued from the original of the same motion, to the original of vital motion, light being nothing but the alteration of vital motion, made by the impression upon it of motion continued from the object. But I give this only for an example, for I shall speak more at large of light, and the generation of it, in its proper place. In the mean time it is manifest, that in the searching out of causes, there is need partly of the analytical, and partly of the synthetical method; of the analytical, to conceive how circumstances conduce severally to the pro-duction of effects; and of the synthetical, for the adding together and compounding of what they can effect singly by themselves. And thus much may serve for the method of invention. It remains that I speak of the method of teaching, that is, of demonstration, and of the means by which we demonstrate.

11. In the method of invention, the use of words consists in this, that they may serve for marks, by which, whatsoever we have found out may be recalled to memory; for without this all our inventions perish, nor will it be possible for us to go on from principles beyond a syllogism or two, by reason of the weakness of memory. For example, if any man, by considering a triangle set before him, should find that all its angles together taken are equal to two right angles, and that by thinking of the same tacitly, without any use of words either understood or expressed; and it should happen afterwards that another triangle, unlike the former, or the same in different situation, should be offered to his consideration, he would not know readily whether the same property were in this last or no, but would be forced, as often as a different triangle were brought before him (and the difference of triangles is infinite) to begin his contemplation anew; which he would have no need to do if he had the use of names, for every universal name denotes the conceptions we have of infinite singular things. Nevertheless, as I said above, they serve as *marks* for the help of our memory, whereby we register to ourselves our own inventions; but not as *signs* by which we declare the same to others; so that a man may be a philosopher alone by himself, without any master; Adam had this capacity. But to teach, that is, to demonstrate, supposes two at the least, and syllogistical speech.

12. And seeing teaching is nothing but leading the mind of him we teach, to the knowledge of our inventions, in that track by which we attained the same with our own mind; therefore, the same method that served for our invention, will serve also for demonstration to others, saving that we omit the first part of method which proceeded from the sense of things to universal principles, which, because they are principles, cannot be demonstrated; and seeing they are known by nature, (as was said above in the 5th article) they need no demonstration, though they need explication. The whole method, therefore, of demonstration, is *synthetical*,

consisting of that order of speech which begins from primary or most universal propositions, which are manifest of themselves, and proceeds by a perpetual composition of propositions into syllogisms, till at last the learner understand the truth of the conclusion sought after.

13. Now, such principles are nothing but definitions, whereof there are two sorts; one of names, that signify such things as have some conceivable cause, and another of such names as signify things of which we can conceive no cause at all. Names of the former kind are, *body*, or *matter*, *quantity*, or *extension*, *motion*, and whatsoever is common to all matter. Of the second kind, are *such a body*, *such and so great motion*, *so great magnitude*, *such figure*, and whatsoever we can distinguish one body from another by. And names of the former kind are well enough defined, when, by speech as short as may be, we raise in the mind of the hearer perfect and clear ideas or conceptions of the things named, as when we define motion to be *the leaving of the place, and the acquiring of another continually*; for though no thing moved, nor any cause of motion be in that definition, yet, at the hearing of that speech, there will come into the mind of the hearer an *idea* of motion clear enough. But definitions of things, which may be understood to have some cause, must consist of such names as express the cause or manner of their generation, as when we define a circle to be a figure made by the circumduction of a straight line in a plane, &c. Besides definitions, there is no other proposition that ought to be called primary, or (according to severe truth) be received into the number of principles. For those *axioms of Euclid*, seeing they may be demonstrated, are no principles of demonstration, though they have by the consent of all men gotten the authority of principles, because they need not be demonstrated. Also, those *petitions*, or *postulata*, (as they call them) though they be principles, yet they are not principles of demonstration, but of construction only; that is, not of science, but of power; or (which is all one) not of *theorems*, which are speculations, but of *problems*,* which belong to practice, or the doing of something. But as for those common received opinions, *Nature abhors vacuity*,

Nature doth nothing in vain, and the like, which are neither evident in themselves, nor at all to be demonstrated, and which are oftener false than true, they are much less to be acknowledged for principles.

To return, therefore, to definitions; the reason why I say that the cause and generation of such things, as have any cause or generation, ought to enter into their definitions, is this. The end of science is the demonstration of the causes and generations of things; which if they be not in the definitions, they cannot be found in the conclusion of the first syllogism, that is made from those definitions; and if they be not in the first conclusion, they will not be found in any further conclusion deduced from that; and, therefore, by proceeding in this manner, we shall never come to science; which is against the scope and intention of demonstration.

14. Now, seeing definitions (as I have said) are principles, or primary propositions, they are therefore speeches; and seeing they are used for the raising of an *idea* of some thing in the mind of the learner, whensoever that thing has a name, the definition of it can be nothing but the explication of that name by speech; and if that name be given it for some compounded conception, the definition is nothing but a resolution of that name into its most universal parts. As when we define man, saying *man is a body animated, sentient, rational*, those names, *body animated, &c.* are parts of that whole name *man*; so that definitions of this kind always consist of *genus* and *difference*;* the former names being all, till the last, *general*; and the last of all, *difference*. But if any name be the most universal in its kind, then the definition of it cannot consist of *genus* and *difference*, but is to be made by such circumlocution, as best explicateth the force of that name. Again, it is possible, and happens often, that the *genus* and *difference* are put together, and yet make no definition; as these words, *a straight line*, contain both the *genus* and *difference*; but are not a definition, unless we should think a straight line may be thus defined, *a straight line is a straight line*: and yet if there were added another name, consisting of different words, but signifying the same thing which these signify, then these might be the definition of that name. From

what has been said, it may be understood how a definition ought to be defined, namely, *that it is a proposition, whose predicate resolves the subject, when it may; and when it may not, it exemplifies the same*.

15. The properties* of a definition are:

First, that it takes away equivocation, as also all that multitude of distinctions, which are used by such as think they may learn philosophy by disputation. For the nature of a definition is to define, that is, to determine the signification of the defined name, and to pare from it all other signification besides what is contained in the definition itself; and therefore one definition does as much, as all the distinctions (how many soever) that can be used about the name defined.

Secondly, that it gives an universal notion of the thing defined, representing a certain universal picture thereof, not to the eye, but to the mind. For as when one paints a man, he paints the image of some man; so he, that defines the name man, makes a representation of some man to the mind.

Thirdly, that it is not necessary to dispute whether definitions are to be admitted or no. For when a master is instructing his scholar, if the scholar understand all the parts of the thing defined, which are resolved in the definition, and yet will not admit of the definition, there needs no further controversy betwixt them, it being all one as if he refused to be taught. But if he understand nothing, then certainly the definition is faulty; for the nature of a definition consists in this, that it exhibit a clear idea of the thing defined; and principles are either known by themselves, or else they are not principles.

Fourthly, that, in philosophy, definitions are before defined names. For in teaching philosophy, the first beginning is from definitions; and all progression in the same, till we come to the knowledge of the thing compounded, is compositive. Seeing, therefore, definition is the explication of a compounded name by resolution, and the progression is from the parts to the compound, definitions must be understood before compounded names; nay, when the names of the parts of any speech be explicated, it is not necessary that the definition should be a name compounded of them. For example, when these names, *equilateral*, *quadrilateral*, *right-*

angled, are sufficiently understood, it is not necessary in geometry that there should be at all such a name as *square*; for defined names are received in philosophy for brevity's sake only.

Fifthly, that compounded names, which are defined one way in some one part of philosophy, may in another part of the same be otherwise defined; as a *parabola* and an *hyperbole* have one definition in geometry, and another in rhetoric; for definitions are instituted and serve for the understanding of the doctrine which is treated of. And, therefore, as in one part of philosophy, a definition may have in it some one fit name for the more brief explanation of some proposition in geometry; so it may have the same liberty in other parts of philosophy; for the use of names is particular (even where many agree to the settling of them) and arbitrary.

Sixthly, that no name can be defined by any one word; because no one word is sufficient for the resolving of one or more words.

Seventhly, that a defined name ought not to be repeated in the definition. For a defined name is the whole compound, and a definition is the resolution of that compound into parts; but no total can be part of itself.

16. Any two definitions, that may be compounded into a syllogism, produce a conclusion; which, because it is derived from principles, that is, from definitions, is said to be demonstrated; and the derivation or composition itself is called a demonstration. In like manner, if a syllogism be made of two propositions, whereof one is a definition, the other a demonstrated conclusion, or neither of them is a definition, but both formerly demonstrated, that syllogism is also called a demonstration, and so successively. The definition therefore of a demonstration is this, *a demonstration is a syllogism, or series of syllogisms, derived and continued, from the definitions of names, to the last conclusion*. And from hence it may be understood, that all true ratiocination, which taketh its beginning from true principles, produceth science, and is true demonstration. For as for the original of the name, although that, which the Greeks called ἀποδέιξις, and the

Latins *demonstratio*, was understood by them for that sort
only of ratiocination, in which, by the describing of certain
lines and figures, they placed the thing they were to prove, as
it were before men's eyes, which is properly ἀποδεικνύειν, or
to *shew* by the figure; yet they seem to have done it for this
reason, that unless it were in geometry, (in which only there
is place for such figures) there was no ratiocination certain,
and ending in science, their doctrines concerning all other
things being nothing but controversy and clamour; which,
nevertheless, happened, not because the truth to which they
pretended could not be made evident without figures, but
because they wanted true principles, from which they might
derive their ratiocination; and, therefore, there is no reason
but that if true definitions were premised in all sorts of
doctrines, the demonstrations also would be true.

17. It is proper to methodical demonstration,

First, that there be a true succession of one reason to
another, according to the rules of syllogizing delivered above.

Secondly, that the premises of all syllogisms be demonstrated from the first definitions.

Thirdly,* that after definitions, he that teaches or demon-
strates any thing, proceed in the same method by which he
found it out; namely, that in the first place those things
be demonstrated, which immediately succeed to universal
definitions (in which is contained that part of philosophy
which is called *philosophia prima*). Next, those things which
may be demonstrated by simple motion (in which geometry
consists). After geometry, such things as may be taught or
shewed by manifest action, that is, by thrusting from, or
pulling towards. And after these, the motion or mutation of
the invisible parts of things, and the doctrine of sense and
imaginations, and of the internal passions, especially those of
men, in which are comprehended the grounds of civil duties,
or civil philosophy; which takes up the last place. And that
this method ought to be kept in all sorts of philosophy, is
evident from hence, that such things as I have said are to
be taught last, cannot be demonstrated, till such as are
propounded to be first treated of, be fully understood. Of
which method no other example can be given, but that

treatise of the elements of philosophy, which I shall begin in the next chapter, and continue to the end of the work.

18. Besides those *paralogisms*, whose fault lies either in the falsity of the premises, or the want of true composition, of which I have spoken in the precedent chapter, there are two more, which are frequent in demonstration; one whereof is commonly called *petitio principii*; the other is the supposing of a *false cause*; and these do not only deceive unskilful learners, but sometimes masters themselves, by making them take that for well demonstrated, which is not demonstrated at all. *Petitio principii* is, when the conclusion to be proved is disguised in other words, and put for the definition or principle from whence it is to be demonstrated; and thus, by putting for the cause of the thing sought, either the thing itself or some effect of it, they make a circle in their demonstration. As for example, he that would demonstrate that the earth stands still in the centre of the world, and should suppose the earth's gravity to be the cause thereof, and define gravity to be a quality by which every heavy body tends towards the centre of the world, would lose his labour; for the question is, what is the cause of that quality in the earth? and, therefore, he that supposes gravity to be the cause, puts the thing itself for its own cause.

Of a *false cause* I find this example in a certain treatise where the thing to be demonstrated is the motion of the earth. He begins, therefore, with this, that seeing the earth and the sun are not always in the same situation, it must needs be that one of them be locally moved, which is true; next, he affirms that the vapours, which the sun raises from the earth and sea, are, by reason of this motion, necessarily moved, which also is true; from whence he infers the winds are made, and this may pass for granted; and by these winds he says, the waters of the sea are moved, and by their motion the bottom of the sea, as if it were beaten forwards, moves round; and let this also be granted; wherefore, he concludes, the earth is moved; which is, nevertheless, a paralogism. For, if that wind were the cause why the earth was, from the beginning, moved round, and the motion either of the sun or the earth were the cause of that wind, then the motion of the sun or the earth was before the wind itself; and if the earth were moved, before the wind was made, then the wind could not be the cause of the earth's revolution; but, if the sun were moved, and the earth stand still, then it is manifest the earth might remain unmoved, notwithstanding that wind; and therefore that motion was not made by the cause which he allegeth. But paralogisms of this kind are very frequent among the writers of *physics*, though none can be more elaborate than this in the example given.

19. It may to some men seem pertinent to treat in this place of that art of the geometricians, which they call *logistica*, that is, the art, by which, from supposing the thing in question to be true, they proceed by ratiocination, till either they come to something known, by which they may demonstrate the truth of the thing sought for; or to something which is impossible, from whence they collect that to be false, which they supposed true. But this art cannot be explicated here, for this reason, that the method of it can neither be practised, nor understood, unless by such as are well versed in geometry; and among geometricians themselves, they, that have most theorems in readiness, are the most ready in the use of this *logistica*; so that, indeed, it is not a distinct thing from geometry itself; for there are, in the method of it, three parts; the first whereof consists in the finding out of equality betwixt known and unknown things, which they call equation; and this equation cannot be found out, but by such as know perfectly the nature, properties, and transpositions of proportion, as also the addition, subtraction, multiplication, and division of lines and superficies, and the extraction of roots; which are the parts of no mean geometrician. The second is, when an equation is found, to be able to judge whether the truth or falsity of the question may be deduced from it, or no; which yet requires greater knowledge. And the third is, when such an equation is found, as is fit for the solution of the question, to know how to resolve the same in such manner, that the truth or falsity may thereby manifestly appear; which, in hard questions, cannot be done without the knowledge of the nature of crooked-lined figures; but he that understands readily the nature and properties of these,

is a complete geometrician. It happens besides, that for the finding out of equation, there is no certain method, but he is best able to do it, that has the best natural wit.

CHAPTER XXV

OF SENSE AND ANIMAL MOTION

1. The connexion of what hath been said with that which followeth.—2. The investigation of the nature of sense, and the definition of sense.—3. The subject and object of sense.—4. The organs of sense.—5. All bodies are not indued with sense.—6. But one phantasm at one and the same time.—7. Imagination the remains of past sense, which also is memory. Of sleep.—8. How phantasms succeed one another.—9. Dreams, whence they proceed.—10. Of the senses, their kinds, their organs, and phantasms proper and common.—11. The magnitude of images, how and by what it is determined.—12. Pleasure, pain, appetite and aversion, what they are.—13. Deliberation and will, what.

1. I HAVE, in the first chapter, defined philosophy to be *knowledge of effects acquired by true ratiocination, from knowledge first had of their causes and generation; and of such causes or generations as may be, from former knowledge of their effects or appearances*. There are, therefore, two methods of philosophy; one, from the generation of things to their possible effects; and the other, from their effects or appearances to some possible generation of the same. In the former of these the truth of the first principles of our ratiocination, namely definitions, is made and constituted by ourselves, whilst we consent and agree about the appellations of things. And this part I have finished in the foregoing chapters; in which, if I am not deceived, I have affirmed nothing, saving the definitions themselves, which hath not good coherence with the definitions I have given; that is to

say, which is not sufficiently demonstrated to all those, that agree with me in the use of words and appellations· for whose sake only I have written the same. I now enter upon the other part; which is the finding out by the appearances or effects of nature, which we know by sense, some ways and means by which they may be, I do not say they are, generated. The principles, therefore, upon which the following discourse depends, are not such as we ourselves make and pronounce in general terms, as definitions; but such, as being placed in the things themselves by the Author of Nature, are by us observed in them; and we make use of them in single and particular, not universal propositions. Nor do they impose upon us any necessity of constituting theorems; their use being only, though not without such general propositions as have been already demonstrated, to show us the possibility of some production or generation. Seeing, therefore, the science, which is here taught, hath its principles in the appearances of nature, and endeth in the attaining of some knowledge of natural causes, I have given to this part the title of PHYSICS, or the *Phenomena of Nature*. Now such things as appear, or are shown to us by nature, we call phenomena or appearances.

Of all the phenomena or appearances which are near us, the most admirable is apparition itself, τὸ φαίνεσθαι; namely, that some natural bodies have in themselves the patterns almost of all things, and others of none at all. So that if the appearances be the principles by which we know all other things, we must needs acknowledge sense to be the principle by which we know those principles, and that all the knowledge we have is derived from it. And as for the causes of sense, we cannot begin our search of them from any other phenomenon than that of sense itself. But you will say, by what sense shall we take notice of sense? I answer, by sense itself, namely, by the memory which for some time remains in us of things sensible, though they themselves pass away. For he that perceives that he hath perceived, remembers.

In the first place, therefore, the causes of our perception, that is, the causes of those ideas and phantasms which are perpetually generated within us whilst we make use of our senses, are to be enquired into; and in what manner their generation proceeds. To help which inquisition, we may observe first of all, that our phantasms or ideas are not always the same; but that new ones appear to us, and old ones vanish, according as we apply our organs of sense, now to one object, now to another. Wherefore they are generated, and perish. And from hence it is manifest, that they are some change or mutation in the sentient.

2. Now that all mutation or alteration is motion or endeavour (and endeavour also is motion) in the internal parts of the thing that is altered, hath been proved (in art. 9, chap. VIII) from this, that whilst even the least parts of any body remain in the same situation in respect of one another, it cannot be said that any alteration, unless perhaps that the whole body together hath been moved, hath happened to it; but that it both appeareth and is the same it appeared and was before. Sense, therefore, in the sentient, can be nothing else but motion in some of the internal parts of the sentient; and the parts so moved are parts of the organs of sense. For the parts of our body, by which we perceive any thing, are those we commonly call the organs of sense. And so we find what is the subject of our sense, namely, that in which are the phantasms; and partly also we have discovered the nature of sense, namely, that it is some internal motion in the sentient.

I have shown besides (in chap. IX, art. 7) that no motion is generated but by a body contiguous and moved: from whence it is manifest, that the immediate cause of sense or perception consists in this, that the first organ of sense is touched and pressed. For when the uttermost part of the organ is pressed, it no sooner yields, but the part next within it is pressed also; and, in this manner, the pressure or motion is propagated through all the parts of the organ to the innermost. And thus also the pressure of the uttermost part proceeds from the pressure of some more remote body, and so continually, till we come to that from which, as from its fountain, we derive the phantasm or idea that is made in us by our sense. And this, whatsoever it be, is that we commonly call *the object*. Sense, therefore, is some internal motion in the sentient, generated by some internal motion of the parts of the object, and propagated through all the media to the innermost part of the organ. By which words I have almost defined what sense is.

Moreover, I have shown (art. 2, chap. XV) that all resistance is endeavour opposite to another endeavour, that is to say, reaction. Seeing, therefore, there is in the whole organ, by reason of its own internal natural motion, some resistance or reaction against the motion which is propagated from the object to the innermost part of the organ, there is also in the same organ an endeavour opposite to the endeavour which proceeds from the object; so that when that endeavour inwards is the last action in the act of sense, then from the reaction, how little soever the duration of it be, a phantasm or idea hath its being; which, by reason that the endeavour is now outwards, doth always appear as something situate without the organ. So that now I shall give you the whole definition of sense, as it is drawn from the explication of the causes thereof and the order of its generation, thus: SENSE *is a phantasm, made by the reaction and endeavour outwards in the organ of sense, caused by an endeavour inwards from the object, remaining for some time more or less.*

3. The *subject* of sense is the *sentient* itself, namely, some living creature; and we speak more correctly, when we say a living creature seeth, than when we say the eye seeth. The object is the thing received; and it is more accurately said, that we see the sun, than that we see the light. For light and colour, and heart and sound, and other qualities which are commonly called sensible, are not objects, but phantasms in the sentients. For a phantasm is the act of sense, and differs no otherwise from sense than *fieri*, that is, being a doing, differs from *factum esse*, that is, being done; which difference, in things that are done in an instant, is none at all; and a phantasm is made in an instant. For in all motion which proceeds by perpetual propagation, the first part being moved moves the second, the second the third, and so on to the last, and that to any distance, how great soever. And in what point of time the first or foremost part proceeded to the place of the second, which is thrust on, in the same point of time the

last save one proceeded into the place of the last yielding part; which by reaction, in the same instant, if the reaction be strong enough, makes a phantasm; and a phantasm being made, perception is made together with it.

4. The *organs* of sense, which are in the sentient, are such parts thereof, that if they be hurt, the very generation of phantasms is thereby destroyed, though all the rest of the parts remain entire. Now these parts in the most of living creatures are found to be certain spirits and membranes, which, proceeding from the *pia mater*,* involve the brain and all the nerves; also the brain itself, and the arteries which are in the brain; and such other parts, as being stirred, the heart also, which is the fountain of all sense, is stirred together with them. For whensoever the action of the object reacheth the body of the sentient, that action is by some nerve propagated to the brain; and if the nerve leading thither be so hurt or obstructed, that the motion can be propagated no further, no sense follows. Also if the motion be intercepted between the brain and the heart by the defect of the organ by which the action is propagated, there will be no perception of the object.

5. But though all sense, as I have said, be made by reaction, nevertheless it is not necessary that every thing that reacteth should have sense. I know there have been philosophers, and those learned men, who have maintained that all bodies are endued with sense. Nor do I see how they can be refuted, if the nature of sense be placed in reaction only. And, though by the reaction of bodies inanimate a phantasm might be made, it would nevertheless cease, as soon as ever the object were removed. For unless those bodies had organs, as living creatures have, fit for the re-taining of such motion as is made in them, their sense would be such, as that they should never remember the same. And therefore this hath nothing to do with that sense which is the subject of my discourse. For by sense, we commonly under-stand the judgment we make of objects by their phantasms; namely, by comparing and distinguishing those phantasms; which we could never do, if that motion in the organ, by which the phantasm is made, did not remain there for some

time, and make the same phantasm return. Wherefore sense, as I here understand it, and which is commonly so called, hath necessarily some memory adhering to it, by which former and later phantasms* may be compared together, and distinguished from one another.

Sense, therefore, properly so called, must necessarily have in it a perpetual variety of phantasms, that they may be discerned one from another. For if we should suppose a man to be made with clear eyes, and all the rest of his organs of sight well disposed, but endued with no other sense; and that he should look only upon one thing, which is always of the same colour and figure, without the least appearance of variety, he would seem to me, whatsoever others may say, to see, no more than I seem to myself to feel the bones of my own limbs by my organs of feeling; and yet those bones are always and on all sides touched by a most sensible membrane. I might perhaps say he were astonished, and looked upon it; but I should not say he saw it; it being almost all one for a man to be always sensible of one and the same thing, and not to be sensible at all of any thing.

6. And yet such is the nature of sense, that it does not permit a man to discern many things at once. For seeing the nature of sense consists in motion; as long as the organs are employed about one object, they cannot be so moved by another at the same time, as to make by both their motions one sincere phantasm of each of them at once. And therefore two several phantasms will not be made by two objects working together, but only one phantasm compounded from the action of both.

Besides, as when we divide a body, we divide its place; and when we reckon many bodies, we must necessarily reckon as many places; and contrarily, as I have shown in the seventh chapter; so what number soever we say there be of times, we must understand the same number of motions also; and as oft as we count many motions, so oft we reckon many times. For though the object we look upon be of divers colours, yet with those divers colours it is but one varied object, and not variety of objects.

Moreover, whilst those organs which are common to all the

senses, such as are those parts of every organ which proceed in men from the root of the nerves to the heart, are vehemently stirred by a strong action from some one object, they are, by reason of the contumacy which the motion, they have already, gives them against the reception of all other motion, made the less fit to receive any other impression from whatsoever other objects, to what sense soever those objects belong. And hence it is, that an earnest studying of one object, takes away the sense of all other objects for the present. For *study* is nothing else but a possession of the mind, that is to say, a vehement motion made by some one object in the organs of sense, which are stupid to all other motions as long as this lasteth; according to what was said by Terence, '*Populus studio stupidus in funambulo animum occuparat.*'* For what is *stupor* but that which the Greeks call ἀναισθησία, that is, a cessation from the sense of other things? Wherefore at one and the same time, we cannot by sense perceive more than one single object; as in reading, we see the letters successively one by one, and not all together, though the whole page be presented to our eye; and though every several letter be distinctly written there, yet when we look upon the whole page at once, we read nothing.

From hence it is manifest, that every endeavour of the organ outwards, is not to be called sense, but that only, which at several times is by vehemence made stronger and more predominant than the rest; which deprives us of the sense of other phantasms, no otherwise than the sun deprives the rest of the stars of light, not by hindering their action, but by obscuring and hiding them with his excess of brightness.

7. But the motion of the organ, by which a phantasm is made, is not commonly called sense, except the object be present. And the phantasm remaining after the object is removed or past by, is called *fancy*, and in Latin *imaginatio*; which word, because all phantasms are not images, doth not fully answer the signification of the word *fancy* in its general acceptation. Nevertheless I may use it safely enough, by understanding it for the Greek Φαντασία.*

IMAGINATION therefore is nothing else but *sense decaying*, or *weakened*, by the absence of the object. But what may be the cause of this decay or weakening? Is the motion the weaker, because the object is taken away? If it were, then phantasms would always and necessarily be less clear in the imagination, than they are in sense; which is not true. For in dreams, which are the imaginations of those that sleep, they are no less clear than in sense itself. But the reason why in men waking the phantasms of things past are more obscure than those of things present, is this, that their organs being at the same time moved by other present objects, those phantasms are the less predominant. Whereas in sleep, the passages being shut up, external action doth not at all disturb or hinder internal motion.

If this be true, the next thing to be considered, will be, whether any cause may be found out, from the supposition whereof it will follow, that the passage is shut up from the external objects of sense to the internal organ. I suppose, therefore, that by the continual action of objects, to which a reaction of the organ, and more especially of the spirits, is necessarily consequent, the organ is wearied, that is, its parts are no longer moved by the spirits without some pain; and consequently the nerves being abandoned and grown slack, they retire to their fountain, which is the cavity either of the brain or of the heart; by which means the action which proceeded by the nerves is necessarily intercepted. For action upon a patient, that retires from it, makes but little impression at the first; and at last, when the nerves are by little and little slackened, none at all. And therefore there is no more reaction, that is, no more sense, till the organ being refreshed by rest, and by a supply of new spirits recovering strength and motion, the sentient awaketh. And thus it seems to be always, unless some other preternatural cause intervene; as heat in the internal parts from lassitude, or from some disease stirring the spirits and other parts of the organ in some extraordinary manner.

8. Now it is not without cause, nor so casual a thing as many perhaps think it, that phantasms in this their great variety proceed from one another; and that the same phantasms sometimes bring into the mind other phantasms like themselves, and at other times extremely unlike. For in the

motion of any continued body, one part follows another by cohesion; and therefore, whilst we turn our eyes and other organs successively to many objects, the motion which was made by every one of them remaining, the phantasms are renewed as often as any one of those motions comes to be predominant above the rest; and they become predominant in the same order in which at any time formerly they were generated by sense. So that when by length of time very many phantasms have been generated within us by sense, then almost any thought may arise from any other thought; insomuch that it may seem to be a thing indifferent and casual, which thought shall follow which. But for the most part this is not so uncertain a thing to waking as to sleeping men. For the thought or phantasm of the desired end brings in all the phantasms, that are means conducing to that end, and that in order backwards from the last to the first, and again forwards from the beginning to the end. But this supposes both appetite, and judgment to discern what means conduce to the end, which is gotten by experience; and experience is store of phantasms, arising from the sense of very many things. For Φανταζεσθαι and *meminisse*, *fancy* and *memory*, differ only in this, that memory supposeth the time past, which fancy doth not. In memory, the phantasms we consider are as if they were worn out with time; but in our fancy we consider them as they are; which distinction is not of the things themselves, but of the considerations of the sentient. For there is in memory something like that which happens in looking upon things at a great distance; in which as the small parts of the object are not discerned, by reason of their remoteness; so in memory, many accidents and places and parts of things, which were formerly perceived by sense, are by length of time decayed and lost.

The perpetual arising of phantasms, both in sense and imagination, is that which we commonly call discourse of the mind, and is common to men with other living creatures. For he that thinketh, compareth the phantasms that pass, that is, taketh notice of their likeness or unlikeness to one another. And as he that observes readily the likenesses of things of different natures, or that are very remote from one another, is said to have a good fancy; so he is said to have a good judgment, that finds out the unlikenesses or differences of things that are like one another. Now this observation of differences is not perception made by a common organ of sense, distinct from sense on perception properly so called, but is memory of the differences of particular phantasms remaining for some time; as the distinction between hot and lucid, is nothing else but the memory both of a heating, and of an enlightening object.

9. The phantasms of men that sleep, are *dreams*. Concerning which we are taught by experience these five things. First, that for the most part there is neither order nor coherence in them. Secondly, that we dream of nothing but what is compounded and made up of the phantasms of sense past. Thirdly, that sometimes they proceed, as in those that are drowsy, from the interruption of their phantasms by little and little, broken and altered through sleepiness; and sometimes also they begin in the midst of sleep. Fourthly, that they are clearer than the imaginations of waking men, except such as are made by sense itself, to which they are equal in clearness. Fifthly, that when we dream, we admire neither the places nor the looks of the things that appear to us. Now from what hath been said, it is not hard to show what may be the causes of these phenomena. For as for the first, seeing all order and coherence proceeds from frequent looking back to the end, that is, from consultation; it must needs be, that seeing in sleep we lose all thought of the end, our phantasms succeed one another, not in that order which tends to any end, but as it happeneth, and in such manner, as objects present themselves to our eyes when we look indifferently upon all things before us, and see them, not because we would see them, but because we do not shut our eyes; for then they appear to us without any order at all. The second proceeds from this, that in the silence of sense there is no new motion from the objects, and therefore no new phantasm, unless we call that new, which is compounded of old ones, as a chimera, a golden mountain, and the like. As for the third, why a dream is sometimes as it were the continuation of sense, made up of broken phantasms, as in men distempered

with sickness, the reason is manifestly this, that in some of the organs sense remains, and in others it faileth. But how some phantasms may be revived, when all the exterior organs are benumbed with sleep, is not so easily shown. Nevertheless that, which hath already been said, contains the reason of this also. For whatsoever strikes the *pia mater*, reviveth some of those phantasms that are still in motion in the brain; and when any internal motion of the heart reacheth that membrane, then the predominant motion in the brain makes the phantasm. Now the motions of the heart are appetites and aversions, of which I shall presently speak further. And as appetites and aversions are generated by phantasms, so reciprocally phantasms are generated by appetites and aversions. For example, heat in the heart proceeds from anger and fighting; and again, from heat in the heart, whatsoever be the cause of it, is generated anger and the image of an enemy, in sleep. And as love and beauty stir up heat in certain organs; so heat in the same organs, from whatsoever it proceeds, often causeth desire and the image of an unresisting beauty. Lastly, cold doth in the same manner generate fear in those that sleep, and causeth them to dream of ghosts, and to have phantasms of horror and danger; as fear also causeth cold in those that wake. So reciprocal are the motions of the heart and brain. The fourth, namely, that the things we seem to see and feel in sleep, are as clear as in sense itself, proceeds from two causes; one, that having then no sense of things without us, that internal motion which makes the phantasm, in the absence of all other impressions, is predominant; and the other, that the parts of our phantasms which are decayed and worn out by time, are made up with other fictitious parts. To conclude, when we dream, we do not wonder at strange places and the appearances of things unknown to us, because admiration requires that the things appearing be new and unusual, which can happen to none but those that remember former appearances; whereas in sleep, all things appear as present.

But it is here to be observed, that certain dreams, especially such as some men have when they are between sleeping and waking, and such as happen to those that have no knowledge of the nature of dreams and are withal superstitious, were not heretofore nor are now accounted dreams. For the apparitions men thought they saw, and the voices they thought they heard in sleep, were not believed to be phantasms, but things subsisting of themselves, and objects without those that dreamed. For to some men, as well sleeping as waking, but especially to guilty men, and in the night, and in hallowed places, fear alone, helped a little with the stories of such apparitions, hath raised in their minds terrible phantasms, which have been and are still deceitfully received for things really true, under the names of *ghosts* and *incorporeal substances*.

10. In most living creatures there are observed five kinds of senses, which are distinguished by their organs, and by their different kinds of phantasms; namely, *sight*, *hearing*, *smell*, *taste*, and *touch*; and these have their organs partly peculiar to each of them severally, and partly common to them all. The organ of sight is partly animate, and partly inanimate. The inanimate parts are the three humours; namely, the watery humour, which by the interposition of the membrane called uvea, the perforation whereof is called the apple of the eye, is contained on one side by the first concave superficies of the eye, and on the other side by the ciliary processes, and the coat of the crystalline humour; the crystalline, which, hanging in the midst between the ciliary processes, and being almost of spherical figure, and of a thick consistence, is enclosed on all sides with its own transparent coat; and the vitreous or glassy humour, which filleth all the rest of the cavity of the eye, and is somewhat thicker then the watery humour, but thinner than the crystalline. The animate part of the organ is, first, the membrane *choroeides*, which is a part of the *pia mater*, saving that it is covered with a coat derived from the marrow of the optic nerve, which is called the *retina*; and this *choroeides*, seeing it is part of the *pia mater*, is continued to the beginning of the *medulla spinalis* within the scull, in which all the nerves which are within the head have their roots. Wherefore all the animal spirits that the nerves receive, enter into them there; for it is not imaginable that they can enter into them anywhere else.

Seeing therefore sense is nothing else but the action of objects propagated to the furthest part of the organ; and seeing also that animal spirits are nothing but vital spirits purified by the heart, and carried from it by the arteries; it follows necessarily, that the action is derived from the heart by some of the arteries to the roots of the nerves which are in the head, whether those arteries be the *plexus retiformis*, or whether they be other arteries which are inserted into the substance of the brain. And, therefore, those arteries are the complement or the remaining part of the whole organ of sight. And this last part is a common organ to all the senses; whereas, that which reacheth from the eye to the roots of the nerves is proper only to sight. The proper organ of hearing is the tympanum of the ear and its own nerve; from which to the heart the organ is common. So the proper organs of smell and taste are nervous membranes, in the palate and tongue for the taste, and in the nostrils for the smell; and from the roots of those nerves to the heart all is common. Lastly, the proper organ of touch are nerves and membranes dispersed through the whole body; which membranes are derived from the root of the nerves. And all things else belonging alike to all senses seem to be administered by the arteries, and not by the nerves.

The proper phantasm of sight is light; and under this name of light, colour also, which is nothing but perturbed light, is comprehended. Wherefore the phantasm of a lucid body is light; and of a coloured body, colour. But the object of sight, properly so called, is neither light nor colour, but the body itself which is lucid, or enlightened, or coloured. For light and colour, being phantasms of the sentient, cannot be accidents of the object. Which is manifest enough from this, that visible things appear oftentimes in places in which we know assuredly they are not, and that in different places they are of different colours, and may at one and the same time appear in divers places. Motion, rest, magnitude, and figure, are common both to the sight and touch; and the whole appearance together of figure, and light or colour, is by the Greeks commonly called εἶδος, and εἴδωλον, and ἰδέα; and by the Latins, *species* and *imago*; all which names signify no more but appearance.

The phantasm, which is made by hearing, is sound; by smell, odour; by taste, savour; and by touch, hardness and softness, heat and cold, wetness, oiliness, and many more, which are easier to be distinguished by sense than words. Smoothness, roughness, rarity, and density, refer to figure, and are therefore common both to touch and sight. And as for the objects of hearing, smell, taste, and touch, they are not sound, odour, savour, hardness, &c., but the bodies themselves from which sound, odour, savour, hardness, &c. proceed; of the causes of which, and of the manner how they are produced, I shall speak hereafter.

But these phantasms, though they be effects in the sentient, as subject, produced by objects working upon the organs; yet there are also other effects besides these, produced by the same objects in the same organs; namely certain motions proceeding from sense, which are called *animal motions*. For seeing in all sense of external things there is mutual action and reaction, that is, two endeavours opposing one another, it is manifest that the motion of both of them together will be continued every way, especially to the confines of both the bodies. And when this happens in the internal organ, the endeavour outwards will proceed in a solid angle, which will be greater, and consequently the idea greater, than it would have been if the impression had been weaker.

11. From hence the natural cause if manifest, first, why those things seem to be greater, which, *cæteris paribus*, are seen in a greater angle; secondly, why in a serene cold night, when the moon doth not shine, more of the fixed stars appear than at another time. For their action is less hindered by the serenity of the air, and not obscured by the greater light of the moon, which is then absent; and the cold, making the air more pressing, helpeth or strengtheneth the action of the stars upon our eyes; in so much as stars may then be seen which are seen at no other time. And this may suffice to be said in general concerning sense made by the reaction of the organ. For, as for the place of the image, the deceptions of sight, and other things of which we have experience in ourselves by sense, seeing they depend for the most part upon the fabric itself of the eye of man, I shall speak of them then when I come to speak of man.

12. But there is another kind of sense, of which I will say something in this place, namely, the sense of pleasure and pain, proceeding not from the reaction of the heart outwards, but from continual action from the outermost part of the organ towards the heart. For the original of life being in the heart, that motion in the sentient, which is propagated to the heart, must necessarily make some alteration or diversion of vital motion, namely, by quickening or slackening, helping or hindering the same. Now when it helpeth, it is pleasure; and when it hindereth, it is pain, trouble, grief, &c. And as phantasms seem to be without, by reason of the endeavour outwards, so pleasure and pain, by reason of the endeavour of the organ inwards, seem to be within; namely, there where the first cause of the pleasure or pain is; as when the pain proceeds from a wound, we think the pain and the wound are both in the same place.

Now vital motion is the motion of the blood, perpetually circulating (as hath been shown from many infallible signs and marks by Doctor Harvey,* the first observer of it) in the veins and arteries. Which motion, when it is hindered by some other motion made by the action of sensible objects, may be restored again either by bending or setting strait the parts of the body; which is done when the spirits are carried now into these, now into other nerves, till the pain, as far as is possible, be quite taken away. But if vital motion be helped by motion made by sense, then the parts of the organ will be disposed to guide the spirits in such manner as conduceth most to the preservation and augmentation of that motion, by the help of the nerves. And in animal motion this is the very first endeavour, and found even in the embryo; which while it is in the womb, moveth its limbs with voluntary motion, for the avoiding of whatsoever troubleth it, or for the pursuing of what pleaseth it. And this first endeavour, when it tends towards such things as are known by experience to be pleasant, is called *appetite*, that is, an approaching; and when it shuns what is troublesome, *aversion*, or flying from it. And little infants, at the beginning and as soon as they are born, have appetite to very few things, as also they avoid very few, by reason of their want of experience and memory; and therefore they have not so great a variety of animal motion as we see in those that are more grown. For it is not possible, without such knowledge as is derived from sense, that is, without experience and memory, to know what will prove pleasant or hurtful; only there is some place for conjecture from the looks or aspects of things. And hence it is, that though they do not know what may do them good or harm, yet sometimes they approach and sometimes retire from the same thing, as their doubt prompts them. But afterwards, by accustoming themselves by little and little, they come to know readily what is to be pursued and what to be avoided; and also to have a ready use of their nerves and other organs, in the pursuing and avoiding of good and bad. Wherefore appetite and aversion are the first endeavours of animal motion.

Consequent to this first endeavour, is the impulsion into the nerves and retraction again of animal spirits, of which it is necessary there be some receptacle or place near the original of the nerves; and this motion or endeavour is followed by a swelling and relaxation of the muscles; and lastly, these are followed by contraction and extension of the limbs, which is animal motion.

13. The considerations of appetites and aversions are divers. For seeing living creatures have sometimes appetite and sometimes aversion to the same thing, as they think it will either be for their good or their hurt; while that vicissitude of appetites and aversions remains in them, they have that series of thoughts which is called *deliberation*; which lasteth as long as they have it in their power to obtain that which pleaseth, or to avoid that which displeaseth them. Appetite, therefore, and aversion are simply so called as long as they follow not deliberation. But if deliberation have gone before, then the last act of it, if it be appetite, is called *will*; if aversion, *unwillingness*. So that the same thing is called both will and appetite; but the consideration of them, namely, before and after deliberation, is divers. Nor is that which is done within a man whilst he willeth any thing, different from that which is done in other living creatures, whilst, deliberation having preceded, they have appetite.

Neither is the freedom of willing or not willing, greater in man, than in other living creatures. For where there is appetite, the entire cause of appetite hath preceded; and, consequently, the act of appetite could not choose but follow, that is, hath of necessity followed (as is shown in chapter IX, article 5). And therefore such a liberty as is free from necessity, is not to be found in the will either of men or beasts. But if by liberty we understand the faculty or power, not of willing, but of doing what they will, then certainly that liberty is to be allowed to both, and both may equally have it, whensoever it is to be had.

Again, when appetite and aversion do with celerity succeed one another, the whole series made by them hath its name sometimes from one, sometimes from the other. For the same deliberation, whilst it inclines sometimes to one, sometimes to the other, is from appetite called *hope*, and from aversion, *fear*. For where there is no hope, it is not to be called fear, but *hate*; and where no fear, not hope, but *desire*. To conclude, all the passions, called passions of the mind, consist of appetite and aversion, except pure pleasure and pain, which are a certain fruition of good or evil; as anger is aversion from some imminent evil, but such as is joined with appetite of avoiding that evil by force. But because the passions and perturbations of the mind are innumerable, and many of them not to be discerned in any creatures besides men; I will speak of them more at large in that section which is concerning *man*. As for those objects, if there be any such, which do not at all stir the mind, we are said to contemn them.

And thus much of sense in general. In the next place I shall speak of sensible objects.

THREE LIVES

THE BRIEF LIFE
JOHN AUBREY

AN ABSTRACT OF AUBREY'S NOTES

Introduction. The writers of the lives of the ancient philosophers used, in the first place, to speak of their lineage; and they tell us that in process of time several great families accounted it their glory to be branched from such or such a *Sapiens* [wise man].

Why now should that method be omitted in this *Historiola* [little history] of our Malmesbury philosopher? Who though but of plebeian descent, his renown has and will give brightness to his name and family, which hereafter may arise glorious and flourish in riches and may justly take it an honour to be of kin to this worthy person, so famous, for his learning, both at home and abroad.

His father. Thomas Hobbes, then, whose life I write, was second son of Mr Thomas Hobbes, vicar of Westport *juxta* Malmesbury, who married Middleton of Brokinborough (a yeomanly family). He was also vicar of Charlton (a mile hence): they are annexed, and are both worth £60 or £80 per annum. Thomas, the father, was one of the ignorant 'Sir Johns' of Queen Elizabeth's time; could only read the prayers of the church and the homilies; and disesteemed learning (his son Edmund told me so), as not knowing the sweetness of it.

His father's brother. He had an elder brother whose name was Francis, a wealthy man, and had been alderman of the borough; by profession a glover, which is a great trade here, and in times past much greater. Having no child, he contributed much to, or rather altogether maintained, his nephew Thomas at Magdalen Hall in Oxon.; and when he died gave him an *agellum* [a mowing-ground] called the Gastenground, lying near to the horse-fair, worth £16 or £18 per annum; the rest of his lands he gave to his nephew Edmund.

Place and date of his birth. Thomas Hobbes, *Malmes-*

buriensis, *philosophus*, was born at his father's house in Westport, being that extreme house that points into, or faces, the horse-fair; the farthest house on the left hand as you go to Tedbury, leaving the church on your right. To prevent mistakes, and that hereafter may rise no doubt what house was famous for this famous man's birth; I do here testify that in April 1659, his brother Edmund went with me into this house, and into the chamber where he was born. Now things begin to be antiquated, and I have heard some guess it might be at the house where his brother Edmund lived and died. But this is so, as I here deliver it. This house was given by Thomas, the vicar, to his daughter, whose daughter or granddaughter possessed it, when I was there. It is a firm house, stone-built and tiled, of one room (besides a buttery, or the like, within) below, and two chambers above. 'Twas in the innermost where he first drew breath.

The day of his birth was April the fifth, Anno Domini 1588, on a Friday morning, which that year was Good Friday. His mother fell in labour with him upon the fright of the invasion of the Spaniards [see 'Verse Life' p. 254].

His school and college life. At four years old he went to school in Westport church, till eight; by that time he could read well, and number four figures. Afterwards he went to school to Malmesbury, to Mr Evans, the minister of the town; and afterwards to Mr Robert Latimer, a young man of about nineteen or twenty, newly come from the University, who then kept a private school in Westport, where the broad place is, next door north from the smith's shop, opposite to the Three Cups (as I take it). He was a bachelor and delighted in his scholar, T.H.'s company, and used to instruct him, and two or three ingenious youths more, in the evening till nine a clock. Here T.H. so well profited in his learning, that at fourteen years of age, he went away a good school-scholar to Magdalen Hall, in Oxford. It is not to be forgotten, that before he went to the University, he had turned Euripides' *Medea* out of Greek into Latin iambics, which he presented to his master. Mr H. told me that he would fain have had them, to have seen how he did grow in [ability]. Twenty-odd years ago I searched all old Mr

Latimer's papers, but could not find them; the good house-wives had devoured them.

I have heard his brother Edmund and Mr Wayte (his schoolfellow) say that when he was a boy he was play-some enough, but withal he had even then a contemplative melancholyness; he would get him into a corner, and learn his lesson by heart presently. His hair was black, and his schoolfellows were wont to call him 'Crow'.

This Mr Latimer was a good Graecian, and the first that came into our parts hereabout since the Reformation. He was afterwards minister of Malmesbury, and from thence preferred to a better living.

At Oxford Mr T.H. used, in the summer-time especially, to rise very early in the morning, and would tie the leaden-counters (which they used in those days at Christmas, at post and pair) with strings, which he did besmear with birdlime, and bait them with parings of cheese, and the jackdaws would spy them a vast distance up in the air, and as far as Osney Abbey,* and strike at the bait, and so be harled in the string, which the weight of the counter would make cling about their wings. He did not much care for logic, yet he learned it, and thought himself a good disputant. He took great delight there to go to the bookbinders' shops, and lie gaping on maps, of which he takes notice in his life written by himself in verse [see p. 255].

He came to Magdalen Hall in the beginning of 1603, at what time, Dr James Hussey LL D was principal. This James Hussey was afterwards knighted by King James and was made Chancellor of Sarum. This Dr Hussey was a great encourager of towardly youths. But he resigning his princi-pality about 1605, Mr John Wilkinson succeeded him: so that Mr Hobbes was under the government of two principals— Thomas Hobbes was admitted to the reading of any book of logic (*ad lecrionem cujuslibet libri logices*), that is, he was admitted to the degree of Bachelor of Arts, 5 Feb., 1607, and in the Lent that then began did determine, that is, did his exercise for the completion of that degree.

Enters the Earl of Devonshire's service. After he had taken his Bachelor of Arts degree, the then principal of Magdalen

Hall (Sir James Hussey) recommended him to his young lord* when he left Oxon., who did believe that he should profit more in his learning if he had a scholar of his own age to wait on him than if he had the information of a grave doctor. He was his lordship's page, and rode a-hunting and hawking with him, and kept his privy purse.

By this way of life he had almost forgot his Latin. He therefore bought him books of an Amsterdam print that he might carry in his pocket (particularly Caesar's *Commentaries*), which he did read in the lobby, or antechamber, whilst his lord was making his visits.

Is servant to Frances Bacon. The Lord Chancellor Bacon loved to converse with him. He assisted his lordship in translating several of his Essays into Latin, one, I well remember, was the *Of the Greatness of Cities*: the rest I have forgot. His lordship was a very contemplative person, and was wont to contemplate in his delicious walks at Gorambery, and dictate to Mr Thomas Bushell, or some other of his gentlemen, that attended him with ink and paper ready to set down presently his thoughts. His lordship would often say that he better liked Mr Hobbes's taking his thoughts, than any of the other, because he understood what he wrote, which the others not understanding, my lord would many times have hard task to make sense of what they writ.

It is to be remembered that about these times, Mr T.H. was much addicted to music, and practised on the bass viol.

Visits his native county, Wiltshire. 1634: this summer—I remember 'twas in venison season (July or August)—Mr T.H. came into his native country to visit his friends, and amongst others he came then to see his old schoolmaster, Mr Robert Latimer, at Leigh-de-la-mer, where I was then at school in the church, newly entered into my grammar by him. Here was the first place and time that ever I had the honour to see this worthy, learned man, who was then pleased to take notice of me and the next day visited my relations. He was then a proper man brisk, and in very good habit. His hair was then quite black. He stayed at

Malmesbury and in the neighbourhood a week or better. 'Twas the last time that ever he was in Wiltshire.

His mathematical studies. He was (*vide* his life) 40 years old before he looked on geometry; which happened accidentally. Being in a gentleman's library, Euclid's *Elements* lay open, and 'twas the 47th Element [i.e. proposition] at Book I. He read the proposition. 'By G——,' said he, 'this is impossible!' So he reads the demonstration of it, which referred him back to such a proposition; which proposition he read. *Et sic deinceps* [and so on], that at last he was demonstratively convinced of that truth. This made him in love with geometry.

I have heard Sir Jonas Moore (and others) say that 'twas a great pity he had not began the study of the mathematics sooner, for such a working head would have made great advancement in it. So had he done he would not have lain so open to his learned mathematical antagonists. But one may say of him, as one says of Jos Scaliger,* that where he errs, he errs so ingeniously, that one had rather err with him than hit the mark with Clavius.* I have heard Mr Hobbes say that he was wont to draw lines on his thigh and on the sheets, abed, and also multiply and divide. He would often complain that algebra (though of great use) was too much admired, and so followed after, that it made men not contemplate and consider so much the nature and power of lines, which was a great hindrance to the growth of geometry; for that though algebra did surely well and quickly, and easily in right lines, yet 'twould not *bite* in *solid* (I think) geometry.

Memorandum—After he began to reflect on the interest of the King of England as touching his affairs between him and the Parliament, for ten years together his thoughts were much, or almost altogether, unhinged from the mathematics; but chiefly intent on his *De Cive*, and after that on his *Leviathan*: which was a great put-back to his mathematical improvement—for in ten years' (or better) discontinuance of that study (especially) one's mathematics will become very rusty.

Memorandum: he told me that Bishop Manwaring (of St David's) preach'd *his doctrine*; for which, among others, he was sent prisoner to the Tower. Then thought Mr Hobbes, 'tis time now for me to shift for myself, and so withdrew into France, and resided at Paris. As I remember, there were others likewise did preach his doctrine. This little MS treatise [*The Elements of Law*] grew to be his book *De Cive*, and at last grew there to be the so formidable LEVIATHAN; the manner of writing of which book (he told me) was thus. He walked much and contemplated, and he had in the head of his cane a pen and ink-horn, carried always a notebook in his pocket, and as soon as a thought darted, he presently entered it into his book, or otherwise he might perhaps have lost it. He had drawn the design of the book into chapters, etc. so he knew whereabouts it would come in. Thus that book was made.

Residence in Paris. During his stay at Paris he went through a course of chemistry with Dr Davison; and he there also studied Vesalius' *Anatomy*.* This I am sure was before 1648; for that Sir William Petty (then Dr Petty, physician) studied and dissected with him.

Return to England. Anno 1650 or 51 he returned into England, and lived most part in London, in Fetter Lane, where he writ, or finished, his book *De Corpore*, in Latin and then in English; and writ his lessons against the two Savilian professors at Oxon.*

Residence in London. He was much in London till the Restoration of His Majesty, having here convenience not only of books, but of learned conversation, as Mr John Selden, Dr William Harvey, John Vaughan, etc., whereof anon in the catalogue [omitted] of his acquaintance.

I have heard him say, that at his lord's house in Derbyshire there was a good library, and books enough for him, and that his lordship stored the library with what books he thought fit to be bought; but he said, the want of learned conversation was a very great inconvenience, and that though he conceived he could order his thinking as well perhaps as another man, yet he found a great defect.

There was a report (and surely true) that in Parliament, not long after the King was settled, some of the bishops made a motion to have the good old gentleman burn't for a heretic. Which he hearing, feared that his papers might be search't by their order, and he told me he had burn't part of them.—I have received word from his amanuensis and executor that he remembers there were such verses for he wrote them out, but knows not what became of them, unless he presented them to Judge Vaughan, or burned them.

Secures the protection of Charles II. 1660. The wintertime of 1659 he spent in Derbyshire. In March following was the dawning of the coming-in of our gracious sovereign, and in April the Aurora.

I then sent a letter to him in the country to advertise him of the advent of his master the King and desired him by all means to be in London before his arrival; and knowing His Majesty was a great lover of good painting I must needs presume he could not but suddenly see Mr Cowper's curious pieces, of whose fame he had so much heard abroad and seen some of his work, and likewise that he would sit to him for his picture, at which place and time he would have the best convenience of renewing His Majesty's graces to him. He returned me thanks for my friendly intimation and came to London in May following.

It happened, about two or three days after His Majesty's happy return, that, as he was passing in his coach through the Strand, Mr Hobbes was standing at Little Salisbury House gate (where his lord then lived). The King espied him, put off his hat very kindly to him, and asked him how he did. About a week after he had oral conference with His Majesty at Mr S. Cowper's, where, as he sat for his picture, he was diverted by Mr Hobbes's pleasant discourse. Here His Majesty's favours were redintegrated* to him, and order was given that he should have free access to His Majesty, who was always much delighted in his wit and smart repartees.

The wits at Court were wont to bait him. But he feared none of them, and would make his part good. The King would call him *the bear*: 'Here comes the bear to be baited!'

Repartees. He was marvellous happy and ready in his replies, and that without rancour (except provoked)—but now I speak of his readiness in replies as to wit and drollery. He would say that he did not care to give, neither was he adroit at, a present answer to a serious question: he had as lief they should have expected an extemporary solution to an arithmetical problem, for he turned and winded and compounded in philosophy, politics, etc., as if he had been at analytical work. He always avoided, as much as he could, to conclude hastily (*Human Nature*, I. 2).

Re-enters the household of the Earl of Devonshire. Memorandum—from 1660 till the time he last went into Derbyshire, he spent most of his time in London at his lord's (viz. at Little Salisbury House; then, Queen Street; lastly, Newport House), following his contemplation and study. He contemplated and invented (set down a hint with a pencil or so) in the morning, but compiled in the afternoon. 1675, he left London *cum animo nunquam revertendi*, and spend the remainder of his days in Derbyshire with the Earl of Devonshire at Chatsworth and Hardwick, in contemplation and study.

Personal characteristics. Mr Hobbes's person, etc.:— hazel, quick eye, which continued to his last. He was a tall man, higher than I am by about half a head, i.e. I could put my hand between my head and his hat.—When young he loved music and practised on the lute. In his old age he used to sing prick-song every night (when all were gone and sure nobody could hear him) for his health, which he did believe would make him live two or three years longer.

His lord,* who was a waster, sent him up and down to borrow money, and to get gentlemen to be bound for him, being ashamed to speak himself: he took colds, being wet in his feet (then were no hackney coaches to stand in the streets), and trod both his shoes aside the same way. Notwithstanding he was well-beloved: they loved his company for his pleasant facetiousness and good nature.

From forty, or better, he grew healthier, and then he had a fresh, ruddy, complexion. He was *sanguineo-melancholicus*; which the physiologers say is the most ingenious complexion. He would say that 'there might be good wits of all complexions; but good-natured, impossible'.

Head. In his old age he was very bald (which claimed a veneration); yet within door, he used to study, and sit, bare-

headed, and said he never took cold in his head, but that
the greatest trouble was to keep off the flies from pitching
on the baldness. His head was ... inches in compass (I
have the measure), and of a mallet form (approved by the
physiologers).

Skin. His skin was soft and of that kind which my Lord
Chancellor Bacon in his *History of Life and Death* calls a
goose-skin, i.e. of a wide texture:—*Crassa cutis, crassum
cerebrum, crassum ingenium.**

Face. Not very great; ample forehead; whiskers yellowish-
reddish, which naturally turned up—which is a sign of a
brisk wit, e.g. James Howell, Henry Jacob of Merton College. Below he was shaved close, except a little tip under
his lip. Not but that nature could have afforded a venerable beard, but being naturally of a cheerful and pleasant
humour, he affected not at all austerity and gravity and to
look severe. He desired not the reputation of his wisdom to be taken from the cut of his beard, but from his
reason.

Eye. He had a good eye, and that of a hazel colour,
which was full of life and spirit, even to the last. When he
was earnest in discourse, there shone (at it were) a bright
live-coal within it. He had two kind of looks:—when he
laughed, was witty, and in a merry humour, one could
scarce see his eyes; by and by, when he was serious and
positive, he opened his eyes round (i.e. his eyelids). He had
middling eyes, not very big, nor very little.

Stature. He was six foot high, and something better, and
went indifferently erect, or rather, considering his great age,
very erect.

Sight; wit. His sight and wit continued to the last. He had
a curious sharp sight, as he had a sharp wit, which was also
so sure and steady (and contrary to that men call *broadwitted-
ness*) that I have heard him oftentimes say that in multiply-
ing and dividing he never mistook a figure: and so in other
things.

His books. He had very few books. I never saw (nor
Sir William Petty) above half a dozen about him in his
chamber. Homer and Virgil were commonly on his table;

sometimes Xenophon, or some probable history, and Greek Testament, or so.

Reading. He had read much, if one considers his long life; but his contemplation was much more than his reading. He was wont to say that if he had read as much as other men, he should have known no more than other men.

His physic. He seldom used any physic. What 'twas I have forgot, but will enquire of Mr Shelbrooke his apothecary at the Black Spread-eagle in the Strand. Memorandum—Mr Hobbes was very sick and like to die at Bristol House in Queen Street, about 1668. He was wont to say that he had rather have the advice, or take physic from an experienced old woman, that had been at many sick people's bedsides, than from the learnedest but unexperienced physician.

Temperance and diet. He was, even in his youth, (generally) temperate, both as to wine and women. I have heard him say that he did believe he had been in excess in his life, a hundred times; which, considering his great age, did not amount to above once a year. When he did drink, he would drink to excess to have the benefit of vomiting, which he did easily; by which benefit neither his wit was disturbed longer than he was spewing nor his stomach oppressed; but he never was, nor could not endure to be, habitually a good fellow, i.e. to drink every day wine with company, which, though not to drunkenness, spoils the brain.

For his last 30+ years, his diet, etc., was very moderate and regular. After sixty he drank no wine, his stomach grew weak, and he did eat most fish, especially whitings, for he said he digested fish better than flesh. He rose about seven, had his breakfast of bread and butter; and took his walk, meditating till ten; then he did put down the minutes of his thoughts, which he penned in the afternoon.

He had an inch-thick board about 16 inches square, whereon paper was pasted. On this board he drew his lines (schemes). When a line came into his head, he would, as he was walking, take a rude memorandum of it, to preserve it in his memory till he came to his chamber. He was never idle; his thoughts were always working.

His dinner was provided for him exactly by eleven, for he

could not now stay till his lord's hour—that is about two: that his stomach could not bear.

After dinner he took a pipe of tobacco, and then threw himself immediately on his bed, with his band* off, and slept (took a nap of about half an hour). In the afternoon he penned his morning thoughts.

Exercises. Besides his daily walking, he did twice or thrice a year play at tennis (at about 75 he did it); then went to bed there and was well rubbed. This he did believe would make him live two or three years the longer. In the country, for want of a tennis-court, he would walk uphill and downhill in the park, till he was in a great sweat, and then give the servant some money to rub him.

Prudence. He gave to his amanuensis, James Wheldon (the Earl of Devon's baker; who writes a delicate hand), his pension at Leicester, yearly, to wait on him, and take a care of him, which he did perform to him living and dying with great respect and diligence: for which consideration he made him his executor.

Habit. In cold weather he commonly wore a black velvet coat, lined with fur; if not, some other coat so lined. But all the year he wore a kind of boots* of Spanish leather, laced or tied along the sides with black ribbons.

Singing. He had always books of prick-song lying on his table:—e.g. of H. Lawes' etc. *Songs*—which at night, when he was abed, and the doors made fast, and was sure nobody heard him, he sang aloud (not that he had a very good voice) but for his health's sake: he did believe it did his lungs good and conduced much to prolong his life.

Shaking palsy. He had the shaking palsy in his hands; which began in France before the year 1650, and has grown upon him by degrees, ever since, so that he had not been able to write very legibly since 1665 or 1666, as I find by some of his letters to me.

His readiness to help with advice and money. His goodness of nature and willingness to instruct any one that was willing to be informed and modestly desired it, which I am a witness of as to my own part and also to others.

Charity. His brotherly love to his kindred hath already

been spoken of. He was very charitable (*pro suo modulo*)*
to those that were true objects of his bounty. One time, I
remember, going in the Strand, a poor and infirm old man
craved his alms. He, beholding him with eyes of pity and
compassion, put his hand in his pocket, and gave him 6*d*.
Said a divine (that Dr Jaspar Mayne) that stood by—'Would
you have done this, if it had not been Christ's command?'—
'Yea,' said he.—'Why?' quoth the other.—'Because,' said
he, 'I was in pain to consider the miserable condition of the
old man; and now my alms, giving him some relief, doth
also ease me.'

Aspersions and envy. His work was attended with envy,
which threw several aspersions and false reports on him. For
instance, one (common) was that he was afraid to lie alone
at night in his chamber, (I have often heard him say that he
was not afraid of *sprites*, but afraid of being knocked on the
head for five or ten pounds, which rogues might think he
had in his chamber); and several other tales, as untrue.

I have heard some positively affirm that he had a yearly
pension from the King of France,—possibly for having asserted such a monarchy as the King of France exercises, but
for what other grounds I know not, unless it be for that the
present King of France is reputed an encourager of choice
and able men in all faculties who can contribute to his
greatness. I never heard him speak of any such thing; and,
since his death, I have inquired of his most intimate friends
in Derbyshire, who write to me they never heard of any
such thing. Had it been so, he, nor they, ought to have been
ashamed of it, and it had been becoming the munificence of
so great a prince to have done it.

Atheism. For his being branded with atheism, his writings
and virtuous life testify against it. And that he was a Christian 'tis clear, for he received the sacrament of Dr [John]
Pierson, and in his confession to Dr John Cosins, at . . . , on
his (as he thought) death-bed,* declared that he liked the
religion of the Church of England best of all other. He
would have the worship of God performed with music.

Verses by him. The love verses he made not long before
his death:—

1

Tho' I am now past ninety, and too old
T' expect preferment in the court of Cupid,
And many winters made me ev'n so cold
I am become almost all over stupid,

2

Yet I can love and have a mistress too,
As fair as can be and as wise as fair;
And yet not proud, nor anything will do
To make me of her favour to despair.

3

To tell you who she is were very bold;
But if i' th' character your self you find
Think not the man a fool tho he be old
Who loves in body fair a fairer mind.

Now as he had [many] learned friends, so he had many
enemies (though undeserved; for he would not provoke, but
if provoked, he was sharp and bitter): and as a prophet is
not esteemed in his own country, so he was more esteemed
by foreigners than by his countrymen.

His death. To my highly honoured friend, John Aubrey,
Esq., this humbly present:

Hardwick, January the 16th, 1680

Worthy Sir,

Having been abroad about business for some days, I received, at
my coming home, your letter of the third of this month, which
evidences the great esteem you have for Mr Hobbes, for which I
return you my humble thanks, and particularly for the pains you
have been pleased to take in the large account of what you yourself,
Mr Anthony a Wood, and Sir George Ent design for Mr Hobbes
his honour.

I am glad Mr Crooke has received his Life in Prose, which was
the only thing Mr Halleley got possession of, and sent it to him by
my hand. Mr Halleley tells me now, that Mr Hobbes (in the time of
his sickness) told him he had promised it to Mr Crooke, but said he
was unwilling it should ever be published as written by himself; and
I believe it was some such motive, which made him burn those
Latin verses Mr Crooke sent him about that time.

For those Latin verses you mention about ecclesiastical power, I remember them, for I writ them out, but know not what became of them, unless he presented them to Judge Vaughan, or burned them, as you seem to intimate.

He fell sick about the middle of October last. His disease was the strangury,* and the physicians judged it incurable by reason of his great age and natural decay. About the 20th of November, my Lord being to remove from Chatsworth to Hardwick, Mr Hobbes would not be left behind; and therefore with a feather bed laid into the coach, upon which he lay warm-clad, he was conveyed safely, and was in appearance as well after that little journey as before it. But seven or eight days after, his whole right side was taken with the dead palsy, and at the same time he was made speechless. He lived after this seven days, taking very little nourishment, slept well, and by intervals endeavoured to speak, but could not. In the whole time of his sickness he was free from fever. He seemed therefore to die rather for want of fuel of life (which was spent in him) and mere weakness and decay, than by the power of his disease, which was thought to be only an effect of his age and weakness. He was born the 5th of April, in the year 1588, and he died the 4th of December 1679. He was put into a woollen shroud and coffin, which was covered with a white sheet, and upon that a black hearse-cloth, and so carried upon men's shoulders, a little mile to church. The company, consisting of the family and neighbours that came to his funeral, and attended him to his grave, were very handsomely entertained with wine, burned and raw, cake, biscuit, etc. He was buried in the parish church of Hault Hucknall, close adjoining to the rail of the monument of the grandmother of the present Earl of Devonshire, with the service of the Church of England by the minister of the parish. It is intended to cover his grave with a stone of black marble as soon as it can be got ready, with a plain inscription of his name, the place of his birth, and the time of that and of his death.

As to his will, it is sent up to London to be proved there, and by the copy of it, which I here send you, I believe you will judge it fit to make no mention of it in what you design to get written by way of commentary on his life.

As for the palsy in his hands, it began in France, before the year 1650, and has grown upon him by degrees ever since; but Mr Halleley remembers not how long it has disabled him to write legibly.

Mr Halleley never heard of a pension from the French King and believes there was no such thing ever intended. He desires you to accept of his thanks for your favourable remembrance of him, and of the return of his respects to you by me. And if hereafter you should want any thing which we know, that might contribute to the honour of Mr Hobbes's memory, upon the least notice, shall readily be imparted to you.

In the mean time, with much respect, I rest,

Sir, your much obliged and humble servant,

JAMES WHELDON.

Thomas Hobbes's life, by himself. This was the draft that Mr Hobbes first did leave in my hands, which he sent for about five years before he died, and wrote that which is printed in his Life in Latin by Dr Richard Blackburn which I lent to him and he was careless and not reminded it from the printer and so 'twas made waste paper of.

Memorandum. He hath no countryman living hath known him so long (1633) as myself, or any of his friends who doth know so much about him. When he had printed his translation of Thucydides [2nd edn. 1676] his life is writ by himself (at my request) in the third person, a copy whereof I have by me, to publish after his death if it please God I survive him:

THE PROSE LIFE
THOMAS HOBBES

A NEW TRANSLATION

Thomas Hobbes was born on the 5th April 1588, at Malmesbury in Wiltshire. Having already been introduced to Greek and Latin literature, he was sent to Oxford in his fourteenth year. He remained there for five years, undertaking exercises in the study of logic and Aristotelian physics.

Having left Oxford when he attained his twentieth year, he was received, on the recommendation of friends, into the household of Lord William Cavendish, Baron Hardwick, and (shortly afterwards) Earl of Devon. He served as tutor to the Earl's first-born son, an adolescent who was close to him in age, pleasing both the father and the son during that time with his diligence and his cheerfulness.

In the following year, while staying with his noble pupil in the Eternal City [Rome], he realized in the course of teaching that he had lost the greater part of his fluency in Greek and Latin.

Afterwards, travelling through Italy and France with his lord, he taught him the languages of those peoples, in order that he might have a better understanding of them. But in the meantime, he felt that his Greek and Latin were gradually slipping away from him. Seeing that intelligent men had little time for either the philosophy or logic (in which he had been held to be outstandingly proficient), he cast aside both of those empty disciplines, and determined to devote such time as was his own to the study of Greek and Latin.

Then, when he had returned to England, he applied himself with diligence to the historians and the poets (together with the commentaries of the best of the grammarians), not in order that he might write in a florid style, but rather in order that he might write well in Latin, and that he might find the appropriate strength in words and thought. This was in order that he might write prose which was clear and easy to read. Of all of the Greek historians, Thucydides was his source of particular delight. Gradually, in his own time, he translated the works of Thucydides into English. This work received considerable praise when it was published in 1628. In it the weaknesses and eventual failures of the Athenian democrats, together with those of their city state, were made clear.

In the same year, the Earl of Devon, whom he had served for twenty years, died, his father having died two years previously.

In the following year, which was 1629, having attained his own fortieth year, he was asked by that most noble of men, the Lord Gervase Clinton, whether he would be willing to accompany his adolescent son to France. He accepted this proposal. During that journey he began to study Euclid's *Elements*. There he read with the utmost diligence, delighting in his methodology, not only in relation to the theorems, but also in terms of his skilful reasoning.

In 1631 he was recalled to the household of the Countess of Devon, so that he might instruct her son, the Earl of Devon, who was then thirteen years of age, in polite letters. Three years later he accompanied his student to France and Italy, directing both his studies and his travels.

When he was staying in Paris, he began to investigate the principles of natural science. When he became aware of the variety of movement contained in the natural world, he first inquired as to the nature of these motions, to determine the ways in which they might effect the senses, the intellect, the imagination, together with the other natural properties. He communicated his findings on a daily basis to the Reverend Father Marin Mersenne, of the Order of the Minim Brothers, a scholar who was venerated as an outstanding exponent of all branches of philosophy.

He returned to England with his patron in 1637, and remained there, continuing to correspond with Mersenne on the natural sciences.

In the meantime, the Scots, who had deposed their bishops, favouring certain English ministers of religion who are called Presbyterians, took up arms against the King. Then that most notorious Parliament was summoned in England. Its sessions began on the 3rd November 1640. He understood, having consulted with some of those who were of the Parliament during the first three or four days of the session, that civil war was unavoidable. Fearing for his safety, he returned to France. There, in Paris, he became involved in scientific inquiry with Mersenne, Gassendi, and with other men who were all well known for their learning, and their vigour in reasoning—but not with those who are called philosophers, for, as is now apparent, many amongst them have been shown to be vacuous, trite, and corrupt.

While he remained in Paris, he wrote a short book called *De Cive*, which was published in 1646.* By this time there were amongst the Parliamentarians many who took the King's part, and they joined the Prince of Wales (who is now King) in Paris. He [Hobbes] was by then planning to stay on the estates of certain friends of his of the Languedoc nobility, and had already made arrangements to move, taking with him such things as were necessary for his work. However, on being recommended to the Prince of Wales as a teacher of mathematics, he decided to remain in Paris.

He subsequently occupied his spare time in writing the book which is now most well known, not only in England, but also in neighbouring countries, called *Leviathan*. It was seen through the press in England, in 1651, while he remained in Paris. In that work he described the right of kings in both spiritual and temporal terms, using both reason and the authority of sacred scripture. This was done so that it might be made clear to all that it was impossible to establish peace in the Christian world unless that doctrine was accepted, and unless a military force of considerable magnitude could compel cities and states to maintain that concord. He hoped that this work might convince his countrymen, especially those who had rejected the episcopacy, of its truth. He also wished at the same time to deal with theological matters in the text, because the administrative structures and powers of the Church were in abeyance, and of no importance. (This was the power to declare that certain doctrines were heretical. It subverted the power of the King, for when it was exercised, the King's own power was lessened proportionally.) However, he took great care not to write in any way against the sense of sacred scripture, or against the doctrines of the Church in England, as established by royal authority prior to the outbreak of the war. Then as now, he had always preferred ecclesiastical government by bishops to all other forms of administration, as he made clear on two separate occasions.

In the first instance, when [1647] he fell seriously ill in the town of Saint Germain, which is close to Paris, Mersenne came to him, to plead with him on the basis of their common friendship, and to persuade him that he should no longer remain outside the Church of Rome. After some words of comfort, he concluded an exposition on the power of the Church of Rome to forgive any sins, regardless of their nature and severity. Hobbes then responded. 'Father,' he

said, 'although you have acted in good faith, I have already
disproved all of these contentions, although that disputation
is now attacked—when will you be seeing Gassendi?' Afterwards, Mersenne sent word of this conversation to Gassendi.
In the following days, Dr John Cosin (who since became)
Bishop of Durham, came to pray with him and administer
the Communion. Hobbes reacted to this offer with gratitude.
'Yes,' he replied, 'if it shall be done in accordance with the
rites of our Church.' This was signal proof of his reverence
for episcopal power and governance.

In 1651 copies of this book [*Leviathan*], which was published in London, were sent into France, where certain
English theologians condemned doctrines contained in the
text as being heretical, and in opposition to the King's
interest. These calumnies gained wide acceptance, with the
result that he was banished from the King's household.
Stripped of the King's protection, and fearing malicious
attacks by Roman clerics whose teachings he had successfully
attacked, he had little option other than to take refuge in
England.

Returning to England, he found that the Church, as
governed by the Assembly, was full of sedition; there were
unauthorized prayers, and daring which amounted to blas-
phemy; there were no visible symbols of the faith, no reference to the Decalogue, so that, for the first three months,
he was unable to find anyone with whom he could com
municate on sacred matters. At length he was taken by a
friend of his to a church which was more than a mile distant
from his house, where the pastor was a good and learned
man, who administered the Lord's Supper in accordance
with the rites of the Church, from whom he could accept
Communion. This was yet another indication that no man
might take the part of the episcopacy unless he was a sincere
Christian, for in those times most men sought to alter the
laws of the Church. Why, then, would any bishop have
cause to attack Hobbes, unless he were incited by pride to
dissent with him?

In the meantime his doctrines were condemned by almost
all academics and ecclesiastics, but they were praised by

noblemen, and by learned men amongst the laity. No man was able to refute him: those who sought to make such refutation, merely confirmed his tenets. Furthermore, he wrote not merely to be read and heard by scholars, but in order that he might be understood by all thinking men of sound judgement, in prose that was simple and direct, not in rhetoric. Poised as it were in equilibrium between friends and enemies, his doctrines were neither whole-heartedly accepted, nor yet oppressed. Meanwhile, as his analysis became better known, he was with his patron, the Earl of Devon, whose hospitality he enjoyed throughout his life, occupying his spare time in work on geometry and the philosophy of natural science. He edited and revised a book which he had written some years previously called *De Corpore*, dealing with the principles of logic, geometry, physics (both sublunary and celestial), deducing in logic certain premisses of significance, and in geometry and physics natural effects from figures and models.

Therefore I do not write and publish the life of a man in terms of his business, or his involvement in matters of peace and war, but rather in terms of his excellence and virtual singularity in all branches of science. When his abilities became known (as has already been demonstrated), innumerable men gathered about him, both from our own country and from foreign parts, and amongst those who came were the emissaries of princes, as well as others of the highest nobility. It may reasonably be supposed that learned men as yet unborn, and that posterity, will be grateful for this transmission of the text of his life. They will first wish to understand his involvement in the sciences, and then something of the nature of his life.

Above all I recognize and value that which he has written on the natural law, concerning the organization of states, the rights of those who exercise supreme power, and of civil office, in the books *Leviathan* and *De Cive* (which are known and well esteemed both here in England and abroad).

He first demonstrated the nature of the senses in physics. His discoveries of the principles of optics, natural light, the cause of reflection and refraction, had been unknown prior to their publication in his book *De Homine*. In this he also dealt with the perception of colour, sound, heat, and cold. Furthermore, he disproved popular fears concerning sleep and dreams, that had previously been associated with spirits and apparitions of those who were dead. He determined the age of the seas and their derivation of gravity from the motions of the earth. He related all phenomena to motion, but not in terms of the intrinsic power of matter itself, nor yet in terms of hidden qualities, but rather in terms of physics. He wrote most comprehensively and thoroughly on motion in his work *De Corpore*.

Prior to his work, nothing had been written in ethics concerning common or vulgar feelings. But he deduced the customs and practices of men from human nature, virtues and vices from natural law, and good or malicious actions from the laws of states. In mathematics he amended certain principles of geometry, resolving some of the most difficult problems, at the heart of that discipline (which had remained unresolved from the beginnings of geometry), as a result of his careful scrutiny, to wit the following—

1. That the arc of a circle rectilinearally determined divided the area of a circle into equal quadrants, was proved by him using various methods—in several books.
2. That any given angle may be divided in predetermined proportion;
3. Discovering the ratio between a cube and a sphere—in *Problematica Geometricis*.
4. Proving that the median between two lines at right angles maintains proportionality—in *Problematica Geometricis*.
5. Describing a regular polygon with any given number of sides—in *Rosetus*.
6. Establishing the centre of gravity of the quadrant of a circle, and of the two lines which contain the arc of the quadrant, and are dependent from it—in *Rosetus*.
7. Discovering the centre of gravity of all forms of parabola—in the book *De Corpore*.

He was the first to have construed and demonstrated these things, and very many others (which occur in his writings, and are of lesser importance), which I omit.

I am certain that the writing of this life will not be seen as a futile exercise, because it will be communicated both to foreigners, and to future students of science. That is of particular importance in these times, when the lives of obscure and unworthy men, lacking in virtue, tend to be written and popularized.

In or around his eightieth year he wrote a history of the English Civil War between King Charles and his Parliament; and also Latin verse, in two thousand stanzas, on the inordinate rise and growth of the power of the priesthood, but the nature of the times was such that they could not be published.

At length, once his adversaries were silenced, and in his eighty-first year, he edited Homer's *Odyssey*, translating it into English verse, and then, seven years later, he also translated the *Iliad*; and subsequently the *Cyclometria** in his ninety-first year. These had never before been edited as a single body of work.

Once he had attained this position, he preferred to be spoken well of, rather than to be an object of public curiosity. A portrait of him, painted from life when he was seventy, finely executed, is held in the private collection of King Charles the Second. Other portraits of him are extant. These were painted at various times, at the behest not least of his friends in England, but also at the behest of his friends in France.

Such were his inclinations that in his youth he was drawn to read history and poetry; and he himself composed verse, with a considerable degree of success (as many have judged). On a subsequent occasion, when he was in company with certain learned men, and discoursing on the nature of the senses, one of them, speaking contemptuously, asked him 'what might a sense be?' He no sooner heard this, than he responded, wondering how it might be possible that those who had the name of being wise men might so despise the judgement of their own senses, which in ignorance they were unwilling to acknowledge. From that time he devoted himself to determining the nature of the senses, disputing whether corporeal body and all its parts were inert, or in a state of continuous movement, and (in consequence) totally sensate. For that reason, he enquired into the diversity of motion: and this principle is of primary importance. Then, when he had determined the varieties and causes of motion, he turned to geometry and, from his own knowledge and ingenuity, demonstrated those theorems that are listed above, and for which he will always be justly famous. These matters are of importance to those who esteem talent, and to those who shall, in future times, seek out the history of scientific writings in venerable archives.*

In familiar speech he was jocose, especially with those who came to dispute against him concerning that which he had published (which they were unable to refute) on the rights of supreme civil or ecclesiastical power. Nor did he employ more vehemence than was strictly necessary in debate.

He was an open-natured man. Amongst his numerous and powerful adversaries, his innocence outweighed their conspiracies.

He was held to be one of the most skilled of scientists,* and the most honest and forthright of men. It should therefore come as no surprise, given that he was also one of the most negligent of men when it came to managing money, that his personal circumstances were insecure, and did not extend beyond such stipends and benefices as he was given. But he was blessed in the open-handedness of his patrons, and particularly favoured by the generosity of King Charles the Second. That is how he passed through old age, well satisfied, and in easy circumstances.

THE VERSE LIFE
THOMAS HOBBES

A CONTEMPORARY TRANSLATION
(ANONYMOUS)

In Fifteen hundred eighty eight, Old Style,
When that Armada did invade our Isle,
Call'd the *Invincible*; whose Freight was then,
Nothing but Murd'ring Steel, and Murd'ring Men;
Most of which Navy was disperst, or lost,
And had the Fate to Perish on our Coast:
April the fifth (though now with Age outworn)
I'th' early Spring, I, a poor worm, was born.
In *Malmesbury* Baptiz'd, and Named there
By my own Father, then a Minister.
Many things worth relating had this Town;
And first, a Monastery of Renown,
And Castle, or two rather it may seem,
On a Hill seated, with a double Stream
Almost environ'd, from whence still are sent
Two Burgesses to sit in Parliament.
Here lie the Bones of Noble *Athelstane*,
Whose Stone-Effigies does there remain;
Who for reward gave them the Neighbouring Plains,
Which he had moistned with the Blood of *Danes*.
Here was the *Roman* Muse by *Adelm* brought,
Here also the first *Latin* Schole was taught.
My Native place I'm not asham'd to own;
Th'ill Times, and Ills born with me, I bemoan:
For Fame had rumour'd, that a Fleet at Sea,
Wou'd cause our Nations Catastrophe;
And hereupon it was my Mother Dear
Did bring forth Twins at once, both Me, and Fear.
For this, My Countries Foes I e'r did hate,
With calm Peace and my Muse associate.

Did Learn to speak Four Languages, to write
And read them too, which was my sole delight.
Six years i'th' *Greek* and *Latin* Tongue I spent,
And at Fourteen I was to *Oxford* sent;
And there of *Magd'len*-Hall admitted, I
My self to *Logick* first did then apply,
And sedulously I my Tutor heard,
Who Gravely Read, althou' he had no Beard.
Barbara, *Celarent*, *Darii*, *Ferio*, *Baralypton*,
These Modes hath the first Figure; then goes on
Cæsare, *Camestres*, *Festino*, *Baroco*, *Darapti*,
This hath of Modes the same variety.
Felapton, *Disamis*, *Datisi*, *Bocardo*, *Ferison*,*
These just so many Modes are look'd upon,
Which I, tho' slowly Learn, and then dispense
With them, and prove things after my own sense.
The *Physicks* read, and my Tutor Display'd,
How all Things were of Form and Matter made.
The Aëry Particles which make Forms we see,*
Both Visible and Audible, to be
Th'Effects of Sympathy, Antipathy,
And many things above my reach Taught me.
Therefore more pleasant studies I then sought,
Which I was formerly, tho' not well Taught.
My Phancie and my Mind divert I do,
With Maps Celestial and Terrestrial too.
Rejoyce t'accompany *Sol* cloath'd with Rays,
Know by what Art he measures out our Days;
How *Drake* and *Cavendish** a Girdle made
Quite round the World, what climates they survey'd;
And strive to find the smaller Cells of Men,
And painted Monsters in their unknown Den.
Nay there's a Fulness in Geography;
For Nature e'r abhor'd Vacuity.
Thus in due time took I my first Degree
Of Batchelor i'th' University.
Then *Oxford* left; serv'd *Ca'ndish* known to be
A Noble and Conspicuous Family.
Our College-Rector did me Recommend,

Where I most pleasantly my Days did spend.
Thus Youth Tutor'd a Youth; for he was still
Under Command, and at his Father's will:
Serv'd him full twenty years, who prov'd to be,
Not a Lord only, but a Friend to Me.
That my Life's sweetest Comfort was, and made
My Slumbers pleasant in Nights darkest shade.
Thus I at Ease did Live, of Books, whilst he
Did with all sorts supply my Library.
Then I our own Historians did peruse,
Greek, *Latin*, and Convers'd too with my Muse.
Homer and *Virgil*, *Horace*, *Sophocles*,
Plautus, *Euripides*, *Aristophanes*,
I understood, nay more; but of all these,
There's none that pleas'd me like *Thucydides*.
He says Democracy's a Foolish Thing,
Than a Republick Wiser is one King.
This Author I taught *English*, that even he
A Guide to Rhetoricians might be.
To Forrain Countries at that time did I
Travel, saw *France*, *Italy*, *Germany*.
This Debonaire Lord th'Earl of *Devonshire*,
I serv'd complete the space of twenty year.
His Life by Sickness Conquer'd, fled away,
T'exchange it for a better the last day.
But yet provided ere he di'd for me,
Who liv'd with little most contentedly.
I left my pleasant Mansion, went away
To *Paris*, and there eighteen Months* did stay,
Thence to be Tutor I'm cal'd back agen
To my Lord's Son, the Earl of *Devon* then.
This Noble Lord I did instruct when young,
Both how to Speak and Write and *Roman* Tongue;
And by what Arts the Rhetor deceives those
That are Illiterate;* taught him Verse and Prose;
The Mathematick Precepts too, with all
The Windings in the Globe Terrestrial;
The whole Design of Law, and how he must
Judge between that which Equal is and Just,

Seven years to him these Arts I did Explain:
He quickly Learnt, and firmly did retain.
We [studied all] this time in Books alone,
[So that] you'l take the World for to be one;
Travel'd through *Italy* and *France*, did view
The sweet Retirements of *Savoy* too.
Whether on Horse, in Coach, or Ship, still I
Was most Intent on my Philosophy.
One only thing i'th' World seem'd true to me,
Tho' several ways that Falsified be.
One only True Thing, the Basis of all
Those Things whereby we any Thing do call.
How Sleep does fly away, and what things still
By Opticks I can Multiply at will.
Phancie's Internal, th'Issue of our Brain,
Th'internal parts only Motion contain:
And he that studies Physicks first must know
What Motion is, and what Motion can do.*
To Matter, Motion, I my self apply,
And thus I spend my Time in *Italy*.
I scribbled nothing o'er, nor then e'r wrought;
I ever had a Mistriss that me taught.
Then leaving *Italy*, return we do
To *Paris*, and its stately Fabricks view.
Here with *Mersennus** I acquainted grew,
Shew'd him of Motion what I ever knew.
He both Prais'd and Approv'd it, and so, Sir,
I was Reputed a Philosopher.
Eight Months elaps'd, I return'd, and thought good
For to Connect what e'r I understood.
That Principles at second hand more clear,
By their Concatenation might appear.
To various Matter various Motion brings
Me, and the different Species of Things.
Man's inward Motions and his Thoughts to know,
The good of Government, and Justice too,
These were my Studies then,* and in these three
Consists the whole Course of Philosophy:
Man, Body, Citizen, for these I do

Heap Matter up, designing three Books too.
I'th' interim breaks forth a horrid War,
Injurious to my Study, and a Bar.
In the year sixteen hundred forty, then
Brake out a Sickness, whereof many Men
Of Learning, languishing, gave up their breath
At last, and yielded to impartial death.
Wherewith when seized, he reputed was
The Man that knew Divine and Humane Laws.
The War's now hot, I dread to see it so,
Therefore to *Paris* well-belov'd, I go.
Two years elaps'd, I published in Print
My Book *de Cive*; the new Matter in't
Gratifi'd Learned Men, which was the Cause
It was Translated, and with great Applause
By several Nations, and great Scholars read,
So that my Name was Famous, and far spread.
England in her sad Pangs of War, and those
Commend it too, whom I do most oppose.
But what's disadvantageous now, who wou'd,
Though it be Just, ever esteem it Good?
Then I four years spent to contrive which way
To Pen my Book *de Corpore*,* Night and Day;
Compare together each Corporeal Thing,
Think whence the known changes of Forms do spring.
Inquire how I compel this *Proteus* may,
His Cheats and Artifices to Display.
About this time *Mersennus* was (by Name)
A Friar Minorite, yet of Great Fame,
Learned, Wise, Good, whose single Cell might be
Prefer'd before an University.
To him all Persons brought what e'r they found
By Learning, if new Principle, or Ground,
In clear and proper Phrase, without the Dress
Of Gawdy Rhet'rick, Pride, Deceitfulness.
Which he imparts to th'Learned, who might there
Discuss them, or at leisure, any where.
Publish'd some Rare Inventions, to the Fame
Of their own Author, with each Authors Name.

About *Mersennus*, like an Axis, here
Each Star wheel'd round, as in its Orb or Sphere.
England, *Scotland*, and *Ireland* was the Stage
Of Civil War, and with its four years Rage,
Harras'd and wasted was; Perfidious Fate
Exil'd the Good, and Help'd the Profligate.
Nay, *Charles*, the Kingdom's Heir, attended then,
By a Retinue of Brave, Noble Men,
To *Paris* came, in hope Times might amend,
And Popular Fury once be at an end.
My Book *de Corpore* then I design'd
To write, all things being ready to my Mind.
But must desist: such Crimes and Sufferings I
Will not impute unto the Deity.
First I resolv'd Divine Laws to fulfil;
This by Degrees, and carefully I will.
My Prince's studies I then waited on,
But cou'd not constantly attend my own.
Then for six Months was sick; but yet at length,
Though very weak, I did recover strength,
And finish'd it in my own Mother-Tongue,
To be read for the good of old and young.
The Book at *London* Printed was, and thence,
Hath visited the Neighbouring Nations since;
Was Read by many a Great and Learned Man,
Known by its dreadful Name, LEVIATHAN.
This Book Contended with all Kings, and they
By any Title, who bear Royal sway.
In the mean time the King's sold by the *Scot*,
Murder'd by th'*English*, an Eternal Blot.*
King *Charles* at *Paris* who did then reside,
Had right to *England's* Scepter undeny'd.
A Rebel Rout the Kingdom kept in aw,
And rul'd the Giddy Rabble without Law,
Who boldly *Parliament* themselves did call,
Though but a poor handful of men in all.
Blood-thirsty Leeches, hating all that's good,
Glutted with Innocent and Noble Blood.
Down go the Miters, neither do we see

That they Establish the Presbytery.
Th'Ambition of the stateliest Clergie-Men,
Did not at all prevail in *England* then.
Hence many Scholars to the King did go,
Expel'd, Sad, Indigent, Burthensome too.
As yet my Studies undisturbed were,
And my Grand Climacterick* past one year.
When that Book was perus'd by knowing Men,
The Gates of *Janus* Temple opened then;
And they accus'd me to the King, that I
Seem'd to approve *Cromwel's* Impiety,
And Countenance the worst of Wickedness:
This was believ'd, and I appear'd no less
Than a Grand Enemy, so that I was for't
Banish'd both the King's Presence and his Court.
Then I began on this to Ruminate
On *Dorislaus*, and on *Ascham*'s* Fate,
And stood amazed, like a poor Exile,
Encompassed with Terrour all the while.
Nor cou'd I blame th'young King for his Assent
To those Intrusted with his Government.
Then home I came, not sure of safety there,
Though I cou'd not be safer any where.
Th'Wind, Frost, Snow sharp, with Age grown gray,
A plunging Beast, and most unpleasant way.
At *London*, lest I should appear a Spy,
Unto the State my self I did apply;
That done, I quietly retired to
Follow my Study, as I us'd to do.
A Parliament so cal'd did Govern here;
There was no Prelate then, nor Presbyter.
Nothing but Arms and Souldiers, one alone
Design'd to Rule, and *Cromwel* was that one.
What Royalist can there, or Man alive,
Blame my Defence o'th' Kings Prerogative?
All Men did scribble what they wou'd, Content
And yielding to the present Government.
My Book *de Corpore* through this Liberty
I wrote, which prov'd a constant War to me.

The Clergy at *Leviathan* repines,
And both of them oppos'd were by Divines.
For whilst I did inveigh gainst Papal Pride,
These, though Prohibited, were not deny'd
T'appear in Print: 'gainst my *Leviathan*
They rail, which made it read by many a man,*
And did confirm't the more; 'tis hop'd by me,
That it will last to all Eternity.
'Twill be the Rule of Justice, and severe
Reproof of those that Men Ambitious are.
The King's Defence and Guard, the peoples Good,
And satisfaction, read, and understood.
I, two years after, Print a Book to show
How every Reader may himself well know.
Where I Teach Ethicks, the Phantômes of Sense,
How th'Wise with Spectres, fearless may dispense.
Publish'd my Book *de Corpore* withal,
Whose Matter's wholly Geometrical.
With great Applause the *Algebrists* then read
Wallis his *Algebra* now Published.
A Hundred years that Geometrick Pest
Ago began, which did that Age Infest.
The Art of finding out the Numbers sought,
Which *Diophantus* once, and *Gheber* Taught:
And then *Vieta** tells you that by this,
Each Geometrick Problem solved is.
*Suvil** the *Oxford* Reader did supply
Wallis with Principles Noble and High,
That Infinite had end, and Finite shou'd
Have parts, but yet those without end allow'd.
Both which Opinions did Enrage and Scare
All those who Geometricasters were.
This was enough to set me Writing, who
Was then in years no less than Seaventy two,
And in Six Dialogues* I do Inveigh
Against that new and Geometrick way,
But to no purpose, Great Men it doth please,
And thus the Med'cine yields to the Disease.
I Printed then two Treatises* that stung

The Bishop *Bramhal*, in our Mother-Tongue.
The Question at that Time was, and is still,
Whether at God's, or our own Choice We Will.
And this was the Result proceeding thence,
He the Schools follow'd, I made use of Sense.
Six Problems,* not long after, Publish'd I,
A Tract but small, yet pure Philosophy.
Wherein I Teach how Nature does cast down
All weighty Bodies, and huge massy Stone:
How Vapors are exhaled by the Sun;
How Winds engender Cold, when that is done:
The reason of their Levity, and how
The Barren Clouds do hang on Heaven's Brow;
How move, and when that they are pregnant grown
With Moisture, do in violent Showers pour down.
By what Cement hard Matter is conjoyn'd,
And how Hard Things grow Soft, the Cause do find:
Whence Lightning, Snow, Ice do proceed, and Thunder,
Breaking through wat'ry Clouds, even to wonder:
How Loadstones Iron attract: how, and which way
They th'Arctick and Antarctick Poles obey.
Why from the Sea unequal Waves do glide,
I'th' Year, or Month, each Day a double Tide;
And why a Ship doth Sail against the Wind,
In that small Treatise all these things you find,
Which may in time tread with applause the Stage,
As yet unblam'd in such a Carping Age.
The Nature of the Air I do discry
In a small Volume; and most pithily,
Compos'd on purpose for to obviate
An Inanisick Machin form'd of late.
Then, leaving *Physicks*, I return again
To my Beloved *Mathematick* strain:
For now the Barb'rous, Bloody Enemy
Had left the place, where my Estate did ly.
The Truth I cou'd not Teach; for none but Fools
May hope t'Instruct in their declaming Schools.
Another Book of Principles I Print,
Nothing cou'd be more clear than what was in't.

Whereby the Nature of Proportion is
Explain'd so fully, none can say amiss.
Upon this Subject most agreed that I
Of every one had gain'd the Victory;
Others seem in it to find Errors store,
But they are crazy grown, and I the more
Press upon them; then do ascend the high
And lofty Summet of Geometry.*
The Circles Quadrature I publish then;
The *Pythian* God's *Porisma* Teach all Men.
By a new Method I thought to o'rcome,
Though not by the same Reasons neither, some
O'th' Former Demonstrations, but in vain.
Mathematicians Half-Witted complain,
Who blush for to Subscribe; but I'll not lose
My Labour any longer, thinking those
Indocil Brutes will ever master Sense,
Or with good Literature ever dispense.
Then my *Rosetum** was put forth, which I
Stor'd with Rare Flowers of Geometry.
Wallis opposes, and I lost the day,
As both *Divines* and *Algebrists* do say.
The Army then Discamp'd, and gone, thereby
Wallis of nothing thinks, but Victory;
Who having chosen an unpleasant Field,
Which Thick and Troublesome deep Roots did yield,
Liking the Combat, I turn, scatter quite
All in a moment, Numbers Infinite.
These were my Wars; what more have I to say?
Now Rich am I, that is, how wise, I pray?
No matter for my Money or my Land;
If any ask that, let him understand,
A small parcel of Ground I had to show,
My own Inheritance, and let him know,
That This I on my Brother did bestow:
Of small Extent, but a most Fertil Ground,
Which did with store of bladed Wheat abound
Fit for a Prince; and had not ev'ry thing
Run cross, I had been counted a great King.

When I the Civil War approaching find,
And people led by every breath of wind,
I sought than this a more commodious place
To live and study in, and that *Paris* was.
Stock'd with five hundred pounds of Coin before
I did desert, or leave my Native Shore;
To these two hundred added, but withal,
A Weighty Lasting Grief did me befal.
(Thou'rt Dead, *Godolphin*,* who lov'dst Reason, true
Justice and Peace, Soldier Belov'd, Adieu)
Twice forty pounds, a yearly Pension, then
I from my own Country receiv'd; and when
King *Charles* restored was, a hundred more
Was allow'd me out of his private Store.
A Noble Gift: I slight Reproaches, when
I know I'm Good, from other Black-mouth'd Men.
Content with this, desire no more Pelf;*
Who but a Mad-man lives beneath himself?
Let my Estate by yours Computed be,
And greater seem; if not, it's enough for me.
My Sums are small, and yet live happy so,
Richer than *Crœsus* far, and *Crassus* too.
Verdusius, thou know'st my Temper well,
And those who read my Works, and with thee dwell.
My Life and Writings speak one Congruous Sense;
Justice I Teach, and Justice Reverence.
None but the Covetous we Wicked call,
For Avarice can do no good at all.
I've now Compleated my Eighty fourth year,
And Death approaching, prompts me not to fear.

FINIS.

EXPLANATORY NOTES

THE ELEMENTS OF LAW

19 *William, Earl of Newcastle*: (1592–1676.) In 1608 Hobbes entered the employment of Sir William Cavendish, later first Earl of Devonshire. The Earl of Newcastle was also a William Cavendish, a nephew of the Earl of Devonshire, and one of the Royalist generals at the outbreak of fighting in the Civil War in 1642. He was created Earl in 1628 and Duke in 1655. Newcastle was a cultivated and learned man who periodically employed Hobbes, for example in 1634 to search in London for a copy of Galileo's *Dialogue concerning the Two Chief World Systems*. (It was not to be found!)

21 *definition*: this plays a very large part in Hobbes's method of argument in *The Elements of Law* and elsewhere. See Introduction, pp. xxii f., and *De Corpore*, VI. 13–15.

22 *images or conceptions*: the word 'conceptions' has to do a lot of work for Hobbes. Conceptions are (*a*) the contents of our minds when and however they are actually being caused by external objects acting through our senses, *and* (*b*) those contents as they remain accessible to us in memories, dreams, imaginations, and so on, *and* (*c*) whatever it is we have when we understand a 'name' (in Hobbes's sense of that word. See Introduction, p. xxii). In usages (*a*) and (*b*), Hobbes often substitutes the word 'phantasm' for 'conception'. 'Images' appear to be the subclass of phantasms associated with vision. 'Idea' (another word Hobbes sometimes uses) seems to have no use distinct from that of 'conception'. But Hobbes is not entirely clear or consistent in his usages. Similar ambiguities can be found in John Locke's use of the word 'idea' in *An Essay concerning Human Understanding* (1690). In David Hume's *Treatise of Human Nature* (1739) usage (*a*) is distinguished as 'impressions', usage (*b*) as 'ideas'. Hobbes, Locke, and Hume all associate usage (*c*) in some way with (*a*) and (*b*). In Hobbes's terms, the conception we have of a name is usually the phantasms we learn to associate with the name.

23 *species visible and intelligible*: Hobbes is referring to an account of sense perception which is ultimately traceable to Aristotle's *De Anima*, particularly II. 12: 'In general, with regard to sense perception, we must take it that sense is that which can receive perceptible forms without their matter, as wax receives the imprint of the ring without the iron or gold.' In late medieval versions, to which Hobbes is objecting, the 'forms' had taken on quasi-physical characteristics never intended by Aristotle.

four points: for a discussion, see R. Peters, *Hobbes* (Harmondsworth, 1956), 106–10. In point (4), Hobbes is maintaining that conceptions are in the percipient, in us, not in the thing perceived.

24 *all that is real . . . nerve*: this is Hobbes's first appeal to his key thesis that motion is the ultimate property of 'body' (see Introduction, pp. xxiv f.), in terms of which everything that can be explained must be explained. The thesis is developed in II. 8 and 9; paragraph 10 puts it succinctly: 'The things that really are in the world without us, are those motions by which these seemings are caused.'

26 *motion*: Hobbes later introduces the concept 'endeavour' to refer to motion that is very small or insensible. See VII. 2, XII. 1, *De Corpore*, XXV. 2, and Introduction, pp. xxvi f.

27 *The causes of Dreams*: it is useful to read paragraph 3 in conjunction with *Leviathan*, II, the paragraph 'Dreams'. See also *De Corpore*, XXV. 12.

28 *And I believe . . . it was begotten*: cf. *De Corpore*, XXV. 12.

not in rerum natura: 'not in the nature of things'.

30 *To see at great . . . by decay*: this sentence is an addition by Hobbes to what was probably his primary manuscript.

κριτήριον: 'criterion', a word still foreign enough in 1640 to justify Hobbes's keeping it in the original Greek.

31 *I will (to avoid equivocation) call it discursion*: to avoid ambiguous speech, I will call it mental discourse.

The cause of . . . or consequence: 'consequence' in the literal sense of following in order. Hobbes is opening up the subject which in David Hume (1711–76) and David Hartly (1705–57) is investigated as 'the association of ideas'. The key question is why and how 'the mind may run almost from any thing to any thing' but not randomly? Compare the example Hobbes gives here (1640) with the famous one given in a similar context in *Leviathan*, III, in 1651, *after* the Civil Wars: 'in a Discourse of our present civil war, what could seem more impertinent, than to ask (as one did) what was the value of a Roman Penny? Yet the Coherence to me was manifest enough. For the Thought of the war, introduced the Thought of the delivering up the King to his Enemies; The Thought of that, brought in the Thought of the delivering up of Christ; and that again the Thought of the 30 pence, which was the price of that treason: and thence easily followed that malicious question; and all this in a moment of time; for Thought is quick'. See also *De Corpore*, XXV. 8.

32 7: this section in particular, and the remainder of Chapter IV in general, contain a significant anticipation of aspects of the seminal account of causation given by David Hume in *A Treatise of Human Nature* (1739) and in *An Enquiry concerning Human Understanding* (1748).

33 *cæteris paribus*: other things being equal.

34 *a sentence given*: a judgement handed down in a court of law, not (as easily read here) merely a proposition uttered: although clearly the usages overlap.

35 *A name or appellation*: a useful discussion of this and other matters arising in Chapter V can be found in J. W. N. Watkins, *Hobbes's System of Ideas* (London, 1965), ch. 8.

36 *the thing it signifieth*: Hobbes is decisively taking sides in a complex and long-running philosophical debate about universals. Universals are 'red', or 'man', or other words that can apply to more than one individual, or can function as a predicate in a sentence. In the view Hobbes is *opposing* (typically associated with Plato) such 'names' do not name an individual like 'the Thames' or 'Charles II', but nevertheless they do name *some* real entity, possibly existing in another world. This Hobbes will not have at any cost.

37 *equivocal*: having two or more significations equally appropriate.

   understanding: i.e. understanding of the speech, not understanding in the sense generally associated with wisdom. Cf. *Leviathan*, IV, 'Understanding being nothing else, but conception caused by speech'.

38 *syllogism*: an argument pattern identified by Aristotle in the *Prior Analytics* having two premises and a conclusion. Valid

forms of the pattern were much the concern of the late medieval logic Hobbes encountered at Oxford and derided in his Verse Life (see note to p. 255).

38 *if I enter further into*: he eventually did; see *De Corpore*, IV.

39 *The passions of man . . . voluntary motions*: see XII. 2–5. Hobbes's thesis will be that it makes no sense ('is insignificant') to talk of a free *will*. But it is significant to talk of a free *action* when the action both proceeds from the passions which *are* the will (fear, anger, love, and the like), and is itself not constrained by external physical force.

and ratio, now, is but oratio: *ratio*, reckoning or computing, verbal thinking; *oratio*, actual speech. Hobbes's point is that we are so accustomed to words that thought and speech are all but identical, and certainly we do not usually think nonverbally and then say what we have thought as a separate act.

paralogism: illogical reasoning, particularly of which the reasoner is unaware.

nosce teipsum: know thyself.

40 *the former . . . the latter . . . in language*: in Hobbes's very aptly chosen illustration the genuinely blind man could immediately have the former, 'knowledge original', but he could not have the latter, or knowledge 'how things are called'.

knowledge: cf. Plato, *Theaetetus*, 201d, for the suggestion that knowledge is belief with a reason, and A. J. Ayer, *The Problem of Knowledge* (Harmondsworth, 1956), 35: 'I conclude then that the necessary and sufficient conditions for knowing that something is the case are first that what one is said to know be true, secondly that one be sure of it, and thirdly that one should have the right to be sure.' Hobbes's remarks are in accord with a long tradition.

41 *what evidence is . . . ratiocination*: a parrot can say 'Come in!' but does not have any evidence (that is to say, understanding) of the noise it makes because it has no conception concomitant with the words.

Knowledge . . . science: cf. *Leviathan*, V, 'Science is the knowledge of Consequences, and dependance of one fact upon another: by which, out of that we can presently do, we know how to do something else when we will, or the like, another time.'

42 *Belief*: Hobbes's account in *Leviathan*, VII, distinguishes between belief in a man (*trust* in him and in the veracity of what he says) and belief in what is said (a favourable *opinion* of the truth of what is said). Hobbes is not concerned with belief as assent proportioned to the evidence, when the evidence falls short of justifying a claim to know, e.g. 'I believe it will rain today.'

44 *final cause*: the objective or purpose for which a thing exists or is done.

45 *Felicity . . . in prospering*: this potential rallying-call for the chairman of a multinational corporation has added to it in *Leviathan*, VI, an even more emphatically here-and-now coda: 'I mean the Felicity of this life. For there is no such thing as perpetual Tranquillity of mind, while we live here; because Life itself is but Motion, and can never be without Desire, nor without Fear, no more than without Sense.'

47 *Galileo, in the first dialogue concerning local motions*: Galileo (1564–1642) published two books in the 1630s whose titles are easily confused, particularly in translation. The first, published in 1632, is usually called *Dialogue concerning the Two Great World Systems* (i.e. the Ptolemaic or fixed-earth system and the Copernican or fixed-sun system). The second, published in 1638, was *Discourses concerning Two New Sciences* (also in dialogue form: the word 'Discorsi' is sometimes translated 'Dialogues'). Hobbes is here referring to the 1638 publication, an item towards the end of the 'First Day' discussion.

50 *for need of little is greater poverty than need of much*: what makes Hobbes so worth reading is partly his flashes of psychological insight. Look, for example, at his remark about delight in delighting (IX. 15), or the profundity of *Leviathan*, XI: 'To have done more hurt to a man, than he can, or is willing to expiate, enclineth the doer to hate the sufferer. For he must expect revenge, or forgiveness; both of which are hateful.'

51 *the fable*: reputedly one of Aesop's.

52 *Hath he escaped me?*: the anecdote is in Suetonius, *The Twelve Caesars*, towards the end of 'Tiberius'—'Cornalus has got away!'

56 *ad hanc*: towards her (towards *this*, where 'this' is a feminine form of the word).

57 *Convivium*: the *Symposium* or *Banquet*, particularly 209–12 (Socrates' speech towards the end).

58 *For example*: the examples are taken from the opening lines of Book II of Lucretius' *De Rerum Natura*, the longest account of Epicureanism surviving from antiquity. In W. H. Mallock's translation:

> When storms blow loud 'tis sweet to watch at ease
> From shore, the sailor labouring with the seas:
>   Because the sense, not that such pains are his,
> But that they are not ours, must always please.
>
> Sweet for the cragsman, from some high retreat
> Watching the plains below where legions meet,
>   To await the moment when the walls of war,
> Thunder and clash together. But more sweet,

And Lucretius continues with a very un-Hobbesian picture of sweet tranquillity which is contrasted with the restless strife of those 'seeking and never finding in the night the road to peace'.

61 *fancy*: to suppose oneself to perceive or conceive something.

62 *if the minds of men were all of white paper*: the metaphor has a venerable history in empiricist accounts of knowledge; thus Aristotle, *De Anima*, III. 4: 'the intellect . . . is nothing before it, thinks . . . [it exists] potentially in the same way as there is writing on a tablet on which nothing actually written exists'. A passage in Aetius, *c.* AD 100, anticipates Hobbes in more ways than one: 'When a man is born, the Stoics say, he has the commanding part of his soul like a sheet of paper ready for writing upon. On this he inscribes each one of his conceptions. The first method of inscription is through the senses. For by perceiving something, e.g. white, they have a memory of it when it has departed. And when many memories of a similar kind have occurred, we then say we have experience. For the plurality of similar impressions is experience' (A. A. Long and D. N. Sedley (eds.), *The Hellenistic Philosophers* (Cambridge, 1987), i. 238).

63 *Amongst the learned madmen . . . prophecy*: Hobbes's acerbic comment was added to his original manuscript. The species of madman is apparently as prevalent now as it was then; only less learned.

   romants: tales of chivalry.

cento: patchwork.

64 2: this paragraph and those following are of the first importance in understanding Hobbes's philosophical account of the limitations of religious understanding. See also XXV. 9, and compare with *Leviathan*, XI, towards the end of the chapter, where Hobbes reuses the example of the warmth of a fire but makes less of the incomprehensibility of God.

66 *tota in toto, and: tota in qualibet parte corporis*: all in all and all in any part you please of the body.

68 *Believe not every spirit . . . and he in God*: Hobbes had a vast and easy familiarity with the Bible on a scale and of an exactness which would now scarcely ever be met with, except among clergy, and rarely then. His numerous citations of scripture, here and elsewhere, are usually close paraphrases or, apparently, his own translations. The result sounds like the Authorized Version of 1611, or other established translation, but seldom is.

70 *It hath been declared already*: II. 9, VII. 2.

71 *Voluntary actions*: see note to p. 39. For a discussion see T. Sorell, *Hobbes* (London, 1986), 92–5, and for the details of Hobbes's own development of his thesis see in particular 'Of Liberty and Necessity', in *English Works of Thomas Hobbes*, ed. W. Molesworth, iv (London, 1840).

73 2: cf. *De Corpore*, VI. 11–12.

76 *Sic volo, sic jubeo . . . Stet pro ratione voluntas*: Thus I will, thus I command . . . let the will stand on behalf of reason.

77 *11: Silence . . . consenteth*: this is the reading of the concluding paragraph as amended by Hobbes in a marginal note to the manuscript. In order to contrive an ending to *Human Nature* as published prior to 1889, the following words were added to old printed texts: 'Conclusion. Thus have we considered the nature of man so far as was requisite for the finding out the first and most simple elements wherein the compositions of politic rules and laws are lastly resolved; which was my present purpose.'

Chapter XIV: this and the following chapter are the core of Hobbes's political theory. The argument is closely paralleled by *De Cive*, I and II. *Leviathan*, XIII and XIV should also be consulted for their masterful literary deployment of the same argument.

77 *In the precedent chapters*: printed editions prior to 1889, treating this as the start of a separately printed book, begin 'In a former treatise of human nature already printed'.

78 *in mere nature*: this could mean 'in our real psychological characters' or 'in a state of nature', i.e. 'without civil organization'. The corresponding passage in *De Cive*, I. 3, makes it clear that Hobbes means that men's physical powers and vulnerability are very similar in 'natural' conditions, that is to say where there is no civil law. Throughout this and following chapters Hobbes's uses of the words 'nature' and 'natural' have to be watched very carefully: (*a*) sometimes he speaks of man's nature, i.e. real character as it actually is all the time, whether we are in or out of civil society, whether we admit to the character or not. This is human nature as real psychology; (*b*) sometimes he speaks of the state of nature as the general condition of the world which would obtain in view of (*a*) if the bonds of civil society had never been formed, or were loosed by civil war; (*c*) sometimes he refers to whatever natural powers (physical, mental, emotional) human beings normally have.

82 *Reason*: it is one of Hobbes's basic contentions that in their passions, and by appeal to conscience, men diverge and war with one another; by appeal to reason they concur. Hence the emphases on the virtues of *mathematici*, XIII. 3–4, and his stated aim in the Epistle Dedicatory to reduce justice and policy 'to the rules and infallibility of reason'.

83 *de præsenti . . . de futuro*: concerning the present, or the past: for concerning the future . . .

84 *Antiochus*: possibly Antiochus IV (*c.*215–163 BC), who had a reputation for eccentricity and figures largely in provoking the Jewish insurrection recorded in the books of Maccabees.

covenant: Hobbes's concern with covenants (9–14) and oaths (15–18) is a product of contemporary events and disputes. Note especially paragraph 11, and refer to the Scottish National Covenant of 1638, which speaks of Christians 'who have renewed their Covenant *with God*' and calls God 'to witness' the declaration.

86 *the action voluntary*: this interesting argument needs to be understood in the terms already set out in XII. 3, where 'the voluntary' is what is done in the absence of external physical compulsion and in accordance with just such passions as fear

and covetousness that are mentioned in the text at this point. Thus, in a sense, we act freely when we walk to the scaffold in preference to being dragged. Hence covenants made in fear, unless they be contrary to law, bind as much as covenants made according to desire. For example, we may not like to pay extra rent, but the agreement to do so binds, despite being made under the fear of being made homeless. For a political application see XIX. 7.

89 *oderunt peccare*: they hate to sin.

90 *For by necessity of nature . . . unto himself*: this is the sort of statement that helps to confirm that in, and particularly in, *The Elements of Law* Hobbes is committed to psychological egoism (the view that people are psychologically programmed to act according to their real desires and aversions) rather than to moral egoism (the view that, in pursuit of the good, people ought to act according to their interests). See also XVII. 14.

That no man suffer . . . for his trusting: this and most of the other precepts of reason that Hobbes identifies in *The Elements* as laws of nature also appear in substantially similar form in *De Cive*, III, and *Leviathan*, XV.

92 *the great war . . . Peloponnesians*: Hobbes's translation of Thucydides' unique history of this war had been published in 1628. It has been reprinted in modern times, ed. R. Schlatter (New Brunswick, NJ, 1975).

93 *1*: Hobbes, always pleased to find fault with Aristotle as a symbol of the old learning he emphatically rejected, is here referring to the thesis about 'natural slaves' in *Politics*, I. 2. 8: 'that some should rule and others be ruled is a thing, not only necessary, but expedient; from the hour of their birth, some are marked out for subjection, others for rule'. Hobbes answers that this is (*a*) at variance with the facts of human nature, and (*b*) a road to dispute. Hence 'for peace sake . . . every man [should] acknowledge other for his equal'.

94 *encroaching*: a fuller rendering of the Greek would be 'a desire of more than their share'. The concept is much in evidence in Thucydides' writing.

96 *Quod tibi fieri non vis, alteri ne feceris*: what you do not want for yourself, don't do for another.

98 *And this is . . . by reason*: one of the few statements in *The Elements of Law* that show Hobbes explicitly differentiating

between general rational good, and an individual's perception of good in terms of his or her desires. The laws of nature are the rational precepts of such general good.

98 *As for the common opinion . . . in extremes*: Aristotle held that good character was a mean between extremes. Thus wit was the mean between buffoonery and boorishness, or liberality was the mean between prodigality and meanness. See *Nicomachean Ethics*, II. 6.

104 *bewrayeth*: betray, reveal.

106 *The making of union . . . command them not to do*: the first major step in Hobbes's political theory was the analysis of the estate of war. The second was the identification in reason of the conditions for its avoidance—the laws of nature. The third is the means of enforcing these laws in a body politic where 'by the fear whereof they may be compelled . . . to keep the peace amongst themselves'. A particular case of the 'making of union', probably known to Hobbes, occurred during the voyage of the *Mayflower* in 1620 when the need for mutual co-operation and order, in a situation where there was no authority to enforce the King's writ, resulted in a written compact or constitution in which the Pilgrim Fathers did 'solemnly and mutually . . . covenant and combine ourselves together into a civil body politic, for our better ordering and preservation; . . . and by virtue hereof to enact, constitute, and frame such just and equal laws, ordinances, acts, constitutions, and offices, from time to time, as shall be thought most meet and convenient for the general good of the colony, unto which we promise all due submission and obedience'. In 1636 a somewhat similar covenant was made at the founding of Hartford (later Connecticut) colony. See also XX. 3.

109 *That part of this treatise which is already past*: in printed editions prior to 1889 this read 'That treatise of Human Nature which was formerly printed' or 'In a former treatise of human nature already printed'.

111 *the estate of security*: note that for Hobbes security means freedom from violence and the fear thereof. Freedom from violence has perhaps a certain priority in terms of human needs to Aristotle's concerns: 'Security may be defined as possession of property in such places and on such conditions that the use of it is in our own hands' (*Rhetoric*, I. 5.7). John Locke, writing in 1690, also felt safe enough from civil

violence to give priority to a citizen's security in his property: 'The great and chief end, therefore, of men uniting into commonwealths, and putting themselves under government, is the preservation of their property; to which in the state of nature there are many things wanting' (*Two Treatises of Civil Government*, II. ix. 124).

112 *For seeing the wills ... there is no fear*: this fundamental Hobbesian belief in the need for fear to maintain the peace within society is perhaps given recent weight by the violence of young persons who are fearless because they are 'juveniles' in a specially defined sense which excludes them from the coercion of law or the *fear* of authority.

113 *10*: The assertion in this paragraph is that the private language of good and evil already described (VII. 3) has a common measure, civil law, superimposed upon it by the sovereign in a body politic. Difficulties immediately arise: (*a*) What about 'good Samaritan' acts and other private acts of kindness which are beyond the reach of a state-imposed 'common measure'? (*b*) What happens when the sovereign power imposes a morally repulsive law? Hobbes's reply to (*a*) is that people, unlike animals, which are driven exclusively by pleasure and pain (XIX. 5), have a non-egoistic *conception* of good and evil (different from, and not driven by, the psychological engines that make every man's end his own good) established by reason and expressed in the laws of nature (XVII. 14). These laws are also the laws of God (XVIII) and the sovereign is bound by them (XXVIII). But the problem (*h*) remains: if the sovereign power (king, council, or whatever) does not act as if bound by them, at what point will the evil and tyrannous body politic be worse than the possibility of a return to the estate of war? Hobbes seems inclined to say never. Most of his critics would be inclined to say sometimes. And the great debate remains—when?

114 *to sovereign power ... there belongeth impunity*: this and the next paragraph sharpen the problem of tyranny discussed in the previous note. In its historical context the argument would be taken to support the personal rule of Charles I *or* Cromwell. The same point is developed in *Leviathan*, XVIII, and *De Cive*, VI. 12.

120 *volenti non fit injuria*: injustice is not done to a willing victim (an old legal maxim).

120 5: In effect Hobbes is here describing Athenian democracy and its defects as seen through the eyes of Thucydides. What follows in this chapter owes quite a bit to Aristotle, *Politics*. III. 5–12, although Hobbes would probably be reluctant to admit it.

121 *optimates*: members of the Patrician order of Roman nobility.

126 *Chapter XXII*: This chapter is addressed to issues of feudalism, master–servant, and master–slave relationships which concern particular structures already in decay when Hobbes wrote and now long departed from any modern state correctly described as liberal-democratic. The interest of the chapter is historical. The content forms no essential part of Hobbes's general theses about human nature and the body politic.

sovereigns: that is to say, whoever or whatever holds sovereign power in the body politic. See XXV. 1.

130 *Chapter XXIII*: as with the previous chapter, this mostly describes social arrangements and discusses issues which are of more historical than current interest (an exception is perhaps the remarks on the care of children) and the argument is not essential to Hobbes's overall political philosophy.

ob præstantiam sexūs: from the superior standing (dominance) of the sex.

137 *conscience*: Hobbes does not allow conscience as some sort of autonomous authority, the word of God within, or the like. It is, as analysed in VI. 8, merely 'opinion of evidence'.

Those levies . . . maintaineth for them: this is about as close as Hobbes gets in *The Elements of Law* to a comment about current politics; in this instance Charles I's attempts to raise taxes for the defence of the realm. The levies are no real grievance, according to Hobbes, 'unless more be exacted than is necessary'. But what then? Hobbes has a clear but widely unacceptable answer: put up with it in the interests of peace. The case for acquiescence in peaceful tyranny has never been put better than by Hobbes in the 1647 Preface to *De Cive*, and particularly in the injunction 'That you will esteeme it better to enjoy your selves in the present state though perhaps not the best, than by waging War, endeavour to procure a reformation for other men in another age, your selves in the meanwhile either killed, or consumed with age.'

138 *eo nomine*: by that name.

139 *every man's end being some good to himself*: this is not mere political cynicism but a consequence of Hobbes's mechanistic psychology. See, for example, XII. 2–5 or XVI. 6, and discussion in my Introduction.

dispensing with the execution of justice: dispensing someone from the provisions of the law in a particular case. In Britain dispute about the monarch's dispensing and suspending powers with regard to law continued until after the revolution of 1688.

140 *Hodie mihi, cras tibi*: today to me, tomorrow to you.

142 *no human law is intended to oblige the conscience of a man*: laws bind what we *do*, not our conscience (our 'opinion' of our own actions). But certain doings may be contrary to conscience. Thus Hobbes proceeds to argue that scripture permits us to obey the sovereign power unless it is contrary to the one essential of Christian salvation—the faith that Jesus is the Christ (XXV. 8) 'and all the explications thereof'. See XXV. 11.

149 *we have huge volumes*: there were indeed huge volumes on this subject and they are still proliferating, but it is not clear to what Hobbes could possibly be referring in relation to the Epicureans and Stoics, most of whose original works survive only in fragments.

160 *Bellarmin*: Cardinal Robert Bellarmine (1542–1621), apologist for the Roman Church, head of the Roman College, and both friend and perforce opponent of Galileo.

161 *the whole effect of excommunicating . . . his dominion*: Hobbes's exceedingly ingenious and scriptural argument has the effect of saying that an ecclesiastical authority, or Pope, merely excludes itself from the company of an excommunicant. If the excommunicant is a sovereign, this leaves his or her position within the body politic exactly as it was before, and (the point Hobbes regards as so important) in no way justifies the disobedience of subjects.

164 *Aristotle saith well*: this is the only word of approval Hobbes finds for Aristotle. The full quotation (*Politics*, VI. 2.1) is: 'The basis of a democratic state is liberty; which, according to the common opinion of men, can only be enjoyed in such a state—this they affirm to be the great end of every democracy.' Since Hobbes is generally unfavourably disposed to what he called democracy (on the grounds that it had proved

an inefficient arrangement for keeping civil peace) even here his praise of Aristotle is somewhat barbed.

165 *supersedeas*: may you desist.

167 *Bodin . . . De Republica*: Jean Bodin (1530–96), French political philosopher whose main work was *Six Books concerning the Republic* (1576) on the definition and limits of sovereignty in general and monarchy in particular.

168 *Seneca*: (*c.*2 BC–AD 65.) Stoic, tutor of Nero, Roman administrator, author of numerous highly readable essays on morality, a work on natural philosophy, and several less readable tragedies. Hobbes gives no source for his observation and it is certainly not true that Seneca frequently maintains that tyrannicide is lawful. There is at most a hint of its propriety with reference to Nero in the historical play *Octavia*; a work, from clear internal evidence, not by Seneca but for long attributed to him. See also *De Ire*, III, 16.

169 *Sallust*: (*c.*86–34 BC.) Roman politician and historian whose writings include a history of the conspiracy of Catiline in 68 BC during the consulship of Cicero.

170 *generally called science*: this definition as it stands gives the impression that Hobbes is committed to what would now be called a conventionalist view of science—that scientific propositions are true in virtue of decisions to give the component words agreed meanings. But this is not a full reading of Hobbes's position. See VI. 4, and *De Corpore*, I. 10. But *De Corpore*, VI. 12–13, seems to favour conventionalism. For a discussion see T. Sorell, *Hobbes* (London, 1986), 45–50.

171 *The daughters of Pelias . . . revive again*: Pelias was responsible for sending his nephew Jason to fetch the Golden Fleece. The unfortunate rejuvenation experiment was attempted by Pelias' daughters after Jason's return with Medea and at Medea's instigation.

173 *against the law of nature*: it is noteworthy that Hobbes is saying that homosexuality, promiscuity, polygamy, and incest are not evidently against 'the law of natural reason', but, because they are antisocial, for the *sovereign* not to forbid them would be against the law of nature.

174 *contribute according to what he spendeth*: an interesting anticipation of arguments against income tax and in favour of customs and VAT.

180   8: The paragraph is in effect a summary of the main points in
      Hobbes's political theory.

DE CORPORE

186   *Philosophy*: in modern terms Hobbes appears to be giving a
      definition of science. Actually he is attempting to specify a
      method which would fit both the natural philosophy (or
      physics) and the civil philosophy he identifies in paragraph 9.

194   διότι . . . ὅτι: because . . . that (i.e. the science of *how*
      things happen, as opposed to the science of observing *what*
      happens).

200   *matter or body*: for an account of Hobbes's conception 'body'
      see Introduction, pp. xxiv f. It is not entirely clear in para-
      graph 8, or below in paragraph 13, whether 'body' and
      'matter' are being given as alternative words for the same
      conception, or as names for two different conceptions.
      Remembering the resounding one-world realism of *Leviathan*,
      XLVI, 'the universe . . . is body . . . also every part of body, is
      likewise body', it is difficult to know what 'matter' could
      mean apart from body, unless 'matter' is a general term for
      the different 'stuffs' that make up body.

203   *we may easily conceive . . . motion to the eye*: Hobbes, in
      company with most other seventeenth-century physicists, felt
      obliged to suppose that the propagation of motion required a
      medium. In giving an account of the senses, the problem of
      motion transferred from object to percipient is straightforward
      in the case of hearing. The medium is air. In the case of
      seeing there appears to be no medium, just light itself. A
      similar problem exists for gravity. Through what connecting
      medium does its pull operate? The problem vexed Sir Isaac
      Newton (1642–1727), who felt *some* medium must exist, but
      also recognized that no observations supported the hypothesis.
      See M. B. Hesse, 'Action at a Distance in Classical Physics',
      Isis (1955).

205   *axioms of Euclid . . . problems*: Euclid's account of geometry
      begins with *definitions* ('A line is length with breadth' etc.),
      five *postulates* (e.g. it is possible 'to draw a straight line from
      any point to any point'), and five or eight—according to
      which manuscript is used—*common notions* or 'axioms' (e.g.
      'Things equal to the same thing are equal to each other').

Hobbes (see paragraph 14) regards definitions as primary propositions, i.e. as axioms.

206 *genus and difference*: definition by genus and difference is one of the oldest-established accounts of definition. It consists in identifying what is being defined (the *definiendum*) with a large class of entities, which is then restricted to a smaller subclass. For example, 'A proposition is a sentence [the genus or large class of entities] capable of being true or false' (the difference which restricts the *definiendum* to a subclass of the genus).

207 *The properties*: Hobbes is here following a tradition started by Aristotle in the *Topics*, VI–VII, and *Posterior Analytics*, II. Some of the properties Hobbes lists (e.g. the sixth) are entirely standard. But he is also giving emphasis to his own concern with the clarity that definitions can bring about.

209 *Thirdly*: what follows is an important justification for the progression—BODY, MAN COMMONWEALTH—in Hobbes's grand system of philosophy.

216 *pia mater*: the innermost membrane enclosing the brain.

217 *phantasms*: a clear instance of Hobbes using the word to mean the actual content of various sense experience (not necessarily images). See note to p. 22.

218 *Terence, 'Populus . . . occuparat'*: Terence (c.190–c.156 BC), Roman writer of comedies. The quotation is from *Hecyra*, The Prologue, line 4: 'From their stupid whim the people devoted their attention to a rope-dancer.'

φαντασία: phantasía, a word much employed by Stoic and Epicurean writers in their accounts of sense perception and knowledge. It is close to Hobbes's 'phantasms' or David Hume's 'impressions of sense'.

226 *Doctor Harvey*: William Harvey (1578–1657), discoverer of the circulation of the blood, first publicized in *De Motu Cordis et Sanguine* (1628). A personal friend of Hobbes.

THE BRIEF LIFE

233 *as far as Osney Abbey*: about a mile and a half from Magdalen Hall as the jackdaw flies, now the desolated site of the former GWR goods yard awaiting new misuse.

234 *his young lord*: the chronology of the Cavendish family is horribly confusing. In 1618 Sir William Cavendish, already one of the richest men in England, was created first Earl of Devonshire. In 1608, when Hobbes was leaving Oxford, the future Earl was father to a son, William, afterwards second earl, two years younger than Hobbes. The first Earl died in 1626. The second Earl died in June 1628. It is not clear from Aubrey whether the son or the father chose Hobbes as companion and tutor to 'his young lord'.

235 *Jos Scaliger*: Joseph Scaliger (1540–1609), greatest European scholar of his time, converted to Calvinism 1562.

   Clavius: Christopher Clavius, distinguished Jesuit astronomer and chief mathematician of the Roman College.

236 *Vesalius' Anatomy*: Andreas Vesalius (1515–64), Belgian anatomist. His *Anatomy* appeared in 1543. Condemned by the Inquisition for dissecting a human body.

   the two Savilian professors at Oxon.: in 1619 Sir Henry Savile founded professorships in geometry and astronomy. After Hobbes's ill-advised attempt in *De Corpore* (1655), Ch. XX, to 'square the circle', John Wallis (Professor of Geometry) and Seth Ward (Professor of Astronomy) mercilessly attacked him. The resulting controversy was ultimately terminated by the death of the participants.

237 *redintegrated*: perfectly re-established.

238 *His lord*: the future second Earl of Devonshire.

239 *Crassa . . . ingenium*: wide skin, wide skull, wide wit.

241 *band*: neckband, a kind of tie or detachable collar.

   boots: leggings.

242 *pro suo modulo*: according to his means.

   death-bed: in Paris in 1647.

244 *the strangury*: an uncomfortably apt-sounding word still used by physicians to indicate any condition that results in retention of urine.

THE PROSE LIFE

247 *De Cive, which was published in 1646*: this is not strictly correct. *De Cive* was written in 1641. It was published in

Latin in a very restricted print run in April 1642. In 1646 Hobbes added notes and the important Preface, and arranged for it to be printed in Amsterdam. The dedication is dated 1 November 1646. The volume was printed early in 1647 and sold out quickly.

252 *Cyclometria*: The Epic Cycle of legends and fragments concerned with the Trojan War, but not by Homer. This sentence must have been added after the year in which Aubrey indicates that the 'Prose Life' was written.

253 *in venerable archives*: Hobbes would surely be disappointed in this matter since the venerable archives of seventeenth-century science, while becoming increasingly venerable, remain to a surprising extent unexplored.

the most skilled of scientists: although Hobbes's somewhat extravagant self-assessment would not be shared by many historians, there is little doubt that if *De Corpore* and *De Homine* were more studied, his place in the history of science would be higher than the footnote he now occupies. What would certainly be much higher is his reputation in the philosophy of science. What is indisputable is that even by seventeenth-century standards he was a polymath of unusual scope.

THE VERSE LIFE

255 *Barbara . . . Ferison*: this is Hobbes's version of an old doggerel mnemonic used to list the valid moods of the syllogism in each of the four figures. The vowels indicate the form of the proposition. For example, A is the form 'All *X*s are *Y*s', E is 'No *X*s are *Y*s'. The figure indicates the position of the term common to both premisses and not present in the conclusion. So 'Celarent' is the first figure valid mood EAE exemplified in such a syllogism as 'No existent thing is spirit: all gods are existent things; therefore no god is a spirit'. A good account of the matter can be found in the entry 'Logic, Traditional' in *The Encyclopedia of Philosophy*, ed. P. Edwards (London, 1967).

Forms we see: see note to p. 23.

Drake and Cavendish: Sir Francis Drake (*c.*1540–96) and Thomas Cavendish (*c.*1555–92). English navigators, explorers, and from the Spanish view, pirates.

256 *eighteen Months*: i.e. 1628–9.

And by what Arts . . . Illiterate: Hobbes regarded mob oratory as a disadvantage in democracy causing confusion of council. See, for example, *Elements of Law*, XXI. 5.

257 *Th'internal parts . . . Motion can do*: Hobbes's fundamental thesis, that reality is body (or matter) in motion. See Introduction, pp. xxiv–xxvii.

Mersennus: Marin Mersenne (1588–1648), a Minim Friar and man of strict but genial orthodoxy whose monastic cell became the heart of a salon of learned men in Paris including Descartes, Pascal, Gassendi, and Hobbes. Hobbes had great affection for him (see below in 'Verse Life') and his death was partly the occasion for Hobbes's plans to return to England after his long sojourn in Paris during the Civil Wars.

To various Matter . . . were my Studies then: this description and the period fit *The Elements of Law*.

258 *To Pen my Book de Corpore*: the implication here and elsewhere in the 'Verse Life' is that Hobbes was working at *De Corpore* on and off over the whole period 1647–55.

259 *Eternal Blot*: having surrendered to the Scots in February 1647, Charles I was 'sold' by them to the English Parliamentarians for the price of half the sum due to the Scots for military services to England. The King was executed by the Parliamentarians in January 1649.

260 *Grand Climacterick*: a, or the, critical epoch of one's life, often associated with 'magic' multiples of the numbers 7 and 9. In 1651, when *Leviathan* was published, Hobbes had been 7 × 9 years old. Thus 1651 was a climaterick year in two senses. The *Latin* text of the 'Verse Life' identifies the following year when he was 8 × 8 years old, the year when possible difficulties with both Royalist and Roman Catholic critics of *Leviathan* sent him back to England.

Dorislaus, and on Ascham's Fate: two of the regicides of 1649. Isaac Dorislaus (1595–1649), assassinated in The Netherlands by Royalists, and Ascham, English envoy sent to Madrid by Cromwell in 1655 and assassinated in his residence by banished Royalists.

261 *made it read by many a man*: Samuel Pepys, in his diary entry for 3 September 1668, remarks 'and so to the Exchequer and several places, calling on several businesses, and particularly

my bookseller's, among others, for Hobbes's *Leviathan*, which is now mightily called for; and what was heretofore sold for 8s [shillings] I now give 24s at the second hand, and is sold for 30s, it being a book the Bishops will not let be printed again'.

261 *Diophantus . . . Gheber . . . Vieta*: mathematicians.

Savil: see note to p. 236.

Six Dialogues: *Examinatio et Emendatio Mathematicae Hodiernae* (1660). Six dialogues between 'A and B', whom Wallis afterwards identified as 'Thomas and Hobbes'.

two Treatises: *Of Liberty and Necessity* (written 1646, published 1654) and *The Questions concerning Liberty, Necessity and Chance . . . Debated between Dr Bramhall . . . and Thomas Hobbes* (1656).

262 *Six Problems*: presumably the Latin *Problemata Physica* (1662), whose seven dialogues fit the description Hobbes gives.

263 *Geometry*: Hobbes's enthusiasm for geometry greatly exceeded his abilities. It is generally agreed that while he appreciated the rigour and clarity required by geometry, he came to it too late in life to be a skilful practitioner—a fact sadly unapparent to Hobbes himself.

Rosetum: *Rosetum Geometricum* (1671), another episode in the hapless controversy with Wallis.

264 *Godolphin*: Sidney Godolphin (1610–43), Royalist member of the Long Parliament killed in a skirmish in 1643. In his will he left £200 to Hobbes. Hobbes dedicated *Leviathan* to Sidney's brother Henry.

Pelf: property, wealth, with overtones of frippery or unnecessary excesses.

THE WORLD'S CLASSICS

A Select List

HANS ANDERSEN: Fairy Tales
Translated by L. W. Kingsland
Introduction by Naomi Lewis
Illustrated by Vilhelm Pedersen and Lorenz Frølich

JANE AUSTEN: Emma
Edited by James Kinsley and David Lodge

Mansfield Park
Edited by James Kinsley and John Lucas

J. M. BARRIE: Peter Pan in Kensington Gardens & Peter and Wendy
Edited by Peter Hollindale

WILLIAM BECKFORD: Vathek
Edited by Roger Lonsdale

CHARLOTTE BRONTË: Jane Eyre
Edited by Margaret Smith

THOMAS CARLYLE: The French Revolution
Edited by K. J. Fielding and David Sorensen

LEWIS CARROLL: Alice's Adventures in Wonderland
and Through the Looking Glass
Edited by Roger Lancelyn Green
Illustrated by John Tenniel

MIGUEL DE CERVANTES: Don Quixote
Translated by Charles Jarvis
Edited by E. C. Riley

GEOFFREY CHAUCER: The Canterbury Tales
Translated by David Wright

ANTON CHEKHOV: The Russian Master and Other Stories
Translated by Ronald Hingley

JOSEPH CONRAD: Victory
Edited by John Batchelor
Introduction by Tony Tanner

DANTE ALIGHIERI: The Divine Comedy
Translated by C. H. Sisson
Edited by David Higgins

A complete list of Oxford Paperbacks, including The World's Classics, OPUS, Past Masters, Oxford Authors, Oxford Shakespeare, and Oxford Paperback Reference, is available in the UK from the Arts and Reference Publicity Department (BH), Oxford University Press, Walton Street, Oxford OX2 6DP.

In the USA, complete lists are available from the Paperbacks Marketing Manager, Oxford University Press, 200 Madison Avenue, New York, NY 10016.

Oxford Paperbacks are available from all good bookshops. In case of difficulty, customers in the UK can order direct from Oxford University Press Bookshop, Freepost, 116 High Street, Oxford, OX1 4BR, enclosing full payment. Please add 10 per cent of published price for postage and packing.